HERALD OF A
RESTLESS WORLD

HERALD OF A
RESTLESS WORLD

HOW HENRI BERGSON BROUGHT
PHILOSOPHY TO THE PEOPLE

EMILY HERRING

BASIC BOOKS

New York

Basic Books
Hachette Book Group
1290 Avenue of the Americas, New York, NY 10104
www.basicbooks.com

Printed in the United States of America

First Edition: October 2024

Published by Basic Books, an imprint of Hachette Book Group, Inc. The Basic Books name and logo is a registered trademark of the Hachette Book Group.

The Hachette Speakers Bureau provides a wide range of authors for speaking events. To find out more, go to hachettespeakersbureau.com or email HachetteSpeakers@hbgusa.com.

Basic books may be purchased in bulk for business, educational, or promotional use. For more information, please contact your local bookseller or the Hachette Book Group Special Markets Department at special.markets@hbgusa.com.

The publisher is not responsible for websites (or their content) that are not owned by the publisher.

Print book interior design by Amy Quinn.

Library of Congress Control Number: 2024005423

ISBNs: 9781541600942 (hardcover), 9781541600935 (ebook)

LSC-C

Printing 1, 2024

For Victor and Maddy

The reason for his stupendous reputation lies, it seems to me, in this: that Bergson is not so much a prophet as a herald in whom the unrest of modern times has found a voice. He is popular because he says with splendid certainty what thousands of people have been feeling vaguely.

—Walter Lippmann, *Everybody's Magazine*, July 1912

CONTENTS

Contents

HERALD OF A
RESTLESS WORLD

INTRODUCTION

THE MOST FAMOUS PHILOSOPHER IN THE WORLD

O f all the lectures on offer at the Collège de France in the early years of the twentieth century, those dispensed by Paul Leroy-Beaulieu were easily the most tedious. Even though his course was open to the public, the professor refused to teach anything even remotely crowd-pleasing. Week after week, the almost seventy-year-old droned on about the organisation of the French financial administration and the economic philosophy of Pierre-Joseph Proudhon. In the three decades Leroy-Beaulieu held the chair of political economy, his lectures had never attracted more than a handful of listeners. But about halfway through the first decade of the new century, something changed.

He started noticing unfamiliar faces emerging alongside his small group of faithful listeners. They were unlike any of the students he had ever taught. In fact, he wondered if they were students at all. Even as young as they were, they did not look like budding economists. The old professor knew he was probably out of touch with the ways of this new generation, but some of these newcomers were so unkempt that they almost looked like servants. Others carried themselves with an aloofness usually found only in introspective artistic types. More perplexing yet, women were now appearing, in large numbers, in the lecture theatre. What business did women, of all people, have learning about the distribution of wealth, public finance, and currency?

To add insult to the professor's bewilderment, he began to suspect that this mysterious phenomenon had little to do with enthusiasm for his lectures. For years, the only sounds he had heard, besides his own monotonous voice, had been the diligent scribbling of notes and the occasional yawn. These had now been replaced with muffled laughter and loud whispers. Once, he could have sworn he saw two rather scruffy men dealing out playing cards at the back of the room. Although his lectures had never been better attended, Leroy-Beaulieu felt that he had lost his audience.

Sadly for the economist, his suspicions were soon confirmed. One day Leroy-Beaulieu entered his lecture theatre to find all the seats occupied. For the first time in his life, he spoke before a full house, and it was the loneliest experience of his life. No one noticed him enter or leave the room that day. As he surveyed the auditorium mid-lecture, he realised with a painful twinge of indignation that not a single person was listening to him. When his hour was up, the old man quietly made his way out into the packed corridor. He was in such a daze that he failed to notice that no one else had followed him out of the lecture theatre, which was now buzzing with an excited murmur. He pushed his way past a group of perfumed women who were talking animatedly: "I told you we should have arrived earlier," one of them sighed. "Not a single seat remains!"

The coup de grâce came in the early months of 1914. One day, before Leroy-Beaulieu could begin his lecture, cries were heard in the corridor. Two men were fighting to get into the room. This time the professor felt emboldened to chastise those who had forgotten he even existed: "Before hearing M. Bergson," he shouted, "I insist that you listen to me in silence." The noise eventually subsided, and the professor arranged his notes on his desk, stroked his long beard, and, ignoring the many women present, began:

"Today, gentlemen, I will only speak briefly . . . "

This statement was met with enthusiastic cheers. Startled, he managed to retain his composure and pursued:

"I will only speak briefly about the classical doctrine of social credit, because there is no need to insist . . . "

He was interrupted by a chorus of sardonic chants:

"Don't insist! Don't insist!"[1]

When he announced the end of the lesson an hour later, several audience members let out unmistakable sighs of relief alongside the sarcastic cheers and claps. Humiliated, the economist dropped his notes and stormed out of the room. The cruel echoes of mocking applause and hysterical laughter followed him down the corridor.

Leroy-Beaulieu's only crime had been to share a lecture theatre with the most famous philosopher in the world.

PHILOSOPHER À LA MODE

In the years leading up to World War I, Henri Bergson's lectures were the most popular in all of Paris. In his books, he took on highly specialised debates, such as the metaphysical status of time, the relationship between memory and the brain, and the evolution of the eye in vertebrates. He illustrated his arguments with complicated examples taken from the psychology, neuroscience, biology, and physics of his day, and he never wrote with a broad readership in mind. Yet week after week, more and more people tried to squeeze inside his Collège de France lecture theatre to hear him speak. The wealthiest members of the audience had started sending their valets to save them a spot. The unsuccessful resorted to climbing onto window ledges to listen in, and inside the room the heat often became so unbearable that people fainted.

By his fiftieth birthday, Bergson had managed what most public figures can only hope to achieve in death: he had become an icon. His fame had skyrocketed with the publication, in 1907, of *Creative Evolution*. With his fourth book, the philosopher, who was already well known in academic circles, became an international celebrity. His notions of "*durée*," "*élan vital*," and "intuition" entered everyday language. His fans believed that he had already earned his place in the philosophy hall of fame, alongside such royalty as Plato, Descartes, and Kant. Pilgrimages were organised to his summer home in Switzerland, and locks of his thinning hair were stolen from his barber.[2]

The crowds of hundreds, sometimes thousands, who flocked to listen to him speak left in a kind of trance, enchanted by the perfectly timed cadence of his speech, the melodic quality of his voice, and his masterful developments, which brought complex philosophical notions together in apparent harmony. Bergson's disciple and friend Jacques Chevalier described the beginning of a lecture with an almost religious emotion:

> A silence descended on the auditorium, a secret quiver ran through our souls, when we saw him silently appear at the back of the amphitheatre and sit under a discreet lamp, his hands free, usually clasped, never needing written notes, with his enormous forehead, his clear eyes that were like two lights beneath his bushy eyebrows, and his delicate features that brought out the power of his forehead and the immaterial radiance of his thought. His speech was slow, noble, and regular, like his writing, extraordinarily confident and surprisingly precise, with caressing, musical intonations.[3]

There was indeed something special about the way the professor spoke. He held as a principle that "there is no philosophical idea, however profound or subtle, that cannot and should not be expressed in everyday language," and that philosophers should "not write for a restricted circle of initiates; they write for humanity in general."[4] And though humanity in general did not attend his lectures, the hundreds who pressed themselves into the Collège de France each week did form a diverse group.

Bergson's lectures had become a weekly rendezvous for a who's who of the capital's trendiest literary, artistic, and political personalities. Week after week, philosophers and philosophy students sat (or stood) next to mathematicians and poets, suffragettes and priests, actors and engineers, socialists and socialites, artists and journalists, aristocrats and anarchists, curious bystanders, and politicians.

The countess and poet Anna de Noailles could often be found in the lecture theatre, adorned in feathers and silk, trailing a flock of devotees. A few rows behind her, one might have seen a large, bearded man, Georges Sorel, a proponent of revolutionary syndicalism. Nearby, one could often glimpse Giovanni Papini, a writer with untamed curls, small round spectacles, and close ties to Futurism, a movement whose manifesto was still fresh off the press. One of Bergson's most ardent followers, Charles Péguy, wearing thick eyeglasses and his distinctive black cape, was there too. Scattered across the room and listening intently, these trendsetters absorbed and transformed Bergson's words, sometimes taking such liberties with them that the philosopher no longer recognised himself in their applications of his ideas.

At first glance, nothing about Bergson screamed avant-garde. At the peak of his fame, he was a peculiar little man in his fifties. It seemed that at any moment his frail body might be crushed under the weight of his massive forehead, which he usually covered in a high crown bowler hat. His light blue, highly expressive eyes, overhung by thick dark brows, gave him a perpetual air of mild astonishment. He spoke softly and moved slowly, with the calculated agility of a large insect or small bird. Although his lectures entranced the most fashionable crowds of the early twentieth century, he was, at heart, a deeply private, almost timid person. Acclaim and flattery left him uncomfortable, and he found the whole situation embarrassing and inconvenient.

On one occasion, Bergson entered the lecture theatre to find his desk entirely covered in flowers. Mortified, he cried: "But ... I am not a ballerina!" He found celebrity "stupid" because it distracted both his followers and him from what mattered the most: his philosophy. Fame, he said, had rapidly become "odious" to him.[5]

Whenever he could, Bergson sought refuge from the madness of the city and the obligations that came with international celebrity in the sanctuaries he had created for himself and his family. He spent his summers in the country home built for him in the cool air of the Swiss mountains. The rest of the year, whenever he could, he enjoyed the quiet of his Parisian home, which sat at the end of a garden in a private residence called the Villa Montmorency. When he looked up from his papers, he could see the neighbours' cats playing amid the trees and flowers, and he could pretend he had left the city. "What I dislike about Paris," he told his friend Jacques Chevalier, "is the lack of sunshine, the lack of air, the lack of silence. . . . People talk about progress. But every new advance is accompanied by the invention of a new kind of noise: trains, cars, aeroplanes. . . . I would have loved to live in the countryside."[6] He envied the peaceful existence of forest rangers, who lived among the trees, breathing in pure air away from the commotion of the city and enjoying levels of freedom he could no longer hope for.[7]

It seemed to Bergson that each stage of his career had pulled him further away from a life that better suited his temperament. Yet he also knew that, step by step, it was a life he had chosen. When he had been assigned his first teaching positions in the smaller and quieter cities of Angers and Clermont-Ferrand, he had grown restless. Although he valued quiet, he had eventually decided to move back to the turbulence of Paris: the gravitational pull of a prestigious academic career in the capital had been too strong. And while he preferred private, meaningful philosophical conversations to what he viewed as the empty chatter of social gatherings, he was adept at networking, playing the career game masterfully, making friends with the right people, and seeking out their support at the right time. His Collège de France position and various Académie elections came as the result of relentless campaigning on his part. The quiet Bergson always had to make concessions to the ambitious Bergson; later, one of his main regrets was that he had not taken better care of himself, that he had not followed the advice he so often gave to his friends—to take time off and rest. In the end, he paid a huge price for not doing so. In 1914, Bergson requested permission to take a break from his Collège de France duties. He never returned to his post: when he finally allowed his body to rest, it broke and never recovered.

On the other side of the First World War, the transgressive appeal of Bergson's philosophy had dissipated. In the 1920s, Bergson received multiple honours and accolades—not least a Nobel Prize in 1927—but those who had found in Bergson's philosophy new ways of thinking about radical change were no longer interested in a figure who had become a living monument. Bergson's fame evaporated almost as rapidly as it had materialised. In 1944, the American philosopher Irwin Edman wrote that "the news of [Bergson's] death, in 1941, was shocking precisely because the world had already fallen into the habit of thinking of him as dead."[8]

UN-BERGSONIAN

Writing a biography is a highly un-Bergsonian exercise. The biographer usually unravels the story of a human life from birth to death. She might give her reader the impression that her subject's life is developing before their very eyes, but in reality she already holds together all the events from start to finish. She looks at portions of a lived experience from the outside, moves them around, and cuts them up into interchangeable pieces. Anyone who is familiar with Bergson's philosophy knows that such a process is at odds with his description of the flow of time as gradually ripening a person's existence from within.

Perhaps the only thing more un-Bergsonian than writing a biography is writing a biography of Henri Bergson. On several occasions, including in the will he started drafting half a decade before he died, the philosopher demanded that he be remembered for his philosophy and nothing else: "I have always asked that my personal life be ignored, and that only my work should be examined. I have invariably maintained that the life of a philosopher sheds no light on his doc-trine and is of no concern to the public."[9] He knew that after he died any traces of himself he left behind would be picked apart, that all manner of tributes (which he viewed as unwarranted) would be paid, and that all sorts of erroneous assumptions and preconceptions about his character and intentions would become set in stone. He knew that the wishes he stated in his testament would not be fully respected, and so, before he died, he made sure to quell all future attempts to study Bergson the man, beyond the work. He instructed his wife Lou-ise, who had shared his life for over four decades, to destroy anything he left unpublished after leaving this world. Correspondence, miscel-laneous papers, lecture notes, drafts of new ideas—Louise threw it all in the fire.[10] A biographer's nightmare.

Bergson often repeated that nothing can be learned about a phi-losopher's ideas by studying their life. But what if it is precisely their life we are interested in?

MY BERGSON

At eighteen, I used the little I knew about Bergson's philosophy in my baccalaureate philosophy exam. We were given four hours to write an essay on a single question: "Does language betray our thoughts?" So much of what I then knew of Bergson's thought felt entirely beyond my reach, but his ideas about language resonated. Words, Bergson said, are mere labels we affix to things. We use concepts to tidy up the overwhelming diversity of reality into neat boxes. But in doing so, we often lose sight of what is special and par-ticular about the different aspects of reality that our words describe, including our own inner lives. Beneath this monochromatic con-ceptual veil, our vibrant, unique self remains hidden out of reach, unless we know how to look for it. Bergson had implanted in me the idea that philosophy could serve as a window into the world beyond what is given.

At the Sorbonne, I majored in philosophy. In an ocean of Western classics, Bergson's name bobbed up once in a while alongside Plato,

Descartes, and Kant, but I wanted to find out more. Towards the end of my third year, I decided to read his works on my own time, in chronological order. I was met with difficult but beautiful texts that delved into scientific debates for which I had little context. Like so many of his contemporaries, I found that his book *Creative Evolution* was the one that stood out to me. I was so fascinated by this early twentieth-century philosophical interpretation of biological evolution that I applied to do a master's degree in the history of science to better understand what was at stake. My curiosity got the better of me, and I ended up writing a PhD thesis at the University of Leeds on the reception of Bergsonian evolution among the biologists of his day. It was only then that I started learning about Bergson's life, beyond his theories, the life the philosopher himself did not want anyone to study.

I was captivated. Parts of his story read like an adventure novel. Other parts reminded me of the most deranged aspects of our current celebrity culture. As I unravelled the various threads of my research, I realised that there was almost no area of early twentieth-century culture that this soft-spoken, bald-headed French philosopher had not touched. For a time he had been the most talked-about person on the planet, but as I would learn, his name meant very little to most of the academics I encountered in the anglophone world. It has always seemed unbelievable to me that such an extraordinary figure and his incredible story could have been almost entirely forgotten.

This book is not an introduction to Bergson's philosophy. There have been many of those, hundreds even. The ones I have found the most helpful throughout my studies and research are listed in the "Beginner's Guide to Bergson" at the end of the book. But naturally, over the course of this book I introduce many of Bergson's key ideas, as they constitute pivotal "moments" in the philosopher's journey. This book is not strictly what one might call an "intellectual biography" either. I do not purport to find within the events of Bergson's life the germs of his ideas. As the philosopher

Gabriel Marcel wrote about Bergson: "Did he not teach us how important it is to be wary of a posteriori reconstructions that so profoundly alter the creative process they claim to describe?"[11]

Instead, I like to think of this book as the product of three intertwined and inseparable portraits. A portrait of a man, with aspirations and contradictions. A portrait of his philosophy, which, in various ways, changed the world around him. And a portrait of the world in which the man and his ideas evolved. A portrait is, by nature, a point of view taken on a subject. My own interests, idiosyncrasies, and blind spots will therefore be reflected in my depiction of Bergson's life, times, and philosophy. But it is my hope that this book will highlight just how profound, interesting, and important Bergson was and why he deserves to be remembered.

It would be a mistake to dismiss Bergson as a mere historical curiosity. In the early years of the twentieth century, his defining of life and consciousness in terms of freedom and creativity reassured those who worried that new discoveries in biology had reduced human existence to a cold mechanical process. His critique of the static symbolism of science resonated deeply with those who had grown suspicious of what they viewed as the excesses of rationality and technology.

The concerns of Bergson's contemporaries echo many of our present-day anxieties, and his philosophy may offer some solutions. The final words of Bergson's 1932 book *The Two Sources of Morality and Religion* could have been written today: "Mankind lies groaning, half-crushed beneath the weight of its own progress. Men do not sufficiently realise that their future is in their own hands. Theirs is the task of determining whether they want to go on living or not."[12]

New facial recognition and artificial intelligence technologies have us fearing for our freedom and humanity. With the current climate crisis, the survival of our species depends on our ability to come up with creative solutions to unprecedented challenges. Who better to turn to than *the* thinker of radical change and creativity?

CHAPTER I

ON THE ORIGIN OF HENRI

In the autumn of 1859, the world changed twice. On October 18, a baby boy was born in Paris, about halfway between the Garnier opera house and the hill of Montmartre. By the turn of the century, everyone would know his name, and the key notions in his philosophy of change would have entered everyday vocabulary. But at the time this event appeared small and unremarkable, and Henri Louis Bergson entered the world quietly.

The second event caused an almost immediate uproar, much louder than the cries of an infant. At the end of November, the first copies of Charles Darwin's *On the Origin of Species* became available to the public, with effects that rippled far beyond biology and into the remotest regions of humankind's collective psyche.

As with any great scientific theory, the philosophical implications of Darwin's theory of natural selection were dizzying. Humans had been pushed out of the spotlight only to find they were standing on shaky ground. Everything they thought they knew about them-selves and their place in the universe had been turned upside down. Palaeontologists, not priests, now held the key to the meaning of life.

Darwin had lent scientific weight to an unsettling idea: humans have not always been human and might one day be nothing more than a distant memory in the fossil record. If humans, like all organisms, are always evolving, then the idea of a fixed, immutable human nature so often depicted in religious and philosophical texts becomes hard to justify. Species can no longer be seen as eternal, unchanging, and created categories, and neither can we.

As evolutionism gained greater acceptance, the world sped up. New discoveries, machines, and modes of transportation were not only profoundly shaking up people's way of life but also altering their basic understanding of reality. The German poet Heinrich Heine chronicled these feelings: "What changes must now occur, in our way of looking at things, in our notions! Even the elementary concepts of time and space have begun to vacillate. Space is killed by the railways, and we are left with time alone."[1]

The world Henri Bergson was born into was one in which aspects of reality once believed stable and eternal were revealed to be sub-ject to continuous and unstoppable change. But change had not always been a popular notion.

OUR OBSESSION WITH ETERNITY

In the fifth century BCE, in the Greek-speaking regions of south-ern Italy, there lived a man called Zeno of Elea. We know very lit-tle about his life, but his ideas have floated down to us along the unpredictable currents of knowledge transmission. Zeno is remem-bered for formulating paradoxes that have perplexed philosophers and mathematicians for over two millennia. One of the paradoxes is based on a familiar story attributed to the fabulist Aesop. A tor-toise is given the apparently insurmountable task of racing a much faster opponent. In this telling, instead of a hare, the tortoise has to face the mythical hero of the Trojan War, Achilles. In the original story, because the arrogant hare underestimates the slow and steady tortoise, he ends up losing the race. But in Zeno's version, no one makes it past the finish line.

The paradox goes something like this. Achilles allows the tortoise a head start, believing he will easily catch up to the slow reptile. But in the time it takes the warrior to run the distance already covered by his opponent, the tortoise has slowly but surely advanced a bit further. Before Achilles can overtake the tortoise, he must first cover this new shorter distance. By the time Achilles arrives at the point most recently reached by the tortoise, it has once again moved slightly further ahead. This process repeats ad infinitum, and Achilles never overtakes his opponent. In fact, according to Zeno's logic, neither Achilles nor the tortoise can ever truly get started. Before they can take their first step, they must take half a step. And before that, a quarter of a step, and so on. The mythical warrior and the heavy-footed reptile remain stuck forever in paradoxical limbo. Defying basic common sense, contradicting what our eyes and ears tell us, the paradox is meant to show that any impression of change we may have is merely an illusion of our senses, the reflection of our own intellectual shortcomings.

Although Zeno never actually proved the impossibility of change, he highlighted a recurring problem encountered by those who wished to understand the universe: change is, by definition, difficult to grasp. If everything is in constant flux, if nothing remains equal to itself—if, as another pre-Socratic philosopher, Heraclitus, put it, one can never bathe in the same river twice—then it seems very difficult to measure, theorise, or even talk about reality with any certainty.

This was precisely Plato's criticism of Heraclitus and of the idea of instability in general. In the *Republic*, he posited a world of "forms": the eternal, abstract counterparts to their changeable and corruptible incarnations in the physical world. The tree we perceive with our senses is subject to the changing of the seasons and to all of life's accidents, from lightning bolts to woodpeckers. This tree is there-fore less reliably knowable than the unchanging idea of a tree, which encompasses all trees and no tree in particular, at all possible stages of development at once. For Plato, the world we perceive with our senses is merely an imperfect and perishable copy of the perfect and eternal ideas.

Plato's student Aristotle divided the universe in two: our own terrestrial realm, a place of change, irregularity, and erosion; and the place beyond the moon, where regular, unchanging, and ethe-real celestial bodies exist. The only motion that exists in the sky is cyclical and predictable. The highest form of being—Aristotle's version of a deity—is the "unmoved mover," or "that which moves without being moved." This most perfect being, the primary cause of all movement, is immortal and unchanging.

Some two millennia later, the French philosopher René Descartes observed a piece of wax change shape under the heat of a flame. He noted that, depending on how close the wax is to the flame, it might be hard or soft to the touch, its smell might change, and it might appear lighter or darker. "Clear and distinct" knowledge is attained by doing away with "those things that do not belong to the wax"—in other words, its fluctuating qualities—and by retaining only the qualities that persist beyond all change.[2] Descartes's abstract idea of wax as something "extended, flexible, and mutable" remains the same no matter the variations of form, texture, and colour any piece of wax may undergo.[3] This is what we can truly know about it beyond the changing data of the senses.

Therefore, some of the most important thinkers in the Western philosophical canon built their philosophy around the idea that in order to know the world it is better to focus on eternal, unchang-ing ideas than on the fluctuations and accidents of everyday life. As Bergson later put it, ancient and modern thinkers alike were "led to seek the reality of things above time, beyond what moves and what changes, and consequently outside what our senses and consciousness perceive."[4] This idea that there is more reality in stability than in change, more truth in eternity than in the passing of time, became one of the most deeply engrained biases of Western thinking.

In the early twentieth century, Bergson would become the most famous philosopher in the world for reversing this trend, for being *the* thinker of change. In the first pages of his international bestseller *Creative Evolution*, he wrote: "For a conscious being, to exist is to change, to change is to mature, to mature is to go on endlessly creating oneself."[5]

BORN INTO AN UNSTABLE WORLD

In the late months of 1859, if you had walked down the rue Lamartine in Paris on a chilly autumn evening, you might have overheard Henri Bergson's father, Michal Bergson, gently playing one of his own compositions to his newborn son—perhaps a mazurka inspired by his old teacher Frédéric Chopin.[6]

The year 1859 had been a good one for the Bergson family. While Michal and his wife Kate had been expecting Henri, their second child and first son, Michal's music was being performed in Paris for the first time.[7] It seemed as though the universe was finally granting the composer some stability, something that had so far been lacking in his life.

Michal was born in 1818 in Poland. His parents, Berek and Tamerl Sonnenberg, had been wealthy Warsaw merchants and renowned benefactors of the Jewish Hasidic community.[8] Their status afforded them rights normally refused to Polish Jews at the time, such as choosing where they lived and how they dressed. After his father's death, however, only the eldest of Michal's brothers was permitted to retain these special rights. Michal and his other brother were forced to leave their home and never return. Everything changed for the young Michal, right down to his last name. With his father gone, he took the name Berksohn (son of Berek), and later Bergson.[9] He went to Dessau and Berlin to study music and later travelled across Europe, finding work where he could.

In Paris in the 1850s, he married an Englishwoman of Irish origins, Kate Levinson. She was also Jewish, twelve years his junior, and the daughter of a Yorkshire doctor.[10] In a charcoal portrait sketched by Mina Bergson, one of Henri's younger sisters, Kate exudes serene wisdom and kindness. She was a rational and calming presence in the Bergson household, contrasting with Michal's sometimes erratic behaviour. She was born in the north of England and spoke in English to all her children.[11] Thus, Henri and his siblings were raised bilingual. Although he did not grow up in Britain, Henri inherited traits stereotypically associated with the British character, like emotional restraint, dry humour, and almost pathological levels of self-deprecation.

Over the years, Kate provided vital support for her husband, caring for their three sons and four daughters through the ups (of which there were some) and downs (of which there were many) of his career. In 1859, Michal happened to be on an all-time career high. A Parisian venue had put on a production of his now-forgotten operetta *Qui va à la chasse perd sa place*, and for a time his music was being played every night.[12] One can imagine that when he gazed at baby Henri, his heart filled with hope, the kind that makes the future scintillate with infinite, smiling possibilities. Unfortunately, this did not last. After the reasonable success of Michal's operetta, the director of the Théâtre Lyrique commissioned another of his works, a full opera this time. But before opening night, the theatre went bankrupt and the project was abandoned.

In 1863, when Henri was four years old, the composer moved his growing family to Switzerland, where he took a professorship at the Geneva Conservatory. The apartment in which Henri learned to read was located on the auspiciously named boulevard des Philosophes.[13] Michal did not get along with his colleagues and did not take well to his new position. Perhaps these tensions stemmed from his difficult character (as the director seemed to think), perhaps they had to do with his being Jewish in an anti-Semitic milieu, or perhaps both were true. In any case, after four years of turmoil, Michal quit his job. With the arrival of each new child putting more financial strain on the family, they returned to Paris.

Michal's music never again occasioned the levels of enthusiasm generated by his 1859 operetta, and by Henri's tenth birthday he had abandoned all hope of a successful public-facing music career. Once again, the Bergsons relocated. This time they moved to Kate's home country, to a house in Shepherd's Bush, London. They hoped that there Michal would be able to find work stable enough to support the family.

Ten-year-old Henri was already showing great academic promise. From a very young age, he obtained multiple scholarships to help his parents finance his studies, first in Switzerland, with the help of the chief rabbi of Geneva, and later from the French government.[14] When his family decided to seek opportunities in London, Henri was all set to attend one of the best secondary schools in France, the Lycée Fontanes (later known as Lycée Condorcet), previously attended by the poet Paul Verlaine and later the novelist Marcel Proust. So Henri, still a small boy, found himself left behind, alone in Paris.

Henri's early life was marked by instability. In his first decade, he moved between countries several times, all the while watching his father wrestle with professional precariousness. At a very young age, he lost the warmth of a family home and grew up apart from his siblings, living instead with a boarding master. He was raised by institutions more so than by his parents. Like the organisms in Darwin's theory, the child Henri had to adapt and build resilience to survive.

At the same time, the world around him was becoming increasingly unpredictable. Left alone in Paris, young Henri found himself in the midst of one of the capital's most violent episodes. In July 1870, a few months before the boy's eleventh birthday, France went to war with Prussia and, within less than a year, was defeated. In the aftermath of this crushing humiliation and the fall of the Second French Empire, a revolutionary insurrection led by thousands of French national guardsmen, as well as by many women, took the capital. The demands of the Commune—the abolition of child labour, the separation of church and state, and fairer working conditions for men and women—and the Communards' capture of some of the government's cannons were met with bloody repression and tens of thousands of casualties. In retaliation against the French government's brutal attacks, the Communards destroyed the president's mansion and set fire to several of the city's landmarks. The Tuileries Palace burned for three days, and for weeks Paris was filled with fire, smoke, and death.

It is hard to imagine what a young child would have made of this upheaval.[15] In an interview he gave many years later, Bergson reflected on the significance of the changes he encountered during his childhood, focussing not on the violent events of the Commune but on the apparently trivial question of his school's name:

> I studied at Condorcet... at a time when the name of the school changed constantly according to political fluctuations. I personally saw these changes occur three times: Condorcet, Bonaparte, then Fontanes, and then back to the original name. As small schoolchildren, we were already meditating on the instability of human affairs.[16]

By the early 1880s, around the time of Darwin's death, Bergson became obsessed with change. It became clear to him that no one had taken the subject seriously enough, not even the leader of the evolutionists. Bergson decided that the trend towards immobility Zeno had set in motion two and a half millennia earlier needed to be reversed once and for all. Bergson's philosophy demanded that we invert what feels like the natural order of things, the habitual direction of our thinking, and step away from our obsession with eternity. In his view, the philosophers of the past had it the wrong way round: permanence is the illusion, and change is the most fundamental reality of all. Throughout his philosophical career, and in different works, Bergson circled back to one fundamental idea:

change is not something that happens on top of a fixed reality; change *is* reality.

Bergson's ideas would eventually make him the most famous person in the world, and for a while in the early twentieth century, his philosophical interpretation of biological evolution would eclipse even Darwinism. But back in 1859, the "City of Light" did not yet have its first electric streetlamps, and the various directions in which Henri Bergson's life would snowball—the weekly riots at the Collège de France, the Nobel Prize, the secret meetings with President Woodrow Wilson—were still impossible to predict.

CHAPTER 2

A "MERE" PHILOSOPHER

O ne afternoon, Adolphe Desboves, the maths teacher at the
Lycée Fontanes, was sitting in his classroom reviewing
his students' homework. Studying one of the papers covered in
unusually neat handwriting, he could not believe his eyes. One of
his teenage pupils had jotted down the solution to a mathematical problem that had remained unanswered for over two hundred
years.

PASCAL'S PROBLEM

At Fontanes, one of the best schools in Paris, Desboves had the
privilege of teaching some of the brightest young minds of his
day. He took comfort in the idea that, as an educator and amateur
researcher, he was fulfilling an important role that unremarkable
but highly competent people like himself had been carrying out for
centuries: the study and propagation of the ideas of geniuses.[1] And

if his efforts could inspire even one of his students to follow in the footsteps of greatness, then it would have all been worth it.

In his spare time, the teacher combed through the private papers of one of the greatest minds of the seventeenth century, Blaise Pascal, hoping to unearth new insights into his mathematical investigations. In the archives, he found an exchange between Pascal and another great French mathematician, Pierre de Fermat. In one of the letters, Pascal had sent Fermat a geometry problem that he claimed to have solved.[2] In the seventeenth century, mathematicians like Pascal often challenged each other to friendly but diabolically difficult mathematical duels. Victory came not to those who found the solution, but to those who managed to come up with a problem so complicated that no one else could solve it. Desboves's research had revealed that, in this instance, Pascal's illustrious friends had been left confounded. In other words, Pascal had won.

Desboves delighted in sharing with his students anything he thought might pique their curiosity. When he presented them with Pascal's problem, he had probably not expected any of his young pupils to succeed where even the great Fermat had failed. But within a few days, and with apparent ease, Henri Bergson, aged seventeen, solved it.

Bergson's solution went beyond what Pascal himself had imagined. Pascal had told Fermat that the problem could only be solved using ruler-and-compass construction. But the seventeen-year-old proved him wrong by making ingenious use of hyperbolas and parabolas. With geometry, Bergson never felt like he was solving a problem; he simply needed to pull on the problem's abstract thread for the solution to reveal itself. In his mind's eye, he could "see" the relationships between the properties of geometric figures as clearly as most people could see objects in space: "I only needed to follow a demonstration on the blackboard once to master it completely; I never had to memorise my lessons at home."[3]

Back then, Bergson was a boy of slight build with striking bright blue eyes. His thick chestnut hair veered towards red in some lights and was always divided neatly over his large, rounded fore-head.[4] He spoke softly and politely in a clear, steady voice. With his teachers, Bergson was modest and deferential, but his attitude never seemed affected, as though his good manners were not learned but simply second nature. Something about the boy's calm seriousness sometimes intimidated the other students. When he turned his attention within rather than outwards, as he often did, he took on an air of introspectiveness and wisdom beyond his years.

It was perhaps not surprising that he had matured faster than his classmates. From the age of ten he had lived several train and boat rides away from his family. His parents and siblings had remained together in London, while Henri lived at the Springer Institution, a Jewish boardinghouse in the north of Paris, with his scholarships covering the cost. There he received everything he needed on a material level to carry out his secondary studies, but the austere care of his boarding masters could replace neither the daily nourishment of parental affection nor the camaraderie of his siblings. Because he did not share daily life with his brothers and sisters, he grew up somewhat estranged from them all. In an essay he wrote as a student at the École normale supérieure, a few years after he left Fontanes, Bergson appeared to reflect back on the loneliness of his childhood. The essay was about the Renaissance writer Étienne de la Boétie, but he might as well have been writing about himself:

> Orphaned at an early age, without parents or friends, abandoned to a large college where he spent his childhood and youth in solitude, he had neither the advice of a father nor that wise governor of whom Montaigne speaks to guide him: all that he is, he owes only to himself: he made himself. This isolation tempered his character and matured him over time. Thrown into a world of strangers, the child learns, in this solitude, to take possession of himself, to reflect and reason about what he does, to shape himself.[5]

Despite his solitary childhood, Henri excelled at school. In 1874, his father proudly wrote to one of his friends that his eldest son was "awarded first place every year." The headmaster described him as "the most distinguished student at the Lycée Fontanes."[6] Bergson amassed an impressive collection of prizes, awarded by both the school (in Latin, Greek, history, and English) and the state. Each year, the Concours général rewarded the best secondary school students in France in each subject. Between 1875 and 1877, Bergson received awards in Latin and French and twice in mathematics. In 1878, one of his demonstrations was even deemed so elegant and original that it was published in an academic journal. The same year, Desboves published his research on Pascal and included his teenage pupil's findings.[7]

Desboves envisioned his star student taking the obvious path laid out in front of him—a shining mathematical career, which could open up a brilliant future. But nothing about this prospect excited Bergson. Unlike geometry problems, philosophical problems did not reveal their solutions to him in an instant; they were not threads that he simply had to unravel. When it came time to decide, in the summer of 1882, to his maths teacher's despair, Bergson chose philosophy.

BROADENING THE MIND

Bergson's decision apparently had very little to do with the philosophical education he had received at school. With a fondness steeped in light sarcasm, he remembered his philosophy teacher, Benjamin Aubé, as "a discreet, erudite, artistic man who was concerned with everything other than philosophy . . . who was happy to talk instead at length about archaeology and history, ancient medals and Christian martyrs."[8] Many years later, Bergson reflected that he was mostly grateful that his first introduction to philosophy had not left much of an imprint on his mind.[9] His teacher's indifference and unorthodox teaching methods had left Bergson with enough room to shape his own philosophical self.

Not committed to any particular school of thought, the young Bergson had been able to develop his own interests and lines of investigation. Outside the classroom, Bergson found thinkers who spoke to his mathematical and scientific inclinations. He read contemporary philosophers like Jules Lachelier, the philosopher and mathematician Antoine Augustin Cournot, and later Herbert Spencer, all of whom showed him a completely different side to philosophy that he had not experienced in school. These thinkers did not speculate in a vacuum but drew instead upon empirical data and scientific theories. Of Lachelier's philosophy, Bergson later wrote that it "gave him the impression of formulating problems the way the problems would formulate themselves."[10] It is not clear when Bergson first encountered these texts, or what role they played in his decision. But at some point they helped him realise that philosophy "could be something serious," something worth pursuing, and not the "merely oratorical amusement" he experienced in school.[11]

A few years after his fateful decision to study philosophy, Bergson started his first teaching job. He was asked to give a speech before an assembly of students and teachers during the traditional end-of-term awards ceremony. Barely out of school himself, the young man invited the students to reflect on the "severe disadvantages of what we call 'specialisation.'"[12] He argued that great men of science of the past, such as the illustrious Frenchmen Blaise Pascal, René Descartes, and Louis Pasteur, had made sure to consider problems from all sorts of different angles and perspectives, using methods from a variety of disciplines. But as the nineteenth century ended, this became more and more difficult to do. The accumulation of knowledge seemed to have reached a tipping point that fragmented the sciences into increasingly narrow fields and subfields and drove a wedge between science and philosophy. In his speech, Bergson warned that this fragmentation, this loss of big-picture, synthetic thinking, impoverished human knowledge as a whole. Bergson conceded that the impulse towards specialisation was a natural one, prompted by the "miserable discovery that the universe is greater than our mind; that life is short, education time-consuming and the truth infinite."[13] But he urged the students to resist this impulse, to put off committing to one specialised subject for as long as possible, and instead to broaden their minds as much as they could.

The young Bergson's aversion to specialisation had started at some point in the late 1870s, when he discovered that, unlike other academic disciplines, philosophy was not limited to a specific object but opened up an infinity of theoretical avenues. It represented an opportunity to encompass all areas of knowledge, to look at the biggest, most important problems, to embrace every aspect of reality in one sweeping gesture. By choosing philosophy, he would not have to abandon any of his interests but could keep them all under investigation. Conceivably, Bergson had also realised in that moment that mathematical problems, though fascinating, were too narrow for his intellectual ambitions. By specialising as a mathematician, he would be willingly cutting himself off from whole areas of human knowledge, whereas, as a philosopher, the entirety of human knowledge would be his subject matter.

A "BAD" SCIENTIST

Desboves was devastated when he found out about Bergson's decision. His young prodigy, the teenager who had bested his hero Pascal, was squandering his incredible mathematical gift, and for what? To pursue his interest in an inferior subject. The teacher wrote to the boy's parents, stating in no uncertain terms that their son was committing an irreparable folly. But Bergson did not budge, and his parents stood by his decision. The next time Desboves caught sight of Henri, he grumbled: "You could have been a mathematician; you will be a mere philosopher."[14] Of course, the teacher could not have foreseen that his student would in fact grow up to be anything but a "mere" philosopher.

Desboves's comment nevertheless ended up haunting Bergson. Throughout his career, Bergson would find himself repeatedly accused of being a philosopher who rejected science because he misunderstood it. As the American journalist Walter Lippmann wrote: "Though his thinking has been about biology, mathematics, and psychology, people call Bergson an artist."[15] Such misconceptions about him would stick. In a scathing article published in the *Monist* in 1912, the British philosopher and mathematician Bertrand Russell would paint Bergson as mathematically illiterate and accuse him of promoting "anti-intellectual philosophy" that led to the absurd view that "incapacity for mathematics is therefore a sign of grace." This view, Russell added sarcastically, was "fortunately a very common one."[16] In 1922, Albert Einstein dismissed Bergson's interpretation of relativity, claiming that the philosopher did not have a sufficient grasp of the physics at play.[17] The following year the evolutionary biologist Julian Huxley wrote that Bergson was a "good poet, but a bad scientist."[18]

Of all the misconceptions about his philosophy, the idea that Bergson was promoting an anti-science agenda was the one that exasperated him the most. Although he was critical of certain aspects of scientific thought, he did not reject science through and through. Just because he found limitations in the methods of science did not mean that his understanding of these methods was limited.

Bergson viewed science and metaphysics as two different but complementary forms of knowledge, each limited in its own way. The perspective on reality offered by science would always be relative to its own symbols. Metaphysics, on the other hand, could aspire to absolute knowledge but would never produce the practical results of science. Yet, if both forms of knowledge came together in a way that recognised their fundamental differences, they could progress by pushing each other forward.

This had not, however, always been Bergson's belief. In 1878, when he became a student at the prestigious École normale supérieure, he leaned towards the side of those who placed absolute faith in the power of science, thanks in large part to the English philosopher Herbert Spencer.

CHAPTER 3

"HE HAS NO SOUL"

A decade before the Eiffel Tower took its place looming impressively over Paris, another, much larger testament to French industrial prowess sat on the Champ de Mars. In 1878, Paris hosted the Exposition Universelle, the biggest exhibition the world had ever seen. For several months, a giant palace of steel and glass, stretching over half a mile, covered the whole park from the École militaire to the Seine. The structure had been erected in just eighteen months by France's best architects and engineers. Inside, visitors admired exhibits sampling the architecture of nearly every country in the world—though, less than a decade after the war against Prussia, Germanic culture was conspicuously absent—as well as a fine arts display and the "Galerie du travail," which presented state-of-the-art French industrial machines, clocks, and even live factory workers in action. Some of the world's newest and most intriguing devices were also on show, including Alexander Graham Bell's telephone and Thomas Edison's phonograph.[1] The Statue of Liberty's head, as big as a house, was paraded around the city, and a hot-air balloon could be seen intermittently floating above the Tuileries Garden. That year, for the first time, electric streetlights were installed along the avenue de l'Opéra. Descartes's seventeenth-century dream of humans becoming "like masters and possessors of nature" had materialised two hundred years later in the machines on display in the temporary palace and in the night sky of Paris. Anything seemed possible, and "progress" was the word on everyone's lips.

The exhibition was France's way of affirming its staying power and technological know-how after the humiliating defeat against Prussia and the chaos of the Commune uprising of 1871. Many French lawmakers felt that France's legitimacy as a powerful state needed to be grounded in an almost religious faith in science. The official philosophy of the new republic was "positivism," which at its core rested upon the ideal of progress. Humans would achieve their full potential only when they stopped asking "why?," the puerile question of children, theologians, and metaphysicians, and concentrated instead on the more serious and scientific question: "How?"

SPENCER IN PARIS

Among the exhibition's millions of visitors, one of the most famous was the English philosopher Herbert Spencer, who felt in his element amid the machines and shiny new inventions. "Progress" was as good as his middle name.

Spencer represents an anomaly in a long history of thinly veiled French hostility towards British culture. France has always celebrated its intellectuals with a keen sense of national pride, and as its longest-standing rival, Britain has produced many targets for French disparagement: over Shakespeare, the French prefer their own Racine, to Newton they oppose Descartes, and for at least a century after Darwin published the *Origin* they hailed the Frenchman Jean-Baptiste de Lamarck as the *true* father of evolution. But for Spencer the French made an exception. His popularity soared to the point that his views about education were cited in the French parliament in debates about secularisation.

Spencer's life trajectory did not resemble that of other highly regarded thinkers of his time. Born in Derby in 1820, he was mostly self-taught and carved out for himself a path that went from school-teacher to railway engineer, to editor of *The Economist*, to one of the most talked about and read thinkers in the world. Before the words "natural selection" had ever appeared in print, Spencer was already defending the idea of evolutionary change inspired by Charles Darwin's grandfather Erasmus Darwin and the French naturalist Lamarck. Spencer is now best remembered (when he is remembered at all) for "social Darwinism," his controversial application of evolutionary theory to moral affairs, but in his day he was celebrated for his sophisticated philosophical system, as detailed in the numerous volumes of his *Synthetic Philosophy*, which was translated into multiple languages and sold thousands of copies worldwide.[2]

In 1878, when Spencer crossed the Channel to visit the Exposition Universelle, the Englishman did his best to remain discreet in a city where he was so famous that his mere presence was sure to cause a commotion. But a few days before he was scheduled to return home, a group of his admirers found out that he was in the country and within hours they had organised a banquet in his honour. The soirée was held chez Brébant, the favourite restaurant of fashionable Parisian society. Politicians, scientists, philosophers, and journalists gathered to celebrate the philosopher of the moment. That night, no doubt aware that his hosts rarely extended this kind of warmth to his countrymen, Spencer raised his glass to *fraternité* between France and Britain. In his toast, he thanked his French audience for their favourable reception of his works and added: "Perhaps it is because the French have such a natural taste for universal ideas and methodical reasoning that they were so well disposed towards the organic whole that is my system of synthetic philosophy."[3]

Spencer's philosophy was "synthetic" precisely because it sought to synthesise, or unify, all of knowledge in one system. Spencer's project was to apply the rigour of science to the study of all levels of reality, from the atoms of physics to the bodies of organisms and the rational choices of moral beings. The unifying principle of Spencer's system was evolution. A few years before the publication of Darwin's *Origin*, Spencer had painted a picture of evolution that was not limited to living things. For him, evolution, or "progress," was woven into the very fabric of reality as a fundamental law of nature that operated throughout the universe at all levels, from cosmos to human society.

In the early twentieth century, Bergson would become an even more influential version of what Spencer had been from the 1860s to the 1890s: an international celebrity. Like Bergson, Spencer was compared to illustrious thinkers such as Aristotle and Kant. Regularly mentioned in newspapers, he was known to the general public outside of universities, and his books sold in huge numbers.

In the late 1870s, the teenage Bergson counted among Spencer's thousands of avid readers. What pleased Bergson the most about the English thinker was "the concrete nature of his philosophy, his desire to always base his philosophy on facts" and to incorporate scientific findings into his theories. Until Bergson's mid-twenties, Spencer remained "the predominant influence" on his mind.[4]

Decades later, Bergson's enemies, like Bertrand Russell, would unfairly dismiss him as an anti-intellectualist who misunderstood scientific theories, while his supporters would hail his philosophy as the answer to the excesses and arrogance of science and rationality. But back in 1878, the year Bergson left school and was admitted to the École normale supérieure in Paris, he could be counted among those who blindly placed their faith in the possibilities of science and progress.

A FRIENDLY RIVALRY

Of all the universities in the world, none have ever boasted a higher concentration of Nobel Prize laureates per capita than the École normale supérieure. When Bergson entered in 1878, the prize did not yet exist, but by 1927 his name too would appear on the long list of alumni Nobelists. To be admitted to the École was to be hand-picked as one of the elite, a student destined for scholarly greatness.

The idea of an "*école normale*" was originally born out of the ideals of the French Revolution. The aim had been to democratise and widen the reach of state-funded education by creating schools to train teachers. But in such tumultuous times, the project was quickly abandoned. A few decades later, the idea of state-sanctioned teachers had been resurrected by Napoleon Bonaparte, minus the egalitarian ideals. The new goal was to train an intellectual elite who would be in charge of educating the country's higher-ups at the university level. The school's selection process was brutal (and remains so to this day), with notoriously difficult entry exams requiring at least two years of preparation after the baccalaureate. Only a small number of students made it through the gruelling competition process each year. After a week of daylong written exams—which, in Bergson's case, included philosophy, Latin, Greek, and French, among others—the prospective students faced a jury who assessed their intellectual abilities as well as their charisma, charm, and wit.

Bergson achieved the (more than respectable) feat of finishing in third place. But when the results were posted on the school walls, his name did not appear on the official list. He had not yet been naturalised as a French citizen, and at the time of the results, as a Polish national (his father's nationality), he was listed separately.[5]

That year, the first place went to a confident boy, with a thick southern accent, called Jean Jaurès. He is remembered today as a remarkable orator who fearlessly led the French Section of the Workers' International in the early years of the twentieth century. After their student days, Bergson and Jaurès both achieved immense fame. In 1913, the same year Bergson caused the first-ever traffic jam on Broadway, Jaurès addressed a crowd of 150,000 antiwar protesters in the north of Paris.[6]

During their time at the École normale supérieure, Bergson and Jaurès emerged as the most remarkable students in their class, so naturally they were pitted against one another as rivals. Though from different backgrounds, the two boys shared similar experiences in their upbringing. They both had a mother they deeply admired and a father who struggled professionally and financially. Neither Bergson nor Jaurès had been socially predestined for the École. For most of Jaurès's childhood, spent on his father's farm in the south of France, his best prospect had been a career in postal administration. But at the age of sixteen, his impeccable Latin verses had impressed a school inspector, who convinced his parents to send him to Paris to prepare for the entry exam for the École. Bergson had also been "discovered" at a young age and ushered, like Jaurès, away from his family and onto the path taken by the French intellectual elite. Character was where the two young men differed. The anthropologist Lucien Lévy-Bruhl, who studied at the École at the same time as Bergson and Jaurès, remembered that

> the contrast between the two figures was striking: Jaurès, stocky, very outspoken, a born orator, improvised superb harangues, with his Southern accent resounding throughout the school. Bergson, slimmer, smaller, with a more delicate appearance, gave an impression of fine and reserved elegance. You should have seen these formidable dialecticians wrestling in a discussion of ideas. People would gather around to hear them. More than once, a simple, sharp and penetrating remark by Bergson counterbalanced Jaurès's broad developments.[7]

One day during their first year, the history professor Ernest Desjardins recounted the famous episode in Roman legal history in which the philosopher Cicero had defended a governor named Fonteius. Perhaps sensing that the topic was a potentially soporific one, the professor decided to liven things up. He had the students arrange the tables and chairs into a semicircle so that the class crudely resembled the layout of a Roman court. The professor then called up his two best students to the front of the class. Jaurès would go first. Acting as the prosecutor, he would have to make a case against Fonteius. Bergson would then come in as the defence, as Cicero had once done. The rest of the class would then vote "A" (*absolvo*) to release the accused, "C" (*condemno*) to find him guilty, or "N.L." (*non liquet*) if they were unable to decide.

Jaurès came to life immediately. He summoned compelling metaphors and seamlessly drew upon what he had already learned about the case, as well as on his extensive understanding of ancient history, to demand retribution against a man accused of embezzlement and other wrongdoings. Although Bergson represented the side of the historical winners of the trial, his task was far from easy. Nevertheless, according to one classmate who witnessed the scene, Bergson handled the assignment "in the most elegant and distinguished way, with arguments where subtlety and irony overlapped."[8]

Back in Cicero's day, the defendant had been acquitted. But in the classroom, both speakers were deemed equally impressive. The students voted unanimously that neither had outshone the other. It was as though they realised that the brilliance on display had been a collaboration, that the humiliation would be too great for the loser, and that the rivals' talents should be recognised together, as one.

BERGSON BEFORE BERGSON

The students' lives were heavily regulated. The young men lived on school premises and were allowed outside only twice a week. Bergson sometimes used this free time to visit the Louvre with Jaurès and others.[9] There were few opportunities for solitude at the École. Students ate, worked, and slept in communal spaces and were expected to be out of bed at six in the morning (five during the summer months) and back in their dormitory by nine. Many students found ways around these strict rules, hosting clandestine evening gatherings to study or to socialise, but Bergson was never among them. He was always in bed before the lights went out.

At a young age, Bergson impressed teachers and classmates with his oratorical skills and the sharpness and refinement of his mind.

But he also often struggled to connect with his peers. He kept himself at a distance, despite yearning for connection. At the end of the summer of 1880, one of his fellow students, Salomon Reinach, had complained about Bergson not responding to his letters. Bergson later confessed that he disliked writing letters and was "afraid of being a burden, of boring people."[10]

In the all-male environment of the École, Bergson did not display the solid bravado and competitive spirit typical of the high-achieving adolescent boys around him. This earned him the nickname "Miss," both a reference to his mother's Yorkshire heritage and a marker of his perceived delicateness. It would not be the last time Bergson found himself on the receiving end of misogynistic jeers. Several decades later, when his lecture theatre filled up with women, his adversaries painted him as an unserious "philosopher for ladies." But at the École the nickname "Miss" was not a dismissal of Bergson as a thinker, nor did Bergson resent it. It pointed at Bergson's difference, but it was also an expression of affection, albeit the kind of affection of which only emotionally stunted and overachieving teenage boys were capable.

Bergson mostly kept to himself. From a young age, what he had valued, and even craved, above anything else was time to himself to meditate in peace. Perhaps this desire sprang from spending the first years of his life either surrounded by noisy younger siblings or sharing accommodations with fellow students. At the École, Bergson found a way around the lack of privacy. Each year one student was chosen to assist the librarian. The position came with some extra work but also the rare luxury of access to a quiet, empty library at times when it was normally closed to students. When he worked alone after closing time, Bergson enjoyed spreading out all his books around him, so he only had to reach out and grab any volume he needed. But when the library was open he was forced to pile them all up in a corner of the desk. On one occasion he had so many books that he placed a few of them at his feet. One of his professors walking by reprimanded him: "Monsieur Bergson . . . surely this must be a painful sight for someone, like you, who has the soul of a librarian!" Without missing a beat, Bergson's classmates cheerfully interjected: "But, sir, he has no soul!"[11] This apparently callous pronouncement was not merely an immature response to everything they found odd about their friend; they were in fact referencing Bergson's distinctive philosophical inclinations.

At the École, Bergson found himself "completely imbued" with Spencer's "mechanistic theories," which he "endorsed almost unconditionally." He religiously read the British philosopher's *First Principles*, which described a universe in constant evolution governed by well-defined laws in which everything from atoms and organisms to societies constantly progressed towards ever-greater complexity. The young Bergson started forming the ambition of following in Spencer's footsteps and becoming a "philosopher of science": "I dreamed of extending his mechanistic explanation to the whole universe, only more accurately and more closely. For this purpose, I had at my disposal all the necessary resources which an assiduous practice of the sciences conferred upon me."[12] His ambitions soon surpassed those of his master. While Spencer did not completely reject the existence of a reality beyond the physical realm, Bergson was interested only in the laws of matter: "I was determined to subject my thought to reality, rather than subject reality to myself. I was a mechanist only because I valued rigour and precision above all else."[13]

Bergson's enthusiasm for Spencer put him at odds with the teachings of some of his professors and the philosophical climate of the school.[14] Around the time Bergson was born, one of the main philosophical movements in France had been spiritualism. In French, *spiritualisme* does not include the supernatural connotations of the English term "spiritualism" but rather designates a set of beliefs that gravitate around the idea that spirit, or consciousness, is a reality distinct from matter and the most important object of study. In the 1860s, however, these ideas were becoming less and less popular because, according to one of spiritualism's main exponents, the philosopher Paul Janet, they were being challenged and replaced by a school of French positivism inspired by Auguste Comte and championed by Ernest Renan and Hippolyte Taine. By the time Bergson was at the École, however, French spiritualism was undergoing a revival under the influence of Kantian transcendental idealism. At the time, Bergson believed that his Spencerism represented a bold stance in favour of positivism and mechanism and against what he viewed as the dominant Kantian position—a stance that earned him another nickname, "the anti-Kantian." Bergson explained: "There were, so to speak, two camps in the University: the much larger group who thought that Kant provided the definitive manner of posing philosophical questions, and the group who rallied behind Spencer's evolutionism. I was part of this second group."[15]

The third and final year at the École was the hardest because students had to prepare for another competitive exam, the *agrégation*. To this day, the *agrégation* determines who will become a state-employed secondary teacher and is a necessary stepping-stone for anyone aspiring to an academic career. Bergson remembered his preparation for the exam as a "nightmare."[16] With both Bergson and Jaurès taking the exam in philosophy, a new competition inevitably arose between the two rivals, one that their École friends thought would be the ultimate tiebreaker. It was obvious to their classmates that one of the two would end up in first place, and so they started taking bets.

On the day of the oral section of the exam, the *leçon*, in which candidates were expected to improvise cogent and compelling answers to deliberately obtuse philosophical problems, Jaurès won the popularity contest. The proceedings were open to the public, and Jaurès's reputation as a great orator was such that not only fellow École students but also students of the neighbouring Sorbonne came to listen. Though a few short decades later Bergson would also be drawing huge crowds, his *agrégation leçon* did not attract as much attention as his rival's. This lower turnout was probably a relief to the young man, who left his presentation feeling he had displeased the examiners. He had entered the auditorium confident that he could tackle any philosophical problem, but he had not been prepared for the question he pulled out of the hat: "What is the value of present-day psychology?" He could not conceal his disappointment:

> I made a full-throated charge not only against present-day psychology, but against psychology in general, to the great displeasure of one of the members of the jury who saw himself as something of a psychologist and had in fact been the one to choose this subject.... But Ravaisson, who was chairing the jury, was satisfied.[17]

Despite having to tackle a topic well outside his mechanistic comfort zone, Bergson scored very highly. But those who had bet that he would beat Jaurès were only partially right. At the top of the leaderboard was Paul Lesbazeilles, whose defeat of the two most brilliant students of his generation would remain his most memorable accomplishment. Bergson believed it was the misfortune of being handed a topic on the inferior subject of psychology that cost him first place. He came in second and Jaurès third. As in their mock Roman debate, neither of them won, and their rivalry remained intact.

In the years after he graduated from the École normale supérieure, Bergson changed his perspective on psychology and the relationship between science and philosophy. He no longer dreamed of becoming a Spencerian philosopher of science; in fact, he completely renounced what had recently been his mechanistic worldview. At some point in the 1880s Bergson the mechanist had a complete change of heart, and he got his soul back.

In 1889, over a decade after Spencer had attended a banquet in his honour chez Brébant, France celebrated the centenary of its revolution with another world's fair. The Eiffel Tower, an impressive new monument to France's advanced industrial savoir faire, now overlooked the Champ de Mars, but the optimism surrounding technological and scientific progress had started to wane. Feelings of disenchantment were rippling through the industrialised world.

What the positivists had hailed as progress was increasingly met with suspicion as many mourned what they saw as a loss of purpose, wonder, and mystery in a mechanically driven world.

Bergson, once a defender of Spencerian mechanism and scientism would become one of the main voices for those who felt that spirit was being ripped out of a world that was starting to feel cold and meaningless. Bergson was about to become a symbol of hope.

CHAPTER 4

TIME IS NOT SPACE

One day in the mid-1910s, as Bergson was gathering his things after lecturing to a packed room at the Collège de France, a woman from the audience marched up to him. Without so much as an introduction, she demanded that he distil the essence of his philosophy in a few words. Bergson was irritated, and not just by the woman's discourteous tone. In so many of his writings and lectures, he had returned to the idea that rigid concepts fail to convey the fluidity of reality. So to be put on the spot and forced to translate the nuances of his finespun developments into a punchy catchphrase felt nothing short of insulting. The woman did not seem to notice his annoyance and impatiently awaited his response.

With his characteristic dry wit disguised as smooth deference, Bergson replied, "I simply argue, Madam, that time is not space," and without another word, he stood up and left.[1]

These four words deliver a concise but accurate characterisation of *durée*, the central notion of Bergson's philosophy. It was the idea to which he returned in all of his works, and the idea that made him famous.

A few years before the woman asked her impertinent question, the American philosopher William James wrote a letter to Bergson, asking him to recall some of the "remarkable events of his career." Bergson did not usually have time to respond to such requests, but for James, a dear friend and an esteemed thinker, he made an exception. Bergson was already a best-selling author, but he opened his letter on a characteristically modest note: "I don't think there have been any objectively remarkable events in my career." But then he added:

> I cannot help but attach great importance to the change in my way of thinking which occurred ... following my graduation from the Ecole Normale.... Until then, I had remained convinced by mechanistic theories which I had been drawn to through Herbert Spencer. I endorsed his ideas almost unconditionally. I had decided to dedicate myself to the "philosophy of science" and I had therefore started, upon leaving the Ecole Normale, examining a few fundamental scientific notions. It was the analysis of the notion of time as it is understood by mechanics or physics that completely revolutionised all my ideas.... This was the starting point of a series of reflections which gradually led me to reject almost everything I had taken for granted up till then and to completely change my point of view.[2]

Bergson's change of heart had only become possible after a long, complicated, and partly unconscious maturation period during which a myriad of thoughts, questions, external influences, and doubts built upon one another, snowballing over time. His internal turmoil had started around 1881, when he moved away from Paris to take on his first teaching position.

TEACHING IN THE PROVINCES

In the first years after Bergson graduated from the École, not much happened on the philosophical front. His new hometown of Angers was described by religious authorities as "one of the most dangerous cities for the youth ... a place of pleasure rather than study."[3] There may have been some truth to this: as Bergson recalled it, there had been no room for thinking in this "prosperous" and "artistic" town because the music had been far too entrancing.[4] After a lifetime spent in close quarters with classmates, Bergson found himself living alone for the first time. Outside the confined and regimented existence of the École, he could do whatever he liked, and for the first couple of years his PhD thesis was low on his priority list.

Some of the liveliest parties Bergson attended were thrown by an octogenarian woman named Marie-Sophie Leroyer de Chantepie. She was seen as eccentric because she had chosen to devote her life not to a husband and family, but to literature, revolutionary politics, and charity work. Bergson reported back to his friend Reinach that "people dance the cancan at her place, and we have a lot of fun."[5]

Despite the joys of his newfound independence, and behind his apparent exuberance, Bergson still yearned for solitude. When he was not dancing, Bergson taught philosophy fourteen hours a week at the *lycée* for boys. In a letter to Reinach, he wrote: "My colleagues are friendly but clingy. Their intimacy frightens me. I don't know how to escape it. I almost regret not having been sent to St. Brieuc, where I would have probably been left alone."[6]

He spent a further three hours a week lecturing girls on "French literature, morality and pedagogy" in a run-down seminary room at the École supérieure de jeunes filles d'Angers. Decades later, women, who were de facto excluded from the Sorbonne, would hurry in droves to Bergson's Collège de France lectures. Here too, Bergson lectured before a female audience thirsty for knowledge they would otherwise have been denied. They were often accompanied by their suspicious *mamans*, who came to keep an eye on the young teacher who was only a few years older than their daughters.

Among Bergson's students was a teenage girl called Mathilde Alanic, who would grow up to author dozens of popular romance novels. Her words in an article titled "The Enchanter" reveal her keen eye for detail and capture the fascination the young girls felt for their teacher:

> Crossing the room with a quick, gliding pace, he reaches the podium, takes possession of the pulpit, empties the portfolio stuffed with books onto the green carpet, his eyelids still lowered. This attitude is perhaps due to a residual youthful shyness. An indecisive smile trembles on his narrow lips. Suddenly the eyes reveal themselves—a blue ray where sparks of joy dance about. The master lifts himself slightly for a courteous bow and begins: "Ladies." As soon as the clear, musical, flexible voice resounds, one can see the mobile physiognomy of the speaker at work, the gaze turning inwards, so to speak, to follow the fluctuations of his thoughts. It is a very young man who is speaking: is he 22? Despite the seductiveness of his delicate features, he imposes a respectful deference upon the young girls listening. He appears intangible and distant: he is all spirit.[7]

Bergson who was once said to have no soul had become "all spirit." During his student days, he would have scoffed at this characterisation of himself. There had been no room in his Spencerian mechanistic worldview for matters of spirit, which he had once viewed as false problems, metaphysical mirages. But outside the sheltered atmosphere of the École normale supérieure, he was exposed to a variety of ideas and questions. His philosophical environment was no longer limited to the very specific theoretical quarrels of the Parisian student elite and their professors. He discovered a whole world of theoretical allegiances beyond Spencer and Kant.

Bergson started to see value in lines of enquiry he had once dismissed, and soon he began doubting everything he had once held as certain. In the two years after leaving the École, he had developed an interest in psychology, the subject he had so publicly reviled during his *agrégation* oral exam. In 1883, he translated the English psychologist James Sully's *Illusions*, a psychological study of the phenomenon. That Bergson chose to publish the translation anonymously is perhaps a sign that he was not ready to fully affiliate himself with such matters. But the patience required to translate the three-hundred-page book showed a willingness to delve deep into a subject matter he had once deemed of no interest. Despite the many distractions of his new environment, Bergson's philosophical interests and theoretical loyalties were undergoing a profound shift: from an almost dogmatic mechanism, Bergson was shifting towards something different and, for him, new.

After two years in Angers, Bergson left "the opulent landscape of the Loire" for the "austere environment of Auvergne."[8] For the next five years, Bergson lived in Clermont-Ferrand, the birthplace of Blaise Pascal, whose mathematical challenge he had so easily solved as a teenager. Perhaps something in the ancient Auvergnat geological formations was conducive to deep philosophical meditation. It had been on top of the Puy de Dôme mountain, visible from inside the city, that Pascal had proved, against Descartes, the existence of a vacuum. And it was there that Bergson's thinking had "collected itself, gathered itself, concentrated" around new and powerful ideas that were slowly coming into focus.[9]

Perhaps more inspiring to Bergson than the town's intellectually charged history was its thriving intellectual scene. He developed a friendship with two of his colleagues at the Lycée Blaise Pascal, both maths teachers, Constantin and Boncenne. Over drawn-out lunch breaks in cosy Clermontois cafés, the three men dissected various issues. Constantin, who stood out by his slightly unkempt look and unconventional approach to most topics, gleefully pointed out anything he took to be a cliché or a paradox. Bergson admired the ease with which he unpacked the metaphysical implications of any mathematical problem. Boncenne, on the other hand, acted as a living, breathing press review, keeping them up to date with political issues.

Bergson also taught at the university of Clermont-Ferrand. On the day of his first lecture, he entered the amphitheatre to see dozens of young men, not much younger than himself, staring back at him. He could feel their eyes following his movements, and he suddenly realised he could not speak. His stage fright was such that he had to leave the room and regroup. A few minutes later, he reentered as though nothing had happened and began his lecture.[10]

Bergson developed a friendship with the university librarian, Albert Maire, who often hosted salon-type gatherings. On some special occasions, Maire's apartment served as the setting for strange experiments. One day Bergson and others witnessed what appeared to be hypnosis-induced telepathy. Bergson was very interested in such phenomena at the time. In 1886, he wrote to Frederic W. H. Myers, the founder of the Society for Psychical Research and the coiner of the term "telepathy," telling him that, though he had no proof, he strongly suspected the phenomenon was real.[11] Bergson had become fascinated with the powers of the mind, and his research was now leading him beyond what positive science usually permitted.

In February 1884, now accustomed to speaking before larger groups and less subject to stage fright, Bergson gave a public lecture at the university on the subject of laughter. His talk delighted the Clermontois audience, who, according to a local newspaper, "came in droves, attracted by the originality of the subject."[12] This foreshadowed the weekly riots at the Collège de France and the future success of Bergson's 1900 book on laughter, whose conclusions differed from those of the 1884 version but enchanted audiences just as much.

Bergson, who could sometimes be seen sporting a monocle, mingled with the most interesting scientists, writers, doctors, journalists, and notables of the region. He had at a young age developed a fierce sense of professional ambition and learned to perfect a social self to fit in with the people who could help him advance his career. He learned how to charm them with his dry wit and his eloquence.

His goal was to return to the capital, where prestigious careers were made. But he also resented these obligations and formalities. When he had first arrived in Clermont-Ferrand, he complained to his friend and former student Albert Kahn:

> I have been extremely busy with all sorts of unpleasant things, finding accommodation, visiting people, and so on. When one arrives in a new town, one is obliged to pay a visit to all the leading figures of the locality; after which one has to stay at home to receive theirs. I'll leave it up to you to imagine how much fun that is.[13]

In a sense, there were two Bergsons: the ambitious social Bergson who was fully familiar with the rules of the career game he was playing and well adapted to the customs of his socio-professional group, and a more reserved, meditative Bergson who preferred the quiet company of his own thoughts. In his PhD thesis, Bergson would distinguish between two selves: a superficial self "that conforms to social conventions and the pressures of language,"[14] and a more profound self, one accessed only at those rare times when the "ego lets itself live."[15]

Outside of his social persona, the young philosopher led a mostly solitary, almost ascetic existence. His only true indulgences were desserts.[16] He lived in modest lodgings and rose every day at six (a habit he had kept from his École days) to work on his thesis before teaching. He kept his body healthy by practicing horseback riding and fencing, impressing his teacher with the "subtlety" of his tactics, a quality that would later translate to his philosophical methodology.[17] He also took long solitary walks during which he meditated on the philosophical issues pressing on his mind.[18] Of these there were many.

BERGSON'S SURPRISE

We have no record of how Bergson arrived at *durée*, a complicated idea, arguably his most important one, that, for the benefit of an impertinent woman at the Collège de France, he would condense down to four words: "time is not space."[19] In Bergson's own telling, all of the doubts, questions, and ideas that had been bubbling up in the years since he left Paris had crystallised in Clermont-Ferrand in one fateful moment: "One day when I was explaining the sophisms of Zeno of Elea to my students on the blackboard, I began to see more clearly in which direction I should look."[20] We can imagine the lesson went something like this.

Outside the classroom window, thick, dark clouds in the distance gathered uninvitingly around the summits of extinct volcanoes. Bergson was still fairly inexperienced as a teacher, but his voice echoed impressively as he paced up and down the room. He spoke slowly, articulating carefully. His pauses were well timed, and he never repeated himself. He unfolded long improvised sentences with remarkable precision, as though reading from a script.

> In the paradox of Achilles and the tortoise, the fastest runner never catches up to his slower opponent. In fact, according to Zeno, neither Achilles nor the tortoise will ever make it past the finish line.

He turned to the blackboard and traced a long horizontal line.

> To run (or in the tortoise's case, crawl) the distance separating the starting line from the finish line, one first has to cover half that distance.

He drew an X at the line's midpoint, separating it into two halves, then continued:

> But before getting to the halfway point, one needs to cover a quarter of the total distance, and before that, one-eighth of the total distance, and before that, one-sixteenth, and so on . . .

He added several more Xs, dividing the line into shorter segments to represent a quarter, an eighth, and a sixteenth of its length.

... such that neither can ever finish the race. In fact, neither can really ever take the first step, and therefore motion is a mere illusion. Or so Zeno claims.

Bergson took a step back and gazed at the board. As he surveyed the crude diagram, a familiar feeling washed over him. An idea was germinating in his mind, pushing its way through the outer crust of his consciousness. Though not yet fully formed, the idea held the colouration and texture of something new and important. It contained the outlines of multiple new pathways suddenly opening up with the promise of all the exciting directions in which they might lead.

After class, Bergson continued to pull on the thread of his new idea. He exited the building, crossed the street, and walked among neat rows of trees, straight past his apartment building on boulevard Trudaine. Ten minutes later, he arrived at one of his favourite spots in Clermont-Ferrand, la Place d'Espagne. He knew that it had briefly been renamed Equality Square during the French Revolution, but later recovered its original name. Since then, it had remained an uneventful and quiet space he could visit when he needed to untie complicated theoretical knots. As he walked around the square, his new idea came more and more into focus. He could see vividly the gigantic, glaring flaw in Zeno's cleverly crafted puzzle. It was so obvious and simple that he could not believe no one else had spotted it yet.

As a student at the École normale supérieure in the late 1870s, Bergson had given himself what he believed to be a straightforward if ambitious mission: to follow in Herbert Spencer's footsteps and become a "philosopher of science." He hoped to consolidate, surpass even, what Spencer had achieved by synthesising the findings of the mechanical sciences into overarching philosophical principles. According to the young Bergson, Spencer had not taken his project far enough, and his grasp of physics was shaky in places. And so, once he had recovered slightly from the excitement of his new-found freedom outside of Paris, he launched into a methodical and meticulous review of the fundamental concepts of mechanics. This review was meant only as a preliminary step, the necessary ground-work upon which he would build his own philosophical system. But when he turned his attention to the scientific definitions of time, he remembered, "a surprise awaited me."[21]

Bergson was shocked to find that the scientific conception of time contained no temporality at all. It soon became clear to him that time as expressed by the letter t in the equations of mechanics in fact represented something quite different.

To theorise about time, scientists and mathematicians first had to stop it in its tracks. Something in constant flux, like time or move-ment, is difficult to talk about, to seize, and to measure. Scientific concepts and mathematical equations require stability. The many symbols and concepts we use to represent time and motion—minutes on a clock, pages on a calendar, points on a graph—are sophisticated ways of freezing time's continuous flow, of cutting it up into identical, solid units in order to measure them. These units are positioned one after the other like objects in space, like inter-changeable beads on a string.

This was particularly apparent in Zeno's paradoxes. The Greek philosopher had intended to prove that the notions of movement and change hold an inherent contradiction. But as Bergson began to understand in front of the blackboard, these contradictions do not arise from movement itself, but from the ways in which we represent and spatialise movement. All Zeno had been able to show was that movement could be represented as a line, and that this line could be divided into as many points as the mathematician wanted. This is a useful way of grasping motion by immobilising it, but it tells us little about how motion is experienced, or about the temporality of time.[22] In Zeno's picture, Achilles's majestic strides are chopped into tiny pieces, mutilated, until nothing is left. The hero stumbles and twitches, eternally convulsing on the spot.

But that is not how people really move. When we leap, run, or dance, when we throw our hands up in the air in frustration, there is no halfway point. There is only movement, fluid and whole.

Previously, Bergson had claimed that he had no interest in psychology, but his discovery forced him to take a closer look at the mind. In a doctor's waiting room an hour can feel like an eternity, but in the company of loved ones an hour seems to slip away before we even notice it was there. It is precisely this experience of the passing of time, the perceived difference in its quality, that is erased in the way science treats time.[23] And it was this qualitative temporality that Bergson called *durée*.

What would happen, Bergson asked, if, through some magic spell, the earth completed a rotation on its own axis every twelve hours instead of every twenty-four? What if every other natural phenomenon accelerated proportionally? To the elaborate equations the astrophysicist devises to predict celestial phenomena this major shift in tempo would make *no difference at all*.[24] The mathematical relations between the terms of the equations would not be impacted by the acceleration in pace; the proportions would remain intact. But for the astrophysicists themselves, for anyone who experiences temporality, a huge change would be perceived:

> Our consciousness would soon inform us of a shortening of the day if we had not experienced the usual amount of duration between sunrise and sunset. No doubt it would not measure this shortening, and perhaps it would not even perceive it immediately as a change of quantity; but it would realise in some way or another a decline in the usual storing up of experience, a change in the progress usually accomplished between sunrise and sunset.[25]

For Bergson, time is not an abstraction. It cannot be reduced to a symbolic notation. It is a real force acting in the world.[26]

During his Spencerian youth, Bergson had believed that science and philosophy are complementary because science is the form of knowledge that best grasps reality, while philosophy, in remaining at a certain degree of generality as it formulates all-embracing principles, is always somewhat removed from reality. But at some point in the early 1880s, through his careful analysis of the scientific notion of time, Bergson realised that it is science that provides a distorted picture of reality.

To measure or even talk about time and movement, science has to borrow from space, a category external to time, thus confusing time with space, movement with immobility. In realising that philosophy, if conducted correctly, is in a position to capture the true, mobile essence of reality, Bergson relegated science to a useful but general and disconnected form of knowledge. This change of heart—Bergson's discovery of *durée*—would resound throughout every theory he would ever formulate and forever transform Western thought.

CHAPTER 5

THE MELODY OF *DURÉE*

Bergson had spent his early childhood immersed in music, both his father's compositions and the piano lessons he received from a young age. To his chagrin, he soon had to give up his musical education to focus on more serious subjects, but for the rest of his life he placed music among the highest arts. His admirers often suggested that despite his incomplete musical training, he had remained a musician of a special kind.

In the early twentieth century, when crowds of hundreds, sometimes thousands, flocked to listen to Bergson speak, they left in a kind of trance, enchanted by the perfectly timed cadence of his speech, the melodic quality of his voice, and his masterful improvisations, which brought complex philosophical notions together in apparent harmony. The professor's words seemed to flow effortlessly, almost as though he sang rather than spoke them. One of his admirers, Raïssa Maritain, recalled: "His eloquent and precise language held us in suspense; distraction was impossible. Our attention did not wander for an instant; nothing could break the precious thread of the discourse. It was like perfect and beautiful music."[1] In his written works as well, Bergson's words resonated like musical instruments. The philosopher and poet André Joussain compared Bergson's writing "to a symphony. . . . It has a flexibility that gives it an inexhaustible power of suggestion and seems to provide it with an almost undefined existence."[2]

It was no accident that Bergson's philosophy had a different ring to it. Ever since he had started formulating his new ideas in Clermont-Ferrand, music had taken on a meaning that went far beyond aesthetic pleasure. Listening to music, he found, was one of the human experiences that best illuminated real time, or as he called it, *durée*.

As Bergson had discovered in Clermont-Ferrand, the representation of time in static symbols and rigid concepts inevitably produces a frozen, empty simulacra of temporality. Thus, by definition, *durée* is almost impossible to define. And so when the American philosopher and intellectual historian Arthur O. Lovejoy wrote to him some years later to ask for clarification about his elusive yet central notion of *durée*, Bergson's response was sympathetic: "The difficulties that you find in my description of *durée* no doubt stem from the fact that it is very difficult, if not impossible, to express in words something that goes against the very essence of language; I can merely attempt to suggest it."[3]

The "suggestion" Bergson was referring to was of the same kind Joussain had mentioned when he compared Bergson to a musician. Music is suggestive and evocative; in the words of the Bergson scholar Suzanne Guerlac, it "influences our attention" and "invites us into its rhythms."[4] Since Bergson could not express *durée* with concepts, or symbols, he had to subvert language itself to put his readers on the right track. Bergson's thought, Joussain writes, "emerges from the rhythm rather than from the words."[5] Like a musician using melody to conjure emotions, Bergson suggested his ideas through images that invited readers to plunge into their own intimate experience of themselves. This was where they could encounter *durée* most immediately.[6]

When we dive deep within our own mind, when we manage to do away with external interference, we find change. In 1907, Bergson wrote: "The first thing I observe is that I pass from one state to another. I am hot or cold, I am happy or sad, I work or do nothing. I look at what is around me or think about something else. . . . I change continuously."[7] However, continued Bergson, "even this does not say enough." The change we sense in ourselves is not as clear-cut as the words we use to describe it might suggest. The "change in question is far more radical than one might have at first believed."[8]

The very language we use tricks us into conceiving our existence as a string of separate events, with a clear-cut "before" and "after." It is hard to resist separating moments in our lived experience from one another and treating them as though each has a clear beginning and ending: "I was hungry, but then I ate and I was no longer hungry," or "I used to be a child, and now I am an adult." But those who are attentive to what is really happening in their inner life will see that the changes occurring within their consciousness are not merely transitions between otherwise stable states; rather, the states themselves are "being modified at each moment." In his letter to Lovejoy, Bergson wrote:

> *Durée* is indivisible; but this does not imply that past and present are simultaneous. On the contrary, *durée* is essentially succession: only it is a succession that does not imply a "before" and an "after" external to each other. You can get a clear sense of this by listening to a melody, letting yourself be lulled by the sound and leaving aside all visual images which, in spite of yourself, distort your auditory perception—visual images of musical notes written on paper, visual images of musical instruments being played and stopping, and so on.[9]

Music can be transcribed into a succession of symbols, juxta-
posed on a series of lines. Each symbol represents a pitch, a tempo,
a chord, and so on. This notation system is useful for recording and
sharing music, but it has little to do with how the music will be experienced. On a sheet of paper, a note can be erased or moved around;
two notes can be interchanged. But when we listen to music, we
do not hear a succession of separate units. The notes melt into one
another, forming an organic whole. We hear a melding, a swelling, a
unity, a harmony. If a single note were to be displaced, if two notes
were to be interchanged, our whole experience of the music would
be altered. It is the same, said Bergson, with our inner life:

> If... we remain absolutely within ourselves, we feel that some-
> thing expands without any divisions, just like the progression of a
> melody. Our inner life, from beginning to end, is thus an indivisi-
> ble continuity, and this is what I call our *durée*. It is succession, but
> succession without numerical and distinct multiplicity, that is, pure
> succession.[10]

No two moments in lived experience are interchangeable because
we are always growing, maturing, changing, even when this change
is difficult to perceive.

Picture yourself in an art gallery. After a few moments of perus-
ing the paintings, one of them stops you in your tracks and you
remain transfixed for a while. Although you are barely moving a
muscle, an important transformation is taking place within you. As
time passes, your appreciation of the painting expands and takes on
new, indescribable forms. The longer you stare at the painting the
more emotional textures, idea associations, and recollections swell
up inside of you, layered on top of your initial impression. Each
moment that passes is slightly different from the one immediately
before. Your impression of the painting evolves as you experience
it, and you will never recapture its initial impact. You could return
to the gallery the next day and experience what might appear to an

outside observer to be the same exact situation as before—looking at the same painting from the exact same vantage point, holding yourself in the exact same position—but the second time would not be the same as the first for the simple reason that you have lived it before.[11]

> *Durée* is the continuous progression of the past, gnawing into the future and swelling up as it advances. ... This survival of the past makes it impossible for a consciousness to pass through the same state twice. ... As such, our personality constantly sprouts, grows, and matures. Each of its moments is something new added onto what came before.[12]

Our personality is like a snowball rolling down a hill, accumulating experience as it grows. Time that passes is not lost but rather it is gained. We carry our whole history with us as we advance.

Rarely, however, do we think of our lived experience as a continuous flow. Instead, we pick out and separate what most draws our attention—a pang of jealousy, a sudden pain—and are blind to the fact that these detached moments are part of a continuously growing whole. "These events," writes Bergson in another musical analogy, "are the [drums] that ring out every now and again in the symphony. Our attention focuses on them because it finds them more interesting, but each one is carried along by the flowing mass of our whole psychological existence."[13]

We have formed the habit of solidifying our inner life into rigidly defined concepts. This is a useful and unavoidable way of making sense of the uninterrupted flux of the multiple interpenetrating qualitative states that constitute our consciousness. How else would we communicate our internal states than by using words that make them accessible to others? But in conforming too heavily to the practical requirements of social life and communication, we miss the symphony for the drums. We lose sight of our real, more profound self.

Of *durée*, his big discovery, of the upending of everything he had once held philosophically dear, Bergson told no one. It was not that worthy interlocutors had been lacking in Clermont-Ferrand. But something compelled him to protect the new ideas pushing up to the surface of his consciousness. Many years later, he told a friend: "I was careful not to reveal any of my ideas for fear of dispelling a kind of dream that was developing inside of me."[14] Perhaps the young Bergson had been all too aware of the paradoxical nature of his discovery, of an idea that was better "suggested," like the emotions evoked by musicians, rather than conceptualised. He knew that, as a philosopher, he could hardly do away with the constraints of language, and yet language was working against him. It was as though putting *durée* into words at such an early stage might somehow compromise it, as though the constraints of language could cost his ideas their novelty and flexibility, strip away their unique nuances, and squash them into ready-made boxes.

Durée was and would remain one of Bergson's most important ideas, but in the late 1880s he struggled to find a way to communicate a notion that was more easily experienced than described. In Clermont-Ferrand, he had spent a lot of time thinking about how to frame his discovery in his PhD thesis. He needed to make his understanding of time intelligible to others, in particular the philosophers who were in charge of evaluating his doctoral research. He hoped that, if he could present his ideas in such a way as to put his examiners on the track of their own experience of *durée*, "the veils would be lifted" and they would see for themselves what he meant. On the day of his PhD defence, however, he realised that he had been "quite mistaken."[15]

CHAPTER 6

THE ENCHANTER

Bergson had grown up in a world in which unbridled optimism about the potential of science seemed to open new avenues in every possible direction. Less than a year after Bergson was born, a German professor called Gustav Fechner tried to radically challenge the way we think about the mind. Despite thousands of years of thorny philosophical debates, the nature of the relationship between mind and body was not, he insisted, as mysterious as it had once seemed. In fact, it could be explained away by a simple mathematical formula.

In his 1860 *Elements of Psychophysics*, Fechner aimed to upgrade psychology from a branch of philosophy to an exact science. In line with other optimistic positivists of the nineteenth century, he hoped it would soon be possible to discover laws of the mind as mechanically regular and reliable as those regulating the movements of the planets. Fechner believed that our internal states can be experimented upon, quantified, and measured as precisely as any other natural phenomenon. Drawing on the works of his mentor, Ernst Heinrich Weber, Fechner used mathematics to describe the proportionality between events in the outside world and our internal perception. In short, he claimed to have come up with a way of quantifying and measuring the mind. Fechner's research represented just one example of the new ways in which, as Bergson was growing up, the methods of science had started to seep into domains where they had not previously dared to venture.

The grand philosophical projects of the century, like those of Comte and Spencer, rested upon the idea that scientific methods can be applied to social and ethical problems to steer humanity towards progress. In France, the anti-metaphysical and anti-religious sentiments of positivists had started seeping into public life and into the texts of lawmakers. Developments in physiology and chemistry fuelled hopes of reducing living phenomena to the regular, predictable laws of matter. In parallel, Darwinism presented the history and fate of all species as subject to chance in a cruel and meaningless environment. If something as mysterious as the origins of life could be made intelligible by the theory of evolution, then there appeared to be little that could escape the meticulous gaze of scientific understanding—not even, according to the positivist philosopher Hippolyte Taine, the human soul:

> Science . . . has gone beyond the visible and palpable world of stars, stones, and plants, to which it had been contemptuously confined— it now challenges the soul, armed with exact and piercing instruments whose precision and whose reach have proved themselves over three hundred years of experience.[1]

But in the second half of the nineteenth century, the optimism of those who were extending the reach of science outside of its habitual domains collided with a growing sense of unease. Some had started to perceive rickety foundations beneath the apparently unassailable façade of scientific progress. What if some questions did not allow for mathematically precise answers? What if not everything could be predicted? What if some aspects of reality were not meant to be quantified at all?

A "BANKRUPTCY OF HOPE"

As Bergson was putting the final touches on his PhD thesis, artists, intellectuals, and even scientists were voicing increasingly loud concerns about what they viewed as the excesses of technology and science. The French novelist and literary critic Paul Bourget spoke of a "bankruptcy of hope" caused by science's empty promise "to unriddle the problems of which revelation offered a solution" that was nothing less than "a war against the spirit."[2] Excessive faith in science and technology was seen as ridding the world of wonder, beauty, and mystery, leaving little room, it seemed, for religious beliefs or the notion of free will. For example, many early twentieth-century thinkers, including some biologists, saw Darwinism as a pessimistic depiction of nature that needed to be combatted. As the American poet and essayist Charles Leonard Moore wrote:

> For fifty years or more, the Gorgon head of Evolution has turned the heart and soul of man to stone. Caught in a mechanical determinism, mankind has lost its freedom—the fluidity which before yielded to all impulses of religion, poetry, and art. If it tried to escape in philosophy, it found that philosophy was fixed in an iron system of concepts which opened only on nescience and nihilism.[3]

It felt as though all sense of purpose and moral bearings was being lost in an increasingly mechanised universe. The world needed an antidote to what the German sociologist Max Weber called, in the early twentieth century, the "disenchantment" of the universe.

These sentiments flowed into the literary and artistic movements of the time. They fed the symbolist poetry of Stéphane Mallarmé, who wrote in 1897: "Poetry is the expression, through human language reduced to its essential rhythm, of the mysterious meanings behind different facets of existence."[4] The will to reenchant the world was also expressed in late nineteenth- and early twentieth-century attempts to modernise the Catholic Church and in a widespread revival of occult and spiritualist movements. In 1888, Bergson's own sister, Moina Mathers, née Mina Bergson, became the first female initiate of a newly founded secret society, the Hermetic Order of the Golden Dawn. Her paintings adorned the society's Tarot cards and temples, and she performed magic rituals and perfected her psychic visions. Soon enough, the Egyptian goddess Isis was appearing to her in dreams to deliver metaphysical messages. This occult revival translated a desire to find meaning beyond, in the words of the poet Anatole France, "the depressing majesty of physical laws."[5] Therefore, said France, "we seek after mystery. . . . We throw ourselves wholeheartedly into psychical research, the last refuge of the marvellous, which astronomy, chemistry, and physiology have driven from their domain."[6]

In the title of his 1889 article, France asked: "Why are we sad?" The culprit, he said, was science: "We have eaten the fruit of the tree of science and the taste of ashes remains in our mouths." He concluded with a plea for help: "Who will bring us new faith and new hope?"[7] The same year, Bergson shared the manuscript of his PhD thesis, "Essai sur les données immédiates de la conscience" (Time and Free Will), and his idea of *durée*, with the world.

TIME AND FREE WILL

Bergson's public PhD defence, a solemn but not humourless four-hour affair, took place on December 27, 1889.[8] In attendance were several of Bergson's high school students, who had come to cheer on their favourite teacher.[9] The examiners, Paul Janet, Émile Boutroux, and Charles Waddington, represented the *crème de la crème* of French philosophy.

The proceedings opened with a discussion of Bergson's secondary thesis, written in Latin, a requirement for all prospective doctors at the time. Bergson had chosen to examine why Aristotle, in book 5 of his *Physics*, had used the rather restrictive concept of "place" instead of the more encompassing concept of space. These reflections had no doubt coincided with Bergson's research into the different objections addressed to Zeno's paradoxes over the centuries, which included Aristotle's. Bergson was lauded for his flawless mastery of Latin and the clarity of his argument. According to a report published in the *Revue de l'enseignement secondaire et de l'enseignement supérieur*, "the Faculty declared that this [was] one of the best theses in philosophy that [had] ever been presented to them."[10] Once the topic had been sufficiently dissected, one of the examiners joked that it was time to "*discedere de loco*" ("leave [this] place").[11] They could now move on to Bergson's main thesis.

When writing *Time and Free Will*, Bergson had to contend not only with the inherent limitations of language and the conceptual slipperiness of *durée* but also the unwritten theoretical requirements of late nineteenth-century French academia. And so his presentation of his most important idea ended up sandwiched between two of the big debates of the day. First, as he wrote to Charles Du Bos, "Fechner and psychophysics were on the agenda, and I hoped that from an analysis of Fechner, there was a chance my examiners would be able to follow and understand me."[12] According to Bergson, psychophysics belonged to a long tradition of theories that inserted space into the nonspatial and quantity into the unquantifiable. Fechner's thinking perfectly embodied the confusion that Bergson had started seeing everywhere between temporal and spatialised realities.

Fechner posited that feelings, perceptions, and sensations could be measured, that our internal life could be explained away in physical terms. In our everyday life, when we talk about the intensity of our feelings, sensations, and emotions, we use the language of physical measurement and quantity. We speak of immense joy, or we say that the pain in our arm is greater than the pain in our leg. Whether we realise it or not, we treat our internal experiences as quantifiable, as though they can be measured against one another. This is spatial thinking.

In space, objects can be placed next to one another. The larger object can contain the smaller one. But mental states do not occupy physical space; they cannot be contained. As Guerlac writes, inner states do not have the same boundaries as external things, but rather "overflow into one another, interpenetrate, even as they succeed one another."[13] Against Fechner, and through detailed analysis of the existing literature, Bergson argued that there is an essential difference, a difference in kind, a complete incommensurability between quantity (something's measurability) and quality (how something feels to us).[14] In other words, for Bergson, despite what Fechner argued, there was no clear relation between how our feelings feel and the measurement of their external cause.

Another strategy Bergson employed to ground *durée* for his examiners was to situate his new ideas within the old philosophical debate concerning freedom and in particular free will—yet another sacred domain into which science had inserted itself. In the early nineteenth century, a French polymath called Pierre-Simon Laplace had imagined a "demon" whose intelligence was vastly superior to ours. Such an intelligence, he said, would be able to know the exact position of all the atoms in the universe at a given time and would therefore be able to determine all their future positions. In other words, "for such an intellect nothing would be uncertain and the future just like the past would be present before its eyes."[15] In a fully Laplacian world, no atom, molecule, event, or even human thought would escape universal determinism. There would be no place for true change or freedom in a universe where everything was determined in advance.

Around the time Bergson defended his PhD thesis, the theoretical fabric of determinism was starting to break down. In the words of the historian Milič Čapek, "the first rumblings under the foundations of classical physics were discernible," from Ludwig Boltzmann's statistical mechanics in the 1870s to the study of spectral lines in the 1880s that would culminate in Niels Bohr's atom model

(1913) and the birth of quantum mechanics.[16] *Durée* represented the antithesis of predictability, yet as Bergson was writing his PhD thesis, many were still clinging to the reassuring certainty of a predictable deterministic picture.[17]

In *Time and Free Will*, Bergson used his discovery of *durée* to argue against determinism and for the reality of free will. For Bergson, mental phenomena cannot be reduced to the laws of physics, no matter how hard the psychophysicists try, and the spontaneity of voluntary actions cannot be boiled down to the predictable effects of clearly defined causes. Prediction relies on repetition and the "projection of past information forward," but in consciousness no two moments are ever the same: "The same cause never presents itself twice."[18] While Bergson argued for the reality of free will, he conceded that true acts of freedom are rare:

> Most of the time, we live outside ourselves; we only perceive the colourless phantom of ourselves.... We live for the external world rather than for ourselves. We speak rather than think; we are acted upon rather than acting ourselves. To act freely is to retake possession of oneself.... It is to place oneself back in pure duration.[19]

In this regard, *durée* invites us to plunge beneath the outer crust of our superficial social self, beneath the rehashed ideas and clichés of everyday life, to discover, in the unique "endless flowing" of our inner life, the "creation of self by the self"—our freedom.[20]

Bergson had hoped that his discussion of the illusions of psychophysics and his new definition of freedom would place his examiners in the right mindset to receive what he viewed as the central and most original idea of his thesis: *durée*. But his plan to situate *durée* within the scholarly preoccupations of the moment had worked too well. It was these contemporary debates, especially the one about psychophysics, that his examiners wanted to talk about.

Bergson was unanimously declared a *doctor ès lettres*, the best possible outcome, and covered in praise. In a sense, the examination had gone better than he could have ever hoped. But he left feeling "furious."[21] Not one of his examiners had even mentioned *durée*. His disruptive idea had gone completely unnoticed.

Bergson's first book was published in a limited run and was noticed in Parisian philosophical circles, but it did not yet propel him to international recognition. It would take a while for Bergson's examiners, and the world, to catch up to the Bergsonian revolution.

One thing the examiners did pick up on was Bergson's remarkable panache as a speaker. In the report on Bergson's public PhD defence, the young philosopher had been credited with "handling public speaking marvellously, with incomparable ease, elegance, confidence and propriety."[22] In the decades that followed, all of those who heard Bergson lecture, even those who did not particularly agree with him, left with a sense of wonderment. Many reported that his voice was so melodious, and the flow of his words so smooth, that he cast a spell on his listeners, many of whom remained entranced long after the lecture had ended. As early as his Clermont-Ferrand days, his teenage student Mathilde Alanic and her friends had called the young professor an "enchanter." Later, as his fame grew, so did his magical powers in the eyes of his followers. One of his students, the poet Léon-Paul Fargue, remembered that "we felt he was reinventing everything, and that he would go even further. He gently fascinated us with that charm, that look, that forehead. . . . He 'captured' us with a kind of mystical jiu-jitsu."[23]

For some admirers, Bergson's written words were enough to evoke the philosopher's mystical charm. In a lecture on Bergson, William James declared: "If anything can make hard things easy to follow, it is a style like Bergson's. . . . The lucidity of Bergson's way of putting things is what all readers are first struck by. It seduces you and bribes you in advance to become his disciple. It is a miracle, and he is a real magician."[24] Bergson, who had once been accused of having no soul by his classmates, was now bringing the soul back into public discourse, becoming the re-enchanter the world so desperately needed.

CHAPTER 7

MEMORY MATTERS

When Bergson got married on January 7, 1892, the best man was a gangly twenty-one-year-old with heavy eyelids and a pencil moustache. Marcel Proust, still a student, was the second cousin of the bride, Louise Neuburger.

Two decades later, while Bergson had reached almost unfathomable levels of notoriety, Proust was still making his way towards literary icon status. In the final months of 1913, the novelist was worried. He had just suffered the sting of several rejections and had to resort to self-publishing the first volume of one of the twentieth century's most imposing literary monuments, *In Search of Lost Time*. Throughout the hundreds of pages of melancholic recollections, sometimes involuntarily summoned by the flavour of small cakes, Proust had developed sophisticated insights into the inner workings of mind and memory. He was convinced that his novel offered a creative new perspective on the matter of memory. But based on the first reviews, he felt that the originality of his work had been overlooked.

The topic was a trendy one. Since the mid-nineteenth century, the ability to recollect, both collectively and individually, had been at the centre of scientific and philosophical interrogations. In an age of accelerating progress in which the past seemed to slip out of reach more rapidly than ever before, at a time when biologists were debating the origins of species, the question of how the past persists into the present was at the forefront of many conversations. And in the early twentieth century, much to Proust's dismay, the notion of memory had become indissociable from his culturally ubiquitous cousin-in-law, Henri Bergson.

In an interview Proust gave to the newspaper *Le Temps*, he tried to set the record straight. He stated that he would have "no shame" in calling his work "Bergsonian," since it was quite natural for literature "to attach itself . . . to the reigning philosophy" of the time. But, he added, "this would not be true."[1]

Back in 1892, neither groom nor groomsman could have imagined how their futures would become intertwined, not only as extended family members but as emblematic thinkers of memory and symbols of their time.

LOUISE BERGSON

As is often the case with the wives of famous men, we know little about Louise Bergson. When she married the man who would become the most talked about philosopher in the world, she was nineteen, barely older than his secondary school students. Of Louise's almost five decades of marriage, her husband's previous biographers have limned only a superficial portrait. Louise Neuburger was born into a Parisian Jewish family. Her father worked for Rothschild, and her mother was the cousin of Jeanne Weil, another woman remembered for being related to a famous man, her son Marcel Proust.

In her role as a wife, Louise has been depicted as a woman of almost saintlike devotion and as even-tempered, graceful, and well mannered in all circumstances. She knew that high virtue was a quality her husband revered, especially in the women in his life. He had once described his mother Kate as "a woman of superior intelligence, a religious soul in the highest sense of the word whose kindness, devotion, serenity—I might even say saintliness—were admired by all who knew her."[2] To Louise's embarrassment, her husband affectionately boasted of her near-absolute faultlessness, once reporting that the only time her parents had ever had to discipline her as a child had been when she had refused to eat her cauliflower.[3]

Louise's main duty in her day-to-day life was to protect her increasingly fatigued husband against the unceasing noises and disturbances of the outside world. She worked tirelessly to provide him with the peaceful environment he needed to think. She carried out the administrative, epistolary, and emotional labour without which the philosopher could not have conducted his research. When, in the 1920s, a telephone was installed in the Bergsons' home, Louise shared their number with no one, not even their closest friends. She knew that the invasive ringing mechanism would become an unbearable nuisance to her husband, who was by then chronically exhausted and had always been allergic to such disturbances.

At the time, telephonic communications were mediated through a central telephonic exchange where human operators, mostly women, manually connected callers by inserting the correct plugs into the corresponding jacks on a huge switchboard. In the 1890s, when Bergson was deep in neurological literature as he researched his book on memory, this mechanism had provided him with an image that helped him understand the role of the brain.

DISPLACING MEMORY

Earlier in the nineteenth century, the physician Paul Broca had wanted not only to understand how memory functions but also to find out *where* memories go. Broca was inspired by the (now long debunked) racist and pseudoscientific theory of phrenology, which correlated measurements of the skull with intellectual ability and other mental traits. Phrenologists believed that various mental faculties could be precisely located in areas of the brain.

Broca took an interest in patients who, through various kinds of accidents, had lost the ability to speak, a condition known as aphasia. Through autopsies of these patients' bodies, Broca was able to link their linguistic memory loss with specific lesions in the brain. He believed that this constituted proof that memories are stored in well-defined sections of the brain. The decades that followed saw the publication of hundreds of papers on cerebral localisation, based on the common assumption that mapping the brain would help us better understand and locate memory.

In 1896, Bergson published *Matter and Memory*, his contribution to the memory debate. In preparation for his second book, Bergson spent half a decade reading all the available literature on psychopathology, in particular research about aphasia. As he condensed this huge mass of information into philosophical lines of enquiry, he became convinced that, despite what the data on aphasia appeared to show, it made no sense to think of memories as "located," or "stored." Bergson wanted to change the way we think about the brain and about memory.

In *Matter and Memory*, Bergson opened a can of worms as old as Western philosophy: How does the relationship between mind and matter, between consciousness and the world, between what we perceive and what is perceived, work? On the "realist" extreme of the debate, the outside world impresses itself upon our passive minds; on the "idealist" side, it is our mind that impresses itself upon the outside world, a world that we cannot know beyond our representations of it. Which one is the correct theory? Neither and both, said Bergson. Both sides, he argued, carry with them insurmountable difficulties because they make the same mistake. They posit that we perceive in order to collect data and reason about the world— in other words, to know. In *Matter and Memory*, Bergson made a radical move by arguing that we do not perceive in order to know, but that we perceive in order to act.

For Bergson, to perceive is essentially to select what is most useful to our present situation out of the overwhelming breadth of what is perceptible. In other words, we do not perceive all there is to be perceived, but only what is relevant to our needs. For example, said Bergson, "It is grass *in general* which attracts the herbivorous animal."[4] The cow that eats grass to survive does not need to distinguish between the differences in each blade of grass; in fact, to do so would probably be detrimental to its survival. Our needs, says Bergson, are "so many search-lights which, directed upon the continuity of sensible qualities, single out in it distinct bodies."[5] Therefore, to return to the realist/idealist debate, what we perceive does not exist solely in our minds, but neither are our perceptions impressed upon us directly by the external world. In other words, external objects exist outside of what I perceive of them, and at the same time I actively participate in producing my perception of them. When we perceive the external world, we select the contours of the objects that best serve our needs.[6]

Bergson stresses that the way our perception works is the result of an evolutionary history:

> In the vision [my senses] furnish me of myself and of things, the differences that are useless to man are obliterated, the resemblances that are useful to him are emphasised, ways are traced out for me in advance along which my activity is to travel. These ways are the ways which all mankind has trod before me.[7]

In unicellular life-forms, with rudimentary nervous systems, there is no separation between perception and action: in such organisms contact with an external object elicits an immediate reflex reaction. In more complex organisms, perceptions are delayed through a central nervous system divided between nerves and brain. Because of this delay in reactivity, these organisms do not have to act in a predetermined, immediate way; they can link present stimuli to past experiences and make choices based on their experience. The separation between nerves and brain allows for action to take place in a "zone of indetermination," with often unpredictable outcomes.[8] The more differentiated the nervous system, the greater the zone of indetermination, and the greater the scope of the organism's choice, creativity, and freedom.

For Bergson, the human brain is nothing more than a sophisticated development within this evolutionary history. Contrary to the claims of Broca and others, Bergson argued that our brains neither "produce" representations of the world nor "store" memories. Rather, in Guerlac's words, the brain is "a centre of action": it "either puts communication through immediately, in which case the result is an automatic action, or it puts the communication on hold, in which case a voluntary action can follow."[9] The brain, wrote Bergson, can therefore be compared to a "central telephonic switchboard": "Its role is to connect communications or put them on hold. It adds nothing to what it receives.... In other words, the brain appears to us to be an instrument of analysis with respect to incoming movements and an instrument of selection in relation to movements ... performed. But in one case as in the other, its role is limited to that of transmitting and dividing movement."[10]

The fact that brain lesions may cause aphasia, as studied by people like Broca, does not prove, said Bergson, that the memories are "stored" in the brain. It simply shows that the mechanism permitting their transmission is severed. According to Bergson, as temporal phenomena, memories cannot be located in space.

In *Matter and Memory*, Bergson elevated the status of memories. They are not, as some psychologists and philosophers suggested, simply copies or dimmed perceptions, but the foundation of our personality, of our consciousness: "What are we, and what is our *character*, if not the condensation of the history that we have lived since our birth?"[11] The very possibility of choice and freedom requires our ability to recollect. We cannot make decisions about the future without having access to the most relevant and useful memories that can inform those decisions:

It may be said that we have no grasp of the future without an equal and corresponding outlook over the past, that the onrush of our activity makes a void behind it into which memories flow, and that memory is thus the reverberation, in the sphere of consciousness, of the indetermination of our will.[12]

TWO KINDS OF MEMORY

One evening in the early 1910s, the American writer Edith Wharton happened to sit next to Bergson at a dinner party. She turned to her neighbour, *the* thinker of time and memory (Proust was not yet a household name), hoping to gain some insights. In her autobiography, she remembered:

I confided to him my distress and perplexity over the odd holes in my memory. How was it, I asked, that I could remember, with exasperating accuracy, the most useless and insignificant things, such as the address of every one I knew, and the author of the libretto of every opera I had ever heard since the age of eighteen while, when it came to poetry, my chiefest passion and my greatest joy, my verbal memory failed me completely, and I heard only the inner cadences, and could hardly ever fill it out with the right words?

I had the impression, before I ended, that my problem did not greatly interest my eminent neighbour; and his reply was distinctly disappointing. *"Mais c'est précisément parce que vous etes éblouie"* ("It's just because you are dazzled"), he answered quietly, turning to examine the dish which was being handed to him, and making no effort to pursue the subject.[13]

Wharton's experience illustrates a distinction that Bergson makes in *Matter and Memory* between two forms of memory. On the one hand, there is "habit informed by memory," or "motor memory."[14] This is the kind of memory that is acquired through repetition and ends up inhabiting our body—for instance, when we repeat a gesture often enough that, without giving it a thought, our muscles seem to retain its steps, or when we repeat a text often enough that we come to know it by heart. On the other hand, as Guerlac summarises, there is the kind of memory "that spontaneously retains the past in the form of images, images that carry the mark of the unique moment in which they were lived."[15] The first kind of memory is "impersonal."[16] It is "habit interpreted by memory rather than memory itself."[17] It differs entirely from the second kind of memory, which retains the uniqueness of each step that was necessary to acquire a new skill or learn something by heart. This form of memory is the opposite of habit in that it can never be repeated.

Most of the time, we are turned towards practical things, towards action, and so what Bergson calls our "attention to life" is at its highest. In everyday life, we rely on our brain to get rid of the background noise of our own consciousness and to only facilitate the passage of the memories that are useful to our actions: "The cerebral mechanism is designed precisely so as to repress almost all of the past into the unconscious and to introduce into consciousness only that which is of a nature as to clarify the present situation, to aid the action that is being prepared."[18] Therefore, only a tiny portion of our past, the part that interests our present situation, is available to us. These are the memories that the brain's central telephonic exchange calls forward. But in reality, wrote Bergson,

> the past preserves itself automatically. It likely follows us around, at each instant, in its entirety. All that we have sensed, thought, and desired since our earliest childhood is there, leaning over the present that is about to join up with it, pressing against the door of consciousness that would prefer to leave it outside.[19]

"This is the sense," said Bergson, "in which we are said to have an *unconscious memory*."[20]

There are situations in which our "attention to life" relaxes itself, for instance, when we are daydreaming. In these cases, memories that have been buried more deeply and are not directly relevant to our everyday actions might resurface. When we are asleep, our attention to life relaxes completely. Awake, we are in a state of "uninterrupted tension" in which perceptions, with some effort, attach themselves to mostly relevant memory images. But when we are asleep, any memory taken from the entirety of our past can attach itself to any external stimulus that happens to make its way into our sleeping state, in any combination and in any order.

When Bergson told Edith Wharton that she could not memorise poetry because she was dazzled by it, he no doubt meant that she was too distracted, almost hypnotised by the beauty of the verses, to call in the kind of habit-forming memory that necessitates the most impersonal and practical attitude. Poetry left her in a dreamlike state that was antithetical to the tension required to be fully attentive to life. In her autobiography, Wharton reflected:

> It was only afterward that I saw he had really said all there was to say: that the gift of precision in ecstasy (the best definition I can find for the highest poetry) is probably almost as rare in the appreciator as in the creator, and that my years of intellectual solitude had made me so super-sensitive to the joys of great talk that precise recording was impossible to me.[21]

PEACE AND QUIET

Proust and Bergson, cousins by marriage, shared a mutual respect but were never truly close. Bergson said that they rarely saw each other because Proust only came out at night. When they did see each other, they bonded over their insomnia. The writer and critic

Edmond Jaloux remembered overhearing a conversation between the two men:

> Both of them studied and analysed their nocturnal afflictions, the uselessness of drugs, and of the procedures generally employed to alleviate them. They had both arrived at the same conclusion; never is the brain more lucid, thought purer, more transparent than in those dark hours of the dark night or at the first stirrings of the morning.[22]

One evening, Proust appeared on Bergson's doorstep holding a small wooden box containing a pair of earplugs. Bergson tried them but disliked the total absence of sound as much as he disliked being disturbed by noise, and he never used them.

The only noise Henri had ever tolerated were the powerful outbursts of his daughter Jeanne. The Bergsons had welcomed her into the world the year after they were wed, and when the child was still small, she liked to erupt into her father's study unannounced, creating the kind of commotion that only toddlers are capable of. In her eyes, there was no philosopher deep in metaphysical meditation, there was only *papa*.

Soon after Jeanne's birth, the Bergsons had realised that their daughter could not hear them. A family friend had recommended a lip-reading technique to teach the little girl to speak, but her parents worried that she seemed "too distracted" to learn anything. In time, she proved to be an extremely talented artist and an ally to her mother in the war against noise. Family friend Jean Guitton later said of Jeanne, "She helped me understand the unspoken law, which I have observed so often in my life, that the suffering, the pain or the brokenness of a loving woman, of a loving daughter, enter as ingredients in the creative work of a man."[23]

Until Henri's death, the three Bergsons lived together, enveloped in the invisible bonds of love and affection that do not need to be said to be felt. Bergson never spoke of their private affairs in public, which meant that not many people realised how greatly his domestic life contrasted with his social and professorial persona. Louise and Jeanne knew a version of Henri that contrasted starkly with what some outsiders took to be his somewhat cold and austere disposition. These outsiders would have been surprised to learn, for instance, that in the intimacy of their home and correspondence Henri called Louise *"mon bon poulet"* (my good chicken) and their daughter *"ma cocotte chérie"* (my darling chick).[24] The select few who sometimes caught fleeting glimpses of the Bergsons' private life perceived a gentle, unspoken harmony. After visiting them, Jean Guitton remembered being struck by the way "the fame and glory of the outside world expired on the doorstep of this home."[25]

With the publication of his second book, Bergson was starting to attract attention, but fame had not yet come to his doorstep. That would soon change. As the twentieth century dawned, the philosopher's life was about to get a lot noisier.

CHAPTER 8

SNOWBALLING

One afternoon in the early years of the twentieth century, a young woman named Raïssa and her fiancé, Jacques, lost the will to live. Standing in the shade of a cedar of Lebanon in the Jardin des plantes in Paris, the two students had come to a grave conclusion: life without meaning was not worth living. They decided that if they could not discover whether existence was "an accident, a blessing, or a misfortune," then "the solution would be suicide; suicide before the years had accumulated their dust, before our youthful strength was spent. We wanted to die by a free act if it were impossible to live according to the truth."[1] Raïssa later attributed their youthful despair to the unbearable dissonance they had perceived between what they had been yearning to understand about the universe and what their institution of learning, the Sorbonne, had been willing to teach them.

At seventeen, bursting with a desire to make sense of existence, Raïssa had enrolled at the Sorbonne's Faculté des sciences, where she was to learn the principles of physiology, geology, and embryology. She was confident that her professors would teach her how to conduct her life based on "faultless truth" and help her understand her place in the universe. She later realised that these ambitions would have called for a more philosophical education, but at the time she "believed that the natural sciences held the key to all knowledge."[2] One day in class she boldly proclaimed that she wanted to understand nature "in its causes, in its essence, in its end," only to hear her professor exclaim, horrified, "But, that is mysticism!" She soon learned that the metaphysical questions that animated her were held in contempt by most of her Sorbonne professors, who maintained either a materialistic philosophy that eliminated spirit from the world entirely or a cautious scepticism that did not allow for any kind of belief beyond empirical observation.

It was at the Sorbonne that she had met her future husband Jacques Maritain, in whom she found a companion in her growing despair. He was studying the natural sciences to complement his philosophy degree, and they had bonded over their search for deeper meaning. Raïssa remembered that the various teachings they received at the Sorbonne had left them feeling desperately empty and hopeless:

> [We] swam aimlessly in the waters of observation like fish in the depths of the sea, without ever seeing the sun whose dim rays filtered down to us. . . . Being too weak to struggle against these giants of science and philosophy, or to defend the rightness of my deepest intuitions, I took refuge in sadness.[3]

But then, when they had almost given up all hope, something miraculous happened. On a Friday afternoon, encouraged by their friend Charles Péguy, a staunch critic of what he saw as the

Sorbonne's sclerotic ways, Raïssa and Jacques exited their official place of learning, crossed the rue Saint-Jacques, took a few steps down the rue des Écoles, and entered the Collège de France. What they heard that day in Bergson's lecture theatre restored their faith in a meaningful existence. In a sense, the philosopher brought them back to life.

It was in the early 1900s that Bergson's teachings started making a noticeable impact. The philosopher started drawing followers who, like Raïssa and Jacques Maritain, felt like life had been lacking meaning and yearned for something more. At the same time, the boost in Bergson's popularity in the years following the publication of *Matter and Memory* began having an adverse effect on his own spiritual and physical well-being.

CAREER CHOICES

The Bergsons spent the first days of 1903 in a clinic, where their daughter Jeanne, who was almost nine years old, was recovering from an appendectomy.[4] The philosopher would have preferred to spare his daughter the stress and pain of the operation, but since she was convalescing with no complications, he welcomed the opportunity to take two weeks of respite from the relentless commotion of Parisian life.

In the years following the publication of *Matter and Memory* in 1896, Bergson had started attracting a lot of attention. While only a handful of specialist publications had recognised his PhD thesis, *Time and Free Will*, as a novel and "profound" contribution, his second book had deeply impressed his peers.[5] In the world of French academic philosophy, Bergson's name had become unavoidable.

Ever since his student days, the philosopher had managed to create pockets of silence for himself in crowded atmospheres. But in the late 1890s, the agitation surrounding his growing renown and the increasing weight of his social obligations had become difficult to tune out. He started suffering from bouts of fatigue coupled with chronic insomnia.

The first time Bergson experienced these unpleasant symptoms had been after he completed the manuscript of *Matter and Memory* in 1896. The book had cost him seven years of intense research during which he had immersed himself in the world of the neurosciences and neuropathology in excruciating detail. His condensation of a huge amount of data into a few hundred pages had taken a great effort of concentration. After he finished writing the book, he found that he could no longer sleep, nor could he focus his attention on any subject for more than a few minutes. No longer able to function, Bergson retired to the Côte d'Azur, where he attempted to "re-educate" his concentration skills: "I would stare at objects and try to describe them."[6]

In his later years, Bergson sometimes wondered what his life might have looked like if he had ignored the advice of two school inspectors and remained hidden amid the dormant volcanoes of Auvergne instead of pursuing a career in Paris. He had always looked back fondly on his time in Clermont-Ferrand. It was there that he had made his big philosophical breakthrough, back when there had been no extraneous noise, no real obligations outside of teaching, philosophising, and occasional socialising.

In Clermont-Ferrand, Bergson had hesitated. Since the age of ten, his life had been dedicated to pursuing the various honours that the French academic system had to offer. Perhaps he had felt indebted to the institutions that had spent more time raising him than his own parents. After entering the most prestigious schools, amassing the most coveted prizes, and completing a few mandatory years of teaching in the provinces, the next logical move for a philosopher of his calibre was to move back to the capital and work his way up the Parisian academic ladder. Had Bergson not pursued a Parisian career, his ideas would certainly not have had the same reach— provincial teachers seldom made the news—though he would have been able to hear himself think. But two of his mentors, the philosophers François Evellin and Jules Lachelier, who were evaluating his teaching at the time, had cautioned their promising young colleague, telling him in no uncertain terms that he needed to go to Paris to make his mark. Otherwise, it would soon be too late, and then he would regret not taking this step. Bergson later remembered: "I trusted them, I followed their advice, although I had always thought that it is best to follow one's inspiration. So I was appointed to Paris, and from that moment on I was caught up in a spiral from which it was impossible to escape."[7]

RAFFALOVICH'S FAVOUR

Russian was Marie Sarah Raffalovich's first language, but she had learned to speak seven others. She and her husband Hermann had moved from Russia to Paris in 1864 to escape anti-Semitic laws in their hometown of Odessa. In Paris, Hermann became a successful and internationally renowned banker, while Marie established herself as one of the most admired and well-connected figures of the Parisian intellectual elite. Endowed with wealth and status that allowed her to nurture her intellectual gifts and explore her interests as she pleased, Marie Raffalovich had first found her way into the capital's most distinguished scholarly circles as an avid learner.

In the late 1860s, the Sorbonne and other institutions of learning were still mostly closed to women. The few places that did allow women to register as students barred them from attending the lectures; they could only sit for the exams.[8] The Collège de France, however, opened its doors to anyone who wished to learn, provided they had the leisure to do so.

The Collège de France was born in the sixteenth century as a rival institution to the already three-hundred-year-old Sorbonne, which the new institution deemed to be out of touch with the Renaissance spirit spreading through Europe. At the Sorbonne, all teaching was dispensed in Latin based on the medieval Quadrivium system, and students learned the scholastic art of disputation, a method of debate that allowed very little departure from tradition and orthodoxy. In 1530, following the advice of fellow humanists, King François I, a patron of the arts (it was he who acquired the *Mona Lisa*), founded the Collège Royal, which later became the Collège de France. It was a place where knowledge could be dispensed freely with none of the constraints of a university. To this day the Collège grants no degrees and has no entry or registration requirements. The dozens of weekly lectures delivered in the sciences and the humanities are open to the public.

In the 1860s, Marie Raffalovich started attending the lectures of the renowned physiologist Claude Bernard, with whom, in time, she formed a strong intellectual and emotional relationship founded on their mutual admiration. She became the scientist's confidant and contributed to the dissemination of his ideas in the rest of Europe by translating his works into multiple languages. In the years following Bernard's death in 1878, Raffalovich became an academic trendsetter. She published a popular weekly column in the francophone Russian newspaper *Le Journal de Saint-Pétersbourg*, covering a wide range of topics from biology to literature. In her salon, politicians, scientists, and writers rubbed shoulders. By the time Bergson was trying to make a name for himself in the cliquish world of Parisian universities, a few words from Madame Raffalovich were enough to make or break a young academic's career.

It may have been Bergson who first sought her out, perhaps following the advice of a colleague who understood the politics of university career making. Or perhaps Raffalovich had become aware of the up-and-coming philosopher through her own networks. After all, in 1892, Théodule Ribot, the founder of *La Revue philosophique de la France et de l'étranger*, had written that it was no longer Bergson's old École professor Émile Boutroux but Bergson himself whose conceptual dexterity was "making the heads of eighteen-year-olds spin."[9] Bergson, he wrote, was one of the "rising stars" of Parisian philosophy, and the one to watch.

A few years later, an article titled "The Philosophy of Yesterday and Today" portrayed Bergson as the "main representative" of the new philosophy, a "first-rate writer," with a "mind of uncommon vigour, penetration, and subtlety."[10] But in the same article the *philosophie nouvelle* for which the philosopher of *durée* had become the figurehead was also harshly criticised for supposedly rejecting the "scientific and logical ideal" and presenting a "singular form of mysticism." The author closed his article by saluting Bergson's philosophy as "a work of genius that we can only hope may attract many admirers, but not a single disciple."[11]

In the 1890s, despite the continuous noise, Bergson feared that his career had started to stagnate. Although his teaching evaluation reports insisted that his place was not in a *lycée* but in a university, he had been teaching in secondary schools for over a decade.[12] Since his return to the capital in 1888, he had held a series of sometimes concurrent positions in various *lycées*, but he had yet to find a position in one of the Parisian institutions of higher education. The only university post he had been offered, and refused, was in Bordeaux, almost six hundred kilometres away from the capital. The Sorbonne did not even consider Bergson the first time he applied, in 1894, and he was rejected a second time four years later.[13] For the materialist Sorbonne, Bergson evidently left too much room for spirit.

Around the time of Bergson's first rejection by the Sorbonne, he and Raffalovich began a decades-long philosophical conversation about "many things, both knowable and unknowable."[14] In Raffalovich, Bergson found both a friend—one close enough to offer advice on how to best educate a deaf child and to recommend the lip-reading techniques she had studied—and a powerful ally.[15] In 1897, a few years after they were introduced, Bergson obtained a semester-long post at the Collège de France to fill in for Charles Lévêque, who held the chair of Greek and Latin philosophy. Raffalovich was close with several important figures who would have been in charge of such a decision—or able to sway those who were, in particular Arsène d'Arsonval, Claude Bernard's old assistant.

This step up was followed by a lecturer position at another prestigious institution, Bergson's alma mater, the École normale supérieure. But Bergson soon found that preparing a new generation of philosophers for the state-sanctioned exams was a tedious and exhausting task that left almost no time for his personal research projects. At the École he taught someone who would become one of his fiercest supporters and greatest friends, Charles Péguy.

During his relatively short life, Péguy acquired and discarded several (sometimes contradictory) labels: socialist, nationalist, agnostic, catholic. Once described as "Bergson's most brilliant pupil; not his most brilliant university, scholastic pupil, but his most brilliant free-lance pupil," his engagement gift to his fiancée was a copy of *Matter and Memory*.[16] Until the end of his life, cut short by World War I, Péguy both revered and resented his master. On several occasions he defended Bergson against his enemies in his publication the *Cahiers de la quinzaine*, often to Bergson's embarrassment. On other occasions, as he struggled to keep the *Cahiers* financially afloat, he vocally deplored that, as a loyal Bergson apologist, he received so little support from his master.

In 1899, the chair of modern philosophy at the Collège de France opened up. Bergson hastened to apply and wrote to Raffalovich: "I would be infinitely grateful for anything you could say or write to M. d'Arsonval."[17] With support for his candidacy from Lévêque and Ribot, who cited "the originality of his methods," his "subtle and vigorous mind," and the fact that he always tied his metaphysical speculation to positive data, Bergson had high hopes.[18] However, not long before the new chair was announced, Charles Lévêque, whom Bergson had previously replaced, died, and the chair of ancient philosophy opened up once again. The position Bergson wanted the most, the one that would allow him to develop his current research rather than propose exegesis of ancient texts, went to another philosopher, Gabriel Tarde, and Bergson was awarded the ancient philosophy chair. Victory was therefore bittersweet, and in the early days of the new century he wrote to Raffalovich of his "sharp disappointment."[19] Nonetheless, he thanked her for having used her influence to help him secure the position.[20]

THE RE-ENCHANTER

Only a few streets separated the Sorbonne from the Collège de France, but the two institutions may as well have been on different planets. On one side, at the distinguished Sorbonne, some students were starting to feel that the well of knowledge and discovery was drying up. Where they had once sought meaning, students were met with exegesis. A decade later, in a pamphlet deploring the direction the Sorbonne had taken, two authors sharing the pen name Agathon wrote: "The disappointment is great for all the young people who come to the Sorbonne looking for something other than a thankless erudition."[21] The authors lamented a teaching that had become obsessed with methods drawn from the physical sciences, that replaced creativity with dry exegesis, bibliographical study, and philology, and conflated the natural and moral sciences, sending the likes of Raïssa and Jacques Maritain into suicidal despair.

Charles Péguy likened Bergson, on the other side of the street, to a "dowser." While the Sorbonne was obsessed with dissecting sources, Bergson used his quasi-magical intuition to find fresh sources of metaphorical water. It was Péguy who led many disenchanted *Sorbonnards* to the other side to hear Bergson, including not only Raïssa and Jacques but also Georges Sorel, who would soon be tying Bergson's philosophy together with his revolutionary syndicalism.

Another of Bergson's most loyal defenders was a mathematician turned philosopher called Edouard Le Roy. Unlike the critics of the *philosophie nouvelle*, Le Roy welcomed the novelty of Bergson's philosophy. In the same way that Péguy and Sorel put Bergson on the radars of the most original minds of the time, Le Roy made Bergson relevant in debates about the conventional, rather than inherently true, nature of mathematical axioms.[22]

In the early 1900s, these young men and women felt a sense of defiance as they crossed the street and entered the Collège de France. To these young minds, Bergson was a fresh spring of creativity in an otherwise dry intellectual environment. Bergson's repeated rejections from the Sorbonne gave him the aura of a transgressor and made him exciting to those who were fed up with rigid institutions.

After an afternoon at the Collège de France, the writer Evelyn Underhill, author of a popular book about mysticism, wrote to a friend, "I'm still drunk with Bergson, who sharpened one's mind and swept one off one's feet both at once."[23] In her memoirs, Raïssa Maritain remembered:

> By means of a wonderfully penetrating critique Bergson dispelled the anti-metaphysical prejudices of pseudo-scientific positivism and recalled to the spirit its real functions and essential liberty. . . .
>
> I was rediscovering the lightheartedness and joy of my childhood, of those days when, with beating heart, I went to the lycée. . . .
>
> We went to Bergson's classes filled with overwhelming curiosity and a sacred expectation. We returned, carrying our little bouquet of truths or of promises, as though vitalised by healthful air—exuberant, prolonging to greater and still greater lengths our commentaries upon the master's teachings. Winter was passing away; spring was coming.[24]

Though in the early 1900s Bergson was gaining hundreds of followers, there was never anything like a Bergsonian school. One reason was that the Collège de France was an institution of learning open to all; it had no registration process and did not deliver diplomas. Bergson therefore did not have doctoral students working under his supervision, nor did he have a group of young people assigned to his classes. Another reason no Bergsonian school emerged was that there was no "Bergsonism" in the same sense that there is Freudianism, Marxism, or Darwinism. To claim that there is such a thing as "Bergsonism" implies that there exists a set of easily identifiable theoretical principles, postulates, or general assumptions that form Bergsonism as a system, theory, or methodology and that Bergsonians can build upon and reinterpret. However, Bergson never formulated such conceptual guidelines that would have enabled a Bergsonian school to form in the first place. In fact, the absence of a Bergsonian "system" was, paradoxically, a defining feature of Bergson's philosophy:

> I have no system in philosophy. I have no simple set of rules from which I could evolve my philosophy. In philosophy there are different problems and each problem must be solved by special methods. The methods employed in solving one problem will not do when you attempt to solve another problem. I cannot always deduce from answers I have already given the answers to other problems. There must be a new answer to every new question.[25]

SPIRALLING

From the start of his Parisian career, Bergson had found himself overwhelmed. He could not spend as much time as he wanted meditating on his philosophy. He had to teach, he had to apply for jobs, he had to campaign. He was told that to be a professor without also being a member of the "Institut" (which grouped the five French *académies*) would reflect poorly on him. So, once again, Bergson, who did not want to disappoint or appear inadequate, had to campaign, visit influential people—in short do his part to honour the institutions that had raised him.

Bergson's hard work definitely paid off. In the early 1900s, in addition to his post at the Collège de France, he received multiple professional accolades, including being elected to the Académie des sciences morales et politiques in 1901—one of the most prestigious learned societies in France, founded in 1795—and receiving the highest French order of merit, the Légion d'honneur, in 1902. Bergson, now one of the most renowned figures in French academia, was not yet an international superstar, but he did attract the attention of at least one notable foreign figure.

In 1902, the American philosopher and psychologist William James responded to a letter Bergson had sent him several years earlier to which he had attached a copy of *Matter and Memory*. James apologised for the late reply, stating:

> I saw its great originality, but found your ideas so new and vast that I could not be sure that I fully understood them, although the style, Heaven knows, was lucid enough. So I laid the book aside for a second reading, which I have just accomplished, slowly and carefully. . . .
>
> It is a work of exquisite genius. It makes a sort of Copernican revolution as much as Berkeley's "Principles" or Kant's "Critique" did, and will probably, as it gets better and better known, open a new era of philosophical discussion. It fills my mind with all sorts of new questions and hypotheses and brings the old into a most agreeable liquefaction. I thank you from the bottom of my heart.[26]

In James, Bergson found not only someone who truly recognised the novelty of his philosophy and would become one of his most powerful allies, but also a dear friend.[27]

Despite all the honours and accolades, Bergson still found himself wondering later in life if it had all been worth it. Part of him yearned for the silence of the dormant volcanoes, but another part wanted to be there for the eruption. When he was in his twenties, he had told a friend that what he wanted most out of life was to be free of boredom. Bergson had always known that no matter how much the noise might inconvenience him, he could never settle for a stagnant career pursued kilometres away from the heart of French philosophy in Paris. This tension inside him, between the shy Bergson and the ambitious Bergson, would earn him the Nobel Prize but cost him his health.

Around the time of his Collège de France appointment, Bergson had a nightmare so vivid that it stayed with him for years. He was standing on a podium before a blurry sea of unfamiliar faces who had filled up the lecture theatre further than he could see. As the words started pouring from his mouth, he realised he was not lecturing about his usual philosophical topics. Rather, he was delivering a speech at a political gathering. He heard a faint murmur growing from the back of the audience but thought nothing of it at first and continued speaking at a steady pace. Gradually, though, the noise became louder. It grew into a rumbling, then a roar, then an awful, all-encompassing howl. It was only then that he understood the words bouncing off the walls around him: "Throw him out! Throw him out!" The chant echoed from all sides of the auditorium, in uniform rhythm, "Throw him out! Throw him out!" The angry cries became so loud that his voice could no longer be heard. Just as he felt he could bear the ear-splitting sound no more, Bergson woke up. The neighbour's dog was barking.[28]

CHAPTER 9

LAUGHTER IS VITAL

Bergson never went to the cinema, but had he attended a screening of the 1936 classic *Modern Times*, he would have recognised in Charlie Chaplin's comedy a virtuosic application of one of his own theories. Chaplin plays a factory worker subjected to the relentless cadence of an assembly line. Under the pressure of the conveyor belt's rapid pace and the alienating monotony of his single task, he loses his grip on reality and causes chaos, disrupting the carefully sequenced mechanical assemblage. He finds himself stuck in the repetitive movement he has been executing all day. He uses his wrenches on anything that remotely resembles a bolt, including coworkers' noses and buttons on women's clothes. Chaplin's performance tapped into many of the anxieties surrounding "modern times"—a loss of soul, of purpose and meaning, and a general mechanisation of life—the very anxieties that had drawn so many to Bergson earlier in the century.

In January 1897, Bergson had written to Raffalovich about his new project, a work in "aesthetics," a "study on the nature of the comic and the causes of laughter."[1] She responded with a picture of a laughing man she had found in Italy that delighted Bergson: "I will place your 'laughing man' in front of me, so as to be constantly imbued with the intense joviality with which the painter and the engraver have so admirably marked his physiognomy."[2]

THE PURPOSE OF LAUGHTER

Before Bergson, few philosophers had theorised laughter.[3] The pre-Socratic thinker Democritus was nicknamed the "laughing philosopher" for espousing cheerfulness as a way of life, but he is better remembered for his thoughts on atomism than on laughter. Similarly, the section of Aristotle's *Poetics* that dealt with comedy has not come down to us. Other major thinkers who have offered passing, often humourless, reflections about humour include Thomas Hobbes and René Descartes, who believed that we laugh because we feel superior; Immanuel Kant and Arthur Schopenhauer, who argued that comedy stems from a sense of incongruity; and Spencer and Freud, who suggested that comedians provide a form of much-needed relief (from, respectively, "nervous energy" and repressed emotions). As Bergson pointed out, however, laughter has "a knack of baffling every effort, of slipping away and escaping only to bob up again, a pert challenge flung at philosophic speculation."[4] His own belief was that laughter should be studied as "a living thing" and treated "with the respect due to life": "We shall not aim at imprisoning the comic spirit within a definition. . . . We shall confine ourselves to watching it grow and expand."[5]

Following this method, in *Le Rire: Un essai sur la signification du comique* (*Laughter: An Essay on the Meaning of the Comic*), Bergson arrived at three general observations. The first one, according to Bergson, was so "important" and "simple" that he was surprised it had not attracted more attention from philosophers: "The comic does not exist outside the pale of what is strictly *human*." If we laugh at an animal, we do so because we "have detected in it some human attitude or expression." If we laugh at an inanimate object, we are laughing at "the shape that men have given it."[6]

Bergson's second observation might appear counterintuitive: "Laughter has no greater foe than emotion." Certain emotional states—such as pity, melancholy, rage, or fear—make it difficult for us to find the humour in things that might otherwise make us laugh. In order to laugh we must shift our perspective to that of a "disinterested spectator." This is not to say that it is impossible to laugh in times of hardship; indeed, humour often appears to serve as a coping mechanism in the face of tragedy or misfortune. Following Bergson's logic, perhaps humour is sometimes cathartic precisely because it forces us to look at things from a detached perspective.[7]

Finally, Bergson's third observation was that laughter "appears to stand in need of an echo." Our laughter "is always the laughter of a group." Even when we are effectively laughing alone—laughing to ourselves, or perhaps at ourselves—laughter always presupposes an imagined audience or community.[8]

Bergson's observations tell us where to find laughter and under what conditions it can emerge, but they don't tell us *why* we laugh. They do nonetheless provide us with important clues. It is no accident that we laugh exclusively at other humans, and that laughter is a communal experience: its purpose, or "function," wrote Bergson, is social.[9]

While researching *Laughter*, Bergson had already been preoccupied with his next big project, a philosophical exploration of biological evolution. Though apparently frivolous in nature, the question of laughter tied in with questions about human evolution. In his 1907 book *Creative Evolution*, Bergson described life as an ever-changing, creative, and spontaneous movement. In this sense, life exhibits the opposite of the mechanical tendencies of inert matter, which is characterised by rigidity, predictability, and repetitiveness. At the same time, life and matter are inexorably intertwined. Using meta-phorical language, Bergson described life as an "effort," a constant striving to break free from material constraints through ever more sophisticated evolutionary innovations. Most often, however, "this effort is cut short," Bergson wrote.[10] Throughout the history of life, organisms that have failed to adapt to environmental challenges have become extinct. At both the individual and the species levels, survival has depended on organisms' ability to demonstrate "a certain elasticity"—that is, enough adaptability to find ways around material obstacles.[11]

These questions were already on Bergson's mind when he was writing *Laughter*. He envisioned the comical, and the laughter it provokes, as a sophisticated solution to a particularly human problem. As a product of biological evolution, human societies are also concerned with the struggle between vital and material (or mechanistic) tendencies. Social life, wrote Bergson, requires a "delicate adjustment of wills" and constant "reciprocal adaptation" between the members of the group. Society therefore needs its members to display "the greatest possible degree of elasticity and sociability," and society itself must guard against "a certain rigidity of body, mind and character." These ossified expressions of human life, according to Bergson, are at the source of the comical, because this is precisely what laughter seeks to correct. Rather than a definition of the comical, Bergson arrived at a "leitmotiv"—a common thread uniting various forms of comedy. In general, we laugh at "something mechanical encrusted on the living."[12]

A man is walking down the street. He slips and falls. Hilarity ensues. Why are benign blunders of this nature almost always funny? According to Bergson, it is the involuntary nature of the action that makes us laugh. Stumbles, gaffes, slipups, bloopers, and general clumsiness indicate a lack of both versatility and awareness: "Where [we] would expect to find the wideawake adaptability and the living pliableness of a human being," we find instead "a certain *mechanical inelasticity*."[13]

We laugh when we see Chaplin, stuck in the repetitive movement he has been executing all day, continuing to tighten imaginary
bolts, because we are seeing someone act out deeply engrained habits even though the circumstances demand otherwise. In both accidental blunders and carefully choreographed slapstick comedy, we
are laughing at figures who lack "elasticity," who are mechanically
following a predetermined trajectory and therefore fail to adapt to
their surroundings.

For Bergson, laughter and comedy do not serve a solely aesthetic purpose. As a specifically human evolutionary strategy,
laughter serves a social function. It allows for the regulation of
certain antisocial attitudes; though not necessarily what society
might consider immoral, these attitudes are either too eccentric to
be viable within a functional society or too inflexible to allow the
society to develop and evolve. For instance, for Bergson, vanity
was one of the most laughable of human traits. In the same way
that a lack of awareness of one's material surroundings can result
in (often comical) physical injuries, an unhealthy obsession with
oneself denotes a lack of awareness of others, which can in turn
damage society. This damage is subtle and therefore, he wrote,
requires a subtle antidote:

> Vanity, though it is a natural product of social life, is an inconve-
> nience to society, just as certain slight poisons, continually secreted
> by the human organism, would destroy it in the long run if they
> were not neutralised by other secretions. Laughter is unceasingly
> doing work of this kind.[14]

The original purpose of laughter is to correct these socially "inconvenient" attitudes gently but firmly. In this sense, according to
Bergson, laughter is punitive: "Society holds suspended over each
individual member, if not the threat of correction, at all events the
prospect of a snubbing, which although it is slight, is none the less
dreaded. Such must be the function of laughter."[15]

When the book was translated into English over a decade later, the *New York Times* hailed it as a "brilliant essay" that

> perhaps explains even better than his most elaborate works the reason why he is the favourite philosopher of the salons of Paris and even of those at Oxford and London. It is both witty and clear while it combines subtlety of observation with a profound knowledge of the ways of society.[16]

Bertrand Russell, on the other hand, accused Bergson's repetitive characterisation of the comical as "something mechanical encrusted upon the living" of becoming laughable in its own terms as he tried to apply the same rigid formula to a complex and spontaneous living phenomenon.[17] But as pointed out earlier, Bergson was claiming that this formula, rather than a clear-cut definition, was a "leitmotiv," that representations of mechanised life constitute a common thread in many different forms of comedy. His theory did not preclude the possibility of laughing at things that are not obviously mechanical, nor did it argue that the mechanical is the only source of laughter. What mattered to Bergson was to understand laughter as a product and a part of life.

THE COMEDY OF BERGSON

Bergson's demeanour often appeared serious, detached, almost austere, but those close to him knew he had a special sense of humour. They knew he specialised in a kind of wit often too dry to be detected by those not attuned to it. Only the philosopher's friends had the privilege of witnessing a flicker of amusement brighten his eyes and of hearing his laughter, which was sometimes silent, sometimes melodious.

Descriptions of Bergson's physical appearance, even by his friends, often read as comical in a very Bergsonian sense. A passage on Bergson's demeanour from Albert Adès, the Egyptian philosopher, could have been used in *Laughter* as an example of the mechanical encrusted on the living:

> And here is Mr. Bergson in the street. You'd say he was the most distracted of all passers-by, so involuntary are his movements. In truth, he's a kind of automaton who swings left and right, leans back excessively, raises his arm unnecessarily. This is not a man who is not paying attention to the outside world, it's a man who has completely forgotten the feeling of being watched.[18]

Others focussed on the size of the philosopher's forehead, which was so large that it seemed to threaten to topple him over, and noted the stiffness of his insectlike, or birdlike, movements.

But when Bergson spoke, no one found him laughable. Compensating for the apparent rigidity of his body was the fluidity of his thought, which enchanted the youth of the late Belle Époque. The writer Tancrède de Visan (the pen name of Vincent Biétrix), who was in his early twenties when he started attending Bergson's lectures at the Collège de France, wrote:

> The influence of Bergson's philosophy on my generation can be compared only to that exerted by Descartes on Malebranche or by Hume on Kant....
>
> At an age when ideas enter the mind in the form of enthusiasms, his dynamic notions of qualitative duration, of heterogeneous continuity, of multiple and mobile states of consciousness... gave us new reasons for exaltation, and very noble ones at that....
>
> Sitting on uncomfortable benches, choirboy benches, using our knees as desks, we listened in religious contemplation to this quiet, mannered voice that rang out to the depths of our troubled lives. Ah, how eagerly we inhaled his words which were laced with poetry![19]

Bergson's debut as a public lecturer in one of the oldest and most prestigious institutions of learning in the country coincided with the publication of *Laughter*. In this short book, Bergson had taken seriously a subject that most philosophers had deemed too trivial to even consider, but that most people knew to be of the utmost importance in their everyday lives. Bergson's discussion of laughter was not steeped in the technical terms of metaphysical or scientific debates and in this sense was a lot more accessible to the general public.

As the first years of the 1900s rolled around, everything was in place for Bergson to become the most famous philosopher in the country—and soon in the world. Bergson was inspiring more and more enthusiastic minds to cross the road to the Collège de France, to let go of the stuffiness that academic philosophy presented both at the Sorbonne and in the works of those who felt above such mundane topics as laughter.

CHAPTER 10

LIFTING THE VEIL

For as long as she could remember, Bergson's daughter Jeanne had enjoyed drawing human figures. With a few simple lines, she managed to imbue her subjects with rich emotional textures. Her own emotions were always visible on her face, and it was not unusual to see tears welling up in her large dark eyes.

Jeanne was taught how to breathe movement into inert matter by the famous sculptor Antoine Bourdelle. In his atelier, he taught hundreds of young men and women in equal numbers. Among them, Jeanne found new ways to express herself. As a child, she had learned lip-reading techniques and how to mimic the movements of the mouth. In Bourdelle's atelier, she could not always follow the master's instructions because he spoke with his face turned towards the ground. But in time, through drawings and gestures they traced in the air with their fingers, Jeanne and Bourdelle invented their own wordless modes of communication. In one of his letters to her, Bourdelle wrote:

> Your drawings carry the *élan* of your gesture.... Their masses vibrate, their detours are pure, so beautifully cursive that they are like thought in the process of being created.... I love the way your drawings are made from the inside, how your sketches are torn from the fleeting moment; your vision is profound, they vibrate with your kindness. They astonish by the purity of the exchange they reveal between reality and your vision, which grasps everything in depth.[1]

Bourdelle was commenting on the fact that artists like Jeanne Bergson seem to share a privileged relationship with reality in their ability to bypass the generalising powers of language to reveal what is singularly unique about their experience and vision.

In the final chapter of *Laughter*, published when Jeanne was still a small child, Bergson reflected on the special kind of vision enjoyed by artists. Most people lose sight of what is singular about the special colouration of their own experience: "Between nature and ourselves, nay, between ourselves and our own consciousness a veil is interposed."[2] It is a veil of generalisations, necessities, and ready-made ideas that we need in order to get things done. This veil is "dense and opaque for the common herd,—thin almost transparent for the artist and the poet":

> Art, whether it be painting or sculpture, poetry or music, has no other object than to brush aside the utilitarian symbols, the conventional and socially accepted generalities, in short, everything that veils reality from us, in order to bring us face to face with reality itself.[3]

One of Bergson's favourite artists was the nineteenth-century British Romantic painter J.M.W. Turner. According to Bergson, we admire artists like Turner because they are able to show us what we have "perceived without seeing."[4] They teach us to see the fog detached from the practical problems it may cause, to see it for itself, for its inherent beauty. Artists are able to isolate "brilliant" but constantly "dissolving" visions from a mass of information that we are usually obliged to dim to be able to function. In a sense, the artist is a distracted figure, one who is detached from the practical requirements of life. But in another sense the artist's gift lies in the ability to perceive and express more than the ordinary person can.

From the 1890s, Bergson himself was portrayed, by his adversaries, as an artist, a poet, a "symbolist writer."[5] In the symbolist manifesto published in *Le Figaro* in 1886, the movement is defined as a reaction against naturalism, against "objective description." One of the main figures of symbolism, Stéphane Mallarmé, upheld the use of suggestion as an aesthetic method: "To name an object is to do away with three quarters of the joy of a poem, made to be divined little by little: to suggest it, that is the dream."[6]

Associations between Bergson and the aesthetic trends of his time were often used to discredit him. As early as 1892, Bergson's old École rival Jean Jaurès had qualified Bergson's philosophy as "the metaphysic of decadent art"—as well as of symbolism and impressionism—because, he wrote, Bergson "thinks that the most annoying thing about words is that they have a meaning."[7] But by the 1910s these associations were being employed by many of Bergson's followers, especially those who were at the forefront of new artistic movements, like the Futurists and the Cubists, to celebrate him and to claim him as one of their sources of inspiration.[8] Bergson's assertion that artists have access to inexpressible ideas also struck a chord with the many members of the broader public who were open to exploring different and more exhilarating ways of seeking meaning beyond the repetitive mundaneness of everyday life.

In 1904, Bergson wrote to Proust: "I believe, as you do, that every form of art sets out to convey certain states of mind that would be inexpressible in any other language: that is the *raison d'être* of that art."[9] Bergson had been thinking a lot about what language could and could not express.

ANALYTIC VS. BERGSONIAN

In 1946, Bertrand Russell published *A History of Western Philosophy*. The book was, and remains, a commercial success, in spite of scholarly criticism. Russell's historical narrative starts around the time of the Greek mathematician Pythagoras and follows an arc that conveniently culminates in his own philosophical school, which he calls "the philosophy of logical analysis."[10]

Russell is often presented as one of the founders of "analytic philosophy," a philosophical movement that originated in the late nineteenth century. What the term encompasses is quite vague, but it often refers to a shift in the practice of philosophy at the turn of the twentieth century. Around this time, philosophers like Russell and G. E. Moore wished to drive philosophy away from what they perceived as the obscure systems popular in British universities— which drew upon nineteenth-century German philosophical systems—and towards more isolated, specialised problems. One of the main ideas associated with analytic philosophy is that philosophical confusions arise from ambiguous language and that all philosophical problems can ultimately be reduced to problems of syntax. Russell argued that misleading or ambiguous propositions should be reexpressed in the formal language of symbolic logic to dispel all confusion and come in contact with the most fundamental truths: "Ordinary language is totally unsuited for expressing what physics really asserts, since the words of everyday life are not sufficiently abstract. Only mathematics and mathematical logic can say as little as the physicist means to say."[11] Russell believed that one of the philosopher's main jobs is to build the rules of this unambiguous ideal language.

Like many thinkers of the late nineteenth and early twentieth century, Bergson was also deeply concerned with the shortcomings of language. But unlike Russell and the other analytic philosophers,

Bergson's worry was not that language leaves too much room for interpretation, but, on the contrary, that it is too restrictive. Bergson did not believe that language needs to be more abstract to become more precise. In fact, according to him, the more abstract the language the further it drifts from reality.

Bergson saw language as an imperfect but essential practical and social tool. In an ever-changing universe, it provides us with solid anchoring points. In a sense, the very purpose of language, concepts, and symbols is to stop *durée* in its tracks. Indeed, communication would be impossible if our definitions of words changed following the constant flow of *durée*. How would we make quantitative predictions about movement other than by immobilising it through symbols? How would we communicate our subjective, ever-evolving internal states if not by using words that delineate them and make them accessible to others?

One of language's most useful features is that it allows us to generalise. Under a single concept, we can file an overwhelming diversity of phenomena. The noun "chair" can fit all existing and imaginary objects that satisfy the general definition of a chair.[12] The adjective "happy" groups infinitely varied subjective emotional experiences.[13] Our actions depend on our ability to anticipate future situations by recognising similar patterns from our past. We therefore sort a vast diversity of phenomena into similar categories that help us make sense of the world and act within it. But as Bergson wrote in *Laughter*, we need to remain aware that, because of our tendency to generalise, "we do not see the actual things themselves; in most cases we confine ourselves to reading the labels affixed to them."[14]

Excessive generalising, the use of ready-made concepts and ideas, is necessary but makes us lose sight of what is truly singular about the unique colouration of our own experience; it leads us to break contact with our profound self. Bergson believed that beyond the practical requirements of scientific knowledge, and of everyday life, a new kind of philosophy could lift the veil of concepts, generalisations, and abstractions sitting between us and reality and thereby reveal the continuous change at work in the universe and put us in direct contact with *durée*: "Beyond the ideas which are chilled and congealed in language, we must seek the warmth and mobility of life."[15]

Bergson, the main representative of *la philosophie nouvelle*, was seen as sharing aspirations with the symbolist poets, who preferred to suggest rather than to say. But the philosopher's ambitions went far beyond poetry. Bergson wanted to give a new impulsion to metaphysics, a domain that he saw as crippled by petty squabbles over terminology. He proposed a practice of philosophy that, he said, had never been attempted before. The metaphysics of the future, he boldly declared, was "the science that claims to dispense with symbols."[16] Although Bergson knew that no science could completely do away with symbols, he nonetheless believed that his new method, which he called "intuition," could bypass the limitations inherent in language.

BERGSON'S INTUITION

In 1900, the year Bergson published *Laughter*, Xavier Léon, one of the founders of the *Revue de métaphysique et de morale*, begged him for an article to publish in his journal. An article by Bergson would serve to promote and legitimise the Société française de philosophie, which he was in the process of founding. Léon asked Bergson for a copy of his inaugural Collège de France lecture, but Bergson refused.

The philosopher had vowed to never commit to writing anything he did not feel he had thoroughly thought through. In addition, he did not like publishing articles on isolated topics, much preferring the long-form shape of a book.[17] In 1901, he once again declined to publish in the *Revue* and admitted to Léon that he did not know where his current research was carrying him:

> The path I have taken in my personal research leads me to even
> greater indecisions. I have to carry out a number of different types

of research at the same time, with the near certainty that they must converge somewhere, but without yet being able to determine where or how.[18]

But in the autumn of 1902, Bergson finally agreed—"after much hesitation"—to submit "a short essay," which he titled "Introduction à la métaphysique" (An Introduction to Metaphysics). It was published in January of the following year.

There are, wrote Bergson, two ways of knowing an object: analysis and intuition. Analysis adopts a series of external viewpoints on its object and translates them into symbols. For instance, we may represent Achilles's race against the tortoise as a linear trajectory divisible into segments—Achilles's trajectory can always be cut up into smaller parts. We can add layers upon layers of complexity to describe each intricate aspect of his movement, pushing the boundaries of abstraction as far as we want.[19] But from this analysis of Achilles's movement, we will never arrive at the movement itself: the simple, indivisible act of running. Analysis, Bergson said, is condemned to be "eternally unsatisfied" in its quest to "embrace the object around which it is compelled to turn."[20]

A more concrete example that Bergson gives is that of "a character whose adventures are related to me in a novel." The novelist may develop description after description and give the reader "many points of view from which I can observe him." These external points of view "give me only what he has in common with others, and not what belongs to him and him alone." But if we could somehow correspond completely with the hero, even if only for an instant, then

out of that indivisible feeling, as from a spring, all the words, gestures, and actions of the man would appear to me to flow naturally. They would no longer be accidents which, added to the idea I had already formed of the character, continually enriched that idea, without ever completing it. The character would be given to me all at once, in its entirety.[21]

Analysis remains external to its object of study, apprehending it through symbols and ready-made concepts. Intuition, on the other hand, "neither depends on a point of view nor relies on any symbol"; instead, it is a form of knowledge that apprehends reality from within.[22] In a sense, intuition is a kind of vision—a direct contact with reality in all its fluidity, beyond the veils interposed by the practical needs of language. Instead of adopting external points of view, intuition "follows the undulations of the real" and coincides with the flow of *durée*.

But if intuition is a vision, it is not a vision that is passively received. Intuition as a philosophical method is an effort to undo some of our most profoundly engrained habits. In the ordinary course of life, our mind "seeks for solid points of support."[23] It demands that we immobilise the continuous flow of *durée* for practical reasons: to help us anticipate, compare, communicate, measure, and generally mould the external world to our advantage. Life requires us to drape a veil between ourselves and the unique particularities and colourations of our temporal experience. It is only when the metaphysician is able to do away with the practical requirements of life that an intuitive vision of *durée* becomes possible. The mind, says Bergson, "has to do violence to itself" and "reverse the direction of the operation by which it habitually thinks."[24] The theologian George Tyrrell, a Bergson admirer, rephrased this requirement:

[Bergson] frankly admits that we must stand on our heads, and seize that brief moment of unstable equilibrium to snatch a hasty glance at things as they really are. We must use our minds in a wholly unaccustomed way, and recognise that its customary use is fatal to speculative truth just in the measure that it is adapted to practical ends. In short, we have to approach philosophy with a new mind and a new method.[25]

This was the thread that Bergson had been pulling on when Léon asked him to produce an article for his journal. "Introduction à la métaphysique" represented a snapshot of where Bergson's thought process was leading him in 1903, when he had yet to discover intuition's full significance. A few years later, in *Creative Evolution*—the book that would transform Bergson into an international superstar—intuition would find its source and its theoretical grounding in the evolutionary history of the mind.

FLUID CONCEPTS

For Bertrand Russell, the language Bergson used to express his theories and his defence of intuition represented the pinnacle of ambiguous discourse. He viewed it as nothing less than an assault on rationality that had to be challenged. At the end of his 1946 book, Russell credited his own philosophy of logical analysis with having "rendered antiquated... a great deal of mysticism such as that of Bergson."[26] Earlier in the century, the French evolutionist Félix Le Dantec had expressed a similar view: "The language [Bergson] uses to express himself is so different to the one I'm used to, that to follow him I would need a translator that I have yet to meet." Then he added, "I do not believe that M. Bergson's narration presents any advantage whatsoever over objective narration." Le Dantec conceded that Bergson's writing had a "poetic appeal," but the risk of such an attractive style was the room it left for readers' "mystical tendencies" to develop. For this reason, Bergson's reflections in "Introduction to Metaphysics," said Le Dantec, were nothing more than "unverifiable poetic considerations."[27]

Bergson later said that he had hesitated a great deal before deciding to use the term "intuition."[28] He worried he might be misread as advocating for a vague feeling, a mere instinct. In fact, he was worried about being read exactly as Russell and Le Dantec had read him. But there was nothing unrigorous about Bergson's vision of intuition. For him, intuition was an effort, a radical upheaval of deeply engrained habits of thought to break through intellectual moulds and come into direct contact with reality. It was also a method that would drive philosophy forward, past old quarrels brought about by the generality of concepts that analysed their objects of study instead of entering directly into them.

Both Bergson's admirers and his critics called him a poet. There was some truth to this characterisation. Bergson needed to be something of a poet to be able to report back on his forays into unveiled reality. Since his philosophy could not dispense with concepts or language, Bergson had to find creative ways to use language to transcend the very limitations of language. Bergson advocated using numerous metaphors that might combine to put the reader on the right track and creating "supple, mobile, and almost fluid" concepts that would be "always ready to mould themselves on the fleeting forms of intuition."[29]

Although Bergson's approach was somewhat artistic, Bergson saw himself as neither an artist nor a poet. His goal was not to reveal, as Turner had done, what most people had not been able to perceive, but to communicate his findings in a manner that could advance philosophical knowledge and transform metaphysics into something like a cumulative science.

To critics like Russell and Le Dantec, Bergson's poetic style was synonymous with ambiguity and lack of rigour. But for Bergson's supporters, his appeal came from his capacity to use language to express what language usually hides and to undo the deeply entrenched habits of thought that had rendered philosophical debates sclerotic. Bergson provided philosophical ammunition to those who wished to see expressions of subjectivity taken seriously at a time when objective methods were making their way into all areas of human experience.

CHAPTER II

THE STRANGE CASE OF EUSAPIA PALLADINO

Nine months before Pierre Curie died, his head crushed under the wheel of a carriage, and two years after he and his wife Marie were awarded the Nobel Prize in Physics for their research on radiation, the physicist took part in a bizarre experiment.

Curie sat at a table with other scientists and scholars in a small, dimly lit room in the centre of Paris. His left hand was wrapped firmly around the right hand of a middle-aged woman sitting next to him, while her right foot rested upon his left shoe. The woman was Eusapia Palladino, a world-famous medium born in the mountains of Abruzzi, at the top of the heel of Italy's boot. In her everyday life, she did not bother to adopt the air of grandiosity of some of her spiritualist peers. But in her element, in the right conditions, she transformed into an impressive and intimidating presence.

That day, her round eyes widened with such intensity that a shiver of anticipation rippled through the room. Because she wore all black, her body blended in with the dark velvet curtain behind her, and her worn, pale face appeared to hover, disembodied, above the table. The flickering of a gas lamp intermittently highlighted a single striking streak of white on her forehead, which contrasted starkly with the rest of her dark grey hair. It was sometimes told that the discolouration was not a sign of advancing age but dated from around the time of her first birthday. Left unsupervised, she had fallen, and blood had gushed out of her tiny head. The hair on the sunken part of her wounded skull had grown white ever since. Some of those who attended her demonstrations said that when she exerted her psychical powers, a cold breeze could be felt emanating from her vestigial cranial cavity, as though her past trauma had become a portal for spirits to travel into our world.

Curie felt Palladino's hand shaking in his. Though she was not touching the table before her, the movements of her body vibrated through the wooden surface, which started rattling uncontrollably. Her face twisted and spasmed in what appeared to be an immense effort of concentration. She was now all grunts, moans, sweat, and convulsions. Some said that in this trancelike state she often appeared to glow an eerie blue, not unlike the radioluminescence emitted by the dangerous decaying substances the Curies studied in their laboratory. Suddenly, the whole table lifted thirty centimetres off the ground and hovered there for seven long seconds. Aside from the hand Palladino held flat on the table's surface, Curie and the other assessors were almost certain that there were no other points of contact between the medium and the heavy object.

The sight they were treated to next was even more implausible. A shadowy arm slowly reached out from behind the curtain in the background, a space that had been empty when they entered the room. The official report later stated that five eyewitnesses, "Messrs Curie, Bergson, de Gramont, Komyakoff and Youriévitch," had all seen it.[1] Curie, who was closest to the curtain, felt the arm hit him, pull his hair, pinch and punch him, and even give him a few sharp slaps when he dared to move his face towards the source of the aggression. After that, objects hidden behind the curtain were thrown about by an invisible force, and one of the heavier ones levitated above the table for all of them to see. To end the session, Palladino tapped Curie's shoulder twice, and a few seconds later two knocks were heard, echoing out of the table, beyond the medium's reach.

In the decades around 1900, it was not uncommon to find people huddled around tables in sitting parlours, in search of a supernatural spectacle. Around this time, occultism and spiritualism were flourishing in Europe and North America, and communicating with the deceased became a popular pastime.

From early on in his career, Bergson had taken an active interest in so-called psychical phenomena like telepathy, though over time he learned to be cautious about how he framed his research into this area, which some of his peers considered highly unserious. But whether he wanted it or not, Bergson found himself at the forefront of the occult revival. He was, after all, known for defending the reality of spirit over the mechanical. In *Matter and Memory*, he provided support for the idea that the mind survives the death of the body in arguing that "only a small part of the work done by the mind is done by the brain" and that "the brain is only a province of the mind."[2] The massive following he was in the process of acquiring came in part from a public eager for a more expansive understanding of the mysteries of the spirit.

PSYCHICAL RESEARCH

Psychical phenomena seeped into all areas of society, and France was no exception. In 1895, a doctor based in Normandy called Joseph Gilbert had enlisted a sleepwalking clairvoyant, Léonie, to help prove the innocence of Alfred Dreyfus, who had been unjustly convicted of treason the previous year. Léonie, who was later hired as a maid by Dreyfus's brother, had allegedly foreseen the existence of the hidden documents that could have cleared Dreyfus's name.

One day, in Bergson's own home, the Polish philosopher Wincenty Lutoslawski had attempted to prove that Bergson was the reincarnation of the poet Adam Mickiewicz, who himself was the reincarnation of the ancient philosopher Plotinus, and that therefore, by some kind of spiritual transitivity, Bergson had been Plotinus in a past life.[3]

Bergson's sister Mina, by this time an important figure in the world of occultism and now known as Moina Mathers, was also said to read people's past lives and to communicate with the dead on various spiritual planes. In the early 1900s, with her husband, Samuel McGregor Mathers, she was performing "the rites of Isis" in a Parisian theatre.[4]

The common thread linking all these beliefs and practices was the idea that there exists something like a soul or a spirit that escapes what William James called "the bounds which science has hitherto set to nature's forces."[5] After attending one of Palladino's demonstrations in New York, James cautiously predicted that these bounds might soon be broken.

With the emergence of experimental psychology in the nineteenth century, the study of unexplained mental phenomena, like hypnosis, telepathy, and somnambulism, started teetering on the edge of scientific respectability. The exploration of these phenomena was no longer reserved to charlatans and performers. Some psychologists and scientists believed that they had the potential to unlock the secrets of the mind and a new understanding of reality. In the 1880s, the neurologist Jean-Martin Charcot presented hypnosis as a potential cure for hysteria. The Collège de France physiologist and Nobel Prize laureate Charles Richet coined the term "ectoplasm," a mysterious substance emanating from the medium's body during séances, in his quest to prove the existence of a "sixth sense" using scientific methods.

Several scientists like Richet wanted to take matters (or spirits) into their own hands. In 1882, a group of psychical researchers in Britain founded the Society for Psychical Research. Their mission statement made their purpose clear: to explain the inexplicable using the methods of scientific experimentation. "It has been widely felt," they wrote, "that the present is an opportune time for making an organised and systematic attempt to investigate that large group of debatable phenomena designated by such terms as mesmeric, psychical, and Spiritualistic."[6] The society's many prestigious members included the co-discoverer of natural selection, Alfred Russel Wallace, the physicist Oliver Lodge, the writer Arthur Conan Doyle, the philosopher and psychologist William James, and the psychoanalysts Sigmund Freud and Carl Jung.

In France, a similar organisation, the Groupe d'étude des phénomènes psychiques, emerged under the respectable umbrella of the Institut général psychologique. The group was mainly composed of physicists, including the Curies, and medical professors like the Collège de France professor Arsène d'Arsonval. All were members of various *académies* and respected figures in their field.[7] Bergson was among the founding members of the Institut and cosigned the group's initial statement, which appeared in 1901 in the *Bulletin de l'Institut général psychologique*:

[The group] proposes to study this region situated on the borders of psychology, biology and physics, where the manifestations of undefined forces have been seen. Between the credulity of some and the indifference of others . . . there is room for strictly scientific research, without any bias to affirm or deny, without any other preoccupation than to ask the following question of experience: What is the share of objective reality and what is the share of subjective interpretation in the facts described under the names of mental suggestion, telepathy, mediumship, levitation, etc.?[8]

The group's statement ended with a call for test subjects of psychical ability and promised volunteers the freedom "to choose the conditions in which the test experiments will be conducted."[9] Unsurprisingly perhaps, very few stepped forward. For mediums whose livelihood often depended on deceit, there was little to be gained by subjecting the veracity of their powers to scientific testing. But this did not worry Eusapia Palladino.

THE MEDIUM'S POWER

The story of Eusapia Palladino's origins is hazy at best. She sometimes claimed that she had first discovered her powers at about fourteen, when she had accidentally made a table levitate. In other accounts, it all started as a terrifying vision during the night, eyes staring at her from the darkness, followed by disembodied hands grabbing at her sheets from beneath her bed. During her early teenage years, a man named Ercole Chiaia had hired her to care for his daughters, and he seems to have been the one who brought Eusapia to the attention of researchers. She was then apparently discovered by a spiritualist called Giovanni Damiani, who had been guided to her by the spirit of a dead man named John King. A fact that she later tried to keep hidden was that, in her youth, she had spent time with magicians, who had presumably taught her a lot of her tricks. From then on, she had travelled across Europe, and later America, demonstrating her incredible powers for a reasonable fee. People gathered to see her levitating tables, playing musical instruments without touching them, and materialising extra limbs.

Between 1905 and 1908, Palladino became the main test subject of the Groupe d'étude des phénomènes psychiques. The members liked to think of their sessions with her less as séances and more as scientific experiments. The room in which they studied Palladino's powers had been conceived as a laboratory. Filled with all sorts of measuring devices and strange equipment, it contained machines to monitor variations in movement and temperature in the room and changes in the medium's blood pressure, temperature, heart rate, and vision. The experimenters even took urine samples from Palladino every forty-eight hours.[10]

Bergson attended at least six sittings. Sometimes he was a simple observer; other times he was given the task of keeping an eye on the whereabouts of Palladino's hands and legs and controlling for trickery. On various occasions, the philosopher saw the medium lift the table without apparently touching it, decrease her weight as it was being measured without apparently moving from the scale, break the equipment being used to measure her various vitals without contact, and materialise extra arms from behind the curtain. Though impressed by the spectacular nature of the experiments, Bergson maintained a position of scepticism.

The final conclusions of the official report on Eusapia Palladino were also mixed and cautious. The conditions of the experiments had been anything but faultless. Palladino would sometimes refuse to perform if the circumstances were not to her liking—for example, if she felt there was too much light in the room. Amazingly, the report also documented several confirmed instances of trickery. Palladino's knee was once found to be in contact with the table she was levitating when it was thought that she had been immobilised by the person monitoring her. She also managed to substitute her own hand for the hand of her monitor, thus freeing her hand to perform all sorts of tricks while maintaining the illusion that she was immobilised. Despite these deceptions, however, Palladino was not entirely dismissed as a fraud. It was widely believed that because the trancelike states of mediums were particularly taxing emotionally and physically, mediums would sometimes unconsciously find ways of preserving their energy and these could involve cheating.[11]

N-RAYS

Pierre Curie did not live to see the conclusions of the Palladino experiments. Though he too had tried his best to maintain a healthy level of scepticism, he could not resist believing. According to one of the psychical research group's founding members and main funders Serge Youriévitch, Curie had decided, after observing Palladino, to "devote the rest of his life to psychical research."[12] In the weeks that followed his first encounter with the medium in 1905, he attended at least two other sessions, and by the end of July that year he would write to his friend and fellow physicist Louis Georges Gouy: "The phenomena we have seen strike us as inexplicable by trickery."[13]

The following year Curie attended at least five more sessions, and in April 1906, less than a week before his fatal accident, he wrote to Gouy again: "These phenomena really do exist and it is no longer possible for me to doubt them. It seems unbelievable, but it is so, and there is no denying it, especially after sessions of such perfectly controlled conditions."[14] It is perhaps not surprising that even eminent scientists like Pierre Curie would be so taken with what many would argue were merely sophisticated parlour tricks. The recent discovery of X-rays and radioactivity had opened up a whole world of previously unknown invisible natural powers. From there, it was quite reasonable to assume that other such powers might soon be uncovered. Pierre Curie was hopeful that undiscovered forms of radiation or energy might one day provide scientific explanations for psychical and supernatural occurrences. But even though respectable scientists like Curie were becoming more and more adventurous with the spiritual world, their reputations were still at stake.

In 1903, the year Pierre and Marie Curie were awarded their Nobel Prize in Physics, another French physicist, René-Prosper Blondlot, announced his discovery of what he had named "N-rays" (after his hometown of Nancy): a new form of radiation emitted by the human body. For a time, this discovery fuelled the hope that there indeed existed a scientific, physical basis for phenomena that, until then, had been considered supernatural, like telepathy or even telekinesis. The "discovery" sent the scientific world into a frenzy. Hundreds of articles were published on the subject, including by some of the members of the French psychical research group, such as Arsène d'Arsonval. A few days after Christmas in 1903, the group discussed the phenomenon at length. Bergson had many questions: Were these radiations emitted by the nervous system or the muscles? Did their emission increase when the human subject was speaking? According to d'Arsonval, the answer to the latter question was yes: when the subject made an intellectual effort, "the brightness of the phosphorescent phenomenon increases."[15]

But soon after Blondlot's discovery, a sceptical American physicist, Robert W. Wood, was sent to the French physicist's laboratory to observe his experiments in action. Wood's suspicions were confirmed after he surreptitiously removed an indispensable aluminium prism and Blondlot claimed he could still see the N-rays. Blondlot's reputation as a scientist never recovered, and his downfall became a cautionary tale for those who felt that the boundaries of scientific acceptability were too restrictive. They learned that, in these matters, it was necessary to proceed with care to avoid alienating oneself from more sceptical colleagues. This was a lesson that Bergson had learned the hard way early in his career.

DANGEROUS EXPERIMENTS

One day in the mid-1880s, when Bergson was still a young man teaching in Clermont-Ferrand, he found himself standing in the living room of the university librarian, Albert Maire. A severe-looking man sporting an impressive handlebar moustache, Dr. Lucien Moutin, invited another young man in attendance to the middle of the room. Without any warning, the doctor rapidly moved forward, his eyes wide open and unblinking, so that his face was hovering only inches away from his subject's. After repeating this strange choreography a few times, the young man's eyes glazed over and he showed all the characteristics of being in a hypnotic trance. The doctor took a few steps back and held a book open in front of his face, making sure he was the only one who could see the pages. He asked his subject to read what was on the page. The young man could not possibly have seen the words hidden from view, but he began, with very little hesitation, to read out loud from the book. It was as though he were reading directly from the doctor's mind.

Later, with one of his friends, André Robinet, a laboratory technician at the university in Clermont-Ferrand, Bergson decided to re-create the experiment. At first, to their amazement, they had obtained results similar to those demonstrated by Moutin. But soon they started noticing that their subjects often made strange mistakes. For instance, when asked to read the number of the page the hypnotist was looking at, their subjects sometimes read it backwards, as though seeing the page through a mirror. So Bergson and Robinet started forming a strange hypothesis. Perhaps the subjects were not reading the hypnotiser's mind but instead they were reading the page as reflected in the eye of the hypnotist. Of course, the reflection would be too small for most people to decipher with the naked eye. But could it be done in a hypnotised state?

Bergson and Robinet believed, following studies available at the time, that in a state of suggestibility like hypnosis, subjects are able to develop heightened sensory capabilities known as hyperesthesia. With this capability, subjects in a trancelike state can perceive things that they would never normally be able to perceive —in this case, tiny images reflected in the hypnotist's pupil. With this in mind, Bergson and Robinet tried the exercise again, this time making sure that the subjects could not see their eyes. Sure enough, the subjects were no longer able to discern the words or numbers on the page. Bergson and his colleague therefore concluded that the phenomenon they had observed was not telepathy, but an incredible kind of unconscious self-deception.[16]

Bergson published the results in the *Revue philosophique de la France et de l'étranger* in 1886, his first published article. He was extremely cautious about the claims he made, adhering as much as possible to an experimental protocol and formulating hypotheses without engaging in empty speculation. He nonetheless attracted the ire of an esteemed French philosopher, Alphonse Darlu, who painted Bergson's experiments with hypnosis and telepathy as dangerous:

These experiments when made public give licence to others. The scientific purpose which inspired them serves as a pretext, in the hypnotic fury which is currently rampant in the provinces as well as in Paris, for unhealthy curiosity, or, worse still, for self-serving and unscrupulous charlatanism. . . . But scientific curiosity alone cannot justify everything.[17]

At such an early stage in his career, Bergson needed more than anything to remain in the good graces of the decision-makers in his field, and this incident taught him that prudence was required when discussing such matters.

Fifteen years later, in 1901, when Bergson was invited to speak at the Institut général psychologique, he chose to talk about dreams. There was a lot of interest in the subject at the time. Freud had just published *The Interpretation of Dreams*, in which he depicted dreams as forms of wish fulfilment. Dreams were also of interest to those interested in the psychical and paranormal, because of phenomena like dream telepathy and premonitions. Even Freud would speculate a little about the possibility of telepathy in dreams.

Bergson's audience therefore had high hopes that the philosopher, speaking on behalf of the French society for psychical research, of which he was a member, would explore some of these topics. Bergson did hint at the idea that any link between telepathy and dreams would no doubt be found in states of the most "profound sleep," but as one psychical researcher noted, this comment came only at the end of the talk, leaving the audience wanting more:

> This promising title had attracted a large number of people who, for an hour and a half, waited for the speaker, M. Bergson, to depart from classical psychology to share the new discoveries of psychical science. The learned professor of the Collège de France had no such audacity, and his lecture, which was otherwise charming, ended at the very point where his audience had hoped to see it begin.[18]

A few years later, when asked directly for his opinion about telepathy, Bergson stated that he was still unsure whether it was a real phenomenon. Though he leaned towards suspecting it was possible, he added, he would never lecture about it, or believe it fully, without definitive evidence.[19] Bergson practiced the same caution in 1913 when he was invited to preside over the Society for Psychical Research. In his presidential address, delivered "before a large and fashionable audience," Bergson was more concerned with the limitations of the methodologies of science in matters of psychical research than with psychical phenomena themselves.[20] This was as far as Bergson was willing to speculate publicly, even before an audience of psychical researchers.

One of the reasons for Bergson's caution was that he did not like to make pronouncements on something about which he did not feel certain: "I neither deny nor believe anything a priori. I am a man who wants to see before he believes, but who only asks to be given many opportunities to see."[21] It is also likely that he did not want to give ammunition to his adversaries, who were already labelling him a poet and an enemy of reason. But despite the care he took to avoid being branded unserious, Bergson had flirted with the supernatural just enough to arouse a great deal of interest from a public already drawn to matters of spirit.

In the middle of the first decade of the twentieth century, attendance at Bergson's lectures had started to increase significantly. In May 1904, the death of Collège de France professor Gabriel Tarde freed up the chair of modern philosophy, a post that Bergson had always coveted, and he asked to be transferred to this post:

During the four years that I have held the Chair of Greek and Latin Philosophy at the Collège de France, I have made every effort to align my teaching and my personal work as closely as possible. But there has always been a considerable gap between my teaching, the essential aim of which is to explore the thought of the ancient philosophers, and my work which deals with the problems of modern philosophy, formulated in their present form and examined in the light of positive science.[22]

Bergson's request was granted, and he became free to explore the problems that most interested him, and in the manner that most suited him. This career move and Bergson's involvement with the French psychical society coincided with an alarming growth in his following.

His popularity was no longer restricted to Paris. In September 1904, Bergson attended the Second International Congress of Philosophy in Geneva, where he gave a talk on the relationship between the brain and thought. In the talk, he expanded upon the problem of the relationship between mind and body, which he had explored both in *Matter and Memory* and in the experiments conducted behind closed doors with Eusapia Palladino. At the last minute, Bergson's talk had to be moved to a larger space because demand to attend was so high.

Bergson had a genius for writing and lecturing on the subjects that the mass audience was most attracted to, and this trend was confirmed in his fourth book, *Creative Evolution*, which dealt with another enticing topic: the meaning of life.

École normale supérieure literary section in 1878. Bergson (bottom left), Jaurès (top right).

Family outing (around 1900). From left to right: Henri Bergson, his wife Louise, his daughter Jeanne, and his father-in-law Gustave Neuburger (family archive).

On écoute aux fenêtres le cours de M. Bergson

ON ÉCOUTE AUX FENÊTRES LE COURS DE M. BERGSON

À L'ENTRÉE DE L'AMPHITHÉÂTRE

M. BERGSON ARRIVANT AU COLLÈGE DE FRANCE

La foule qui s'est rendue hier au cours de M. Bergson était plus dense encore que de coutume. Il s'agissait, pour ses disciples et admirateurs, de lui témoigner leur joie à l'occasion de son élection. On écouta aux fenêtres la leçon du maître!   (Central-Excelsior-Photos.)

Crowds gather at the Collège de France for Bergson's lecture. Front page of *Excelsior*, February 14, 1914 (BNF).

Bergson in 1922 in his holiday home
in Switzerland (family archive).

From left to right: Jeanne, Louise, and Henri Bergson in 1923 (family archive).

Bergson later in life (family archive).

CHAPTER 12

CINEMATOGRAPHIC INTELLIGENCE

On December 28, 1895, thirty-five people gathered in the basement of the Grand Café on the boulevard des Capucines. A mysterious poster on the door that simply read "Cinématographe Lumière" had drawn them downstairs. When they entered the Salon Indien, none of them possessed the frame of reference to understand what a film was, but when they reemerged into the cold Parisian street about half an hour later, they had become the first people in history who could say, "I went to the cinema."

Film projections had already taken place in various contexts, mainly before learned societies, but this handful of curious spectators had just witnessed the first-ever commercial screening. Named *cinématographe*, from the Greek "the writing of movement," and *lumière*, after the brothers who invented it, the machine could be used as both a camera and a projector that rendered it, in the

Lumières' opinion, superior to Edison's combined use of his kineto-graph and kinetoscope.

The Lumière brothers had offered the owner of the Grand Café 20 percent of the proceeds from the event as remuneration for the space, but the man had so little faith in their project that he refused this offer and instead set a fixed rate for a year's rental of the space. He would soon realise what a monumental mistake he had made: within a few weeks of the first showing, through the sheer power of word of mouth, thousands were pressing themselves at the doors to witness the moving images. The first to attend the screenings left in such a daze that they instinctively knew that what they had experienced had to be seen to be believed. Most of them returned with a group of acquaintances they had rounded up so that they too could witness this miracle of technology. The Salon Indien in the basement could hold only about 135 people, and soon security was deployed to contain the crowds.

Projected onto the screen through the Lumières' hand-cranked device, scenes of everyday life—workers hurrying out of a factory, a baby attempting to catch a fish in a bowl, a group of men jumping off a small pier and swimming back to shore—unfolded as though in real time, as though the black-and-white images had truly come to life.

The audience also witnessed the first scripted comedy film in history, an excellent illustration of Bergson's theory of laughter. In the forty-five-second clip "L'arroseur arrosé" ("The Sprinkler Sprin-kled"), we see a gardener watering his plants with a hose. A young boy creeps up behind him and steps on the hose, cutting off the water flow. When the gardener inspects the nozzle, the boy releases the hose, spraying the gardener.

But in its infancy, the main draw of cinema was not its narrative structure. People stood in line for the most lifelike motion they had ever experienced outside of life itself. It was the movement on the screen that enthralled so many audience members. One wrote: "It is impossibly real. The power of illusion! As you gaze at these moving pictures, you wonder if you are not in fact hallucinating. . . . The Lumières are great magicians."[1]

In 1932, several decades after the Lumières' first commercial projection, Bergson was asked what he thought about cinema. That same year the Marx Brothers had released *Horse Feathers*, the Disney studios showed their first-ever colourised cartoon, and Ingrid Bergman graced the silver screen for the first time. "Talkies" had become as common as silent films, and filmmaking techniques had improved in ways that the Lumière brothers could never have foreseen. But Bergson was not impressed. He answered truthfully: "I have never been."[2] Perhaps, like many people of his generation, he did not consider cinema an art form but rather saw it as a gimmick unworthy of his time. As it was, he had neither the leisure nor the energy to go to the theatre or to listen to music, activities he actually enjoyed, so he would not waste his time on this new form of spectacle. Perhaps, also, he was suspicious of a mechanism that purported to convey the movement of life so convincingly.

Although Bergson never went to the cinema, he did study the cinematograph in detail. A machine like the *cinématographe lumière*, he wrote, takes "a series of snapshots" of real-life motion and then projects "these snapshots onto the screen such that they replace each other in quick succession."[3] But the movement does not come from the snapshots. Looked at side by side, they would not come to life, because "we will never make movement out of immobile parts."[4] Bergson pointed out that cinema creates the illusion that the movement is coming from the photographs when in fact it is coming from the machine itself. The machine deceives us into thinking that movement is being recomposed from immobility: "Such is the artifice of the cinematograph. And such is also the artifice of our knowledge. Rather than attaching ourselves to the inner becoming of things, we place ourselves on the outside of them in order to artificially recompose their becoming."[5]

Bergson's rise to fame in the early twentieth century coincided with the advent of cinema, a new art form that completely changed our relationship to images and movement. Though Bergson was not much interested in the medium itself, the mechanism of the cinematograph offered him a perfect analogy to describe the limitations of the human intellect.

PUTTING INTELLIGENCE IN ITS PLACE

In the first years of the twentieth century, Bergson was working on the follow-up to *Matter and Memory*. True to himself, he told almost no one about his new project, and when he did, he remained extremely vague. In a letter to the British philosopher Victoria Welby, he alluded to the fact that he was preparing new and more concrete applications of his method of intuition.[6] But he never mentioned that he was spending all of his free time reading the most cutting-edge biological research of his day, focussing mainly on evolutionary theories but also delving into palaeontology, animal behaviour, and embryology.

The last time Bergson had presented new research to the public had been in his 1903 article, "Introduction to Metaphysics," in which he had argued that philosophy needed to change its course entirely. He had proposed intuition as a method for thinking from the point of view of *durée* itself, a way of looking at reality from within rather than through a collage of static snapshots taken from the outside.

In the early 1900s, Bergson had turned his attention to biology because he wanted to understand why our intellect tends to feel more at home with all things spatial and solid. He had realised that to fully understand both how intuitive knowledge is possible and how conceptual knowledge can be surpassed, he would have to meet cognition at its source and investigate the very origins of the human intellect.

When, Bergson asked himself, did human intelligence appear? What are the signs we can look for that indicate with certainty the presence of an intelligent being? Tools, like flint hatchets, are seen as a common indicator of prehistoric human intellect. This is also, remarked Bergson, how we determine a nonhuman animal's intelligence—by its ability to use a rudimentary tool, like a stone or a stick, to achieve certain ends. "Mechanical invention," Bergson wrote, was the first "essential activity" of the human intellect, and "still today our social life gravitates around the fabrication and utilization of artificial instruments."[7]

We tend to place our intellect on a pedestal of pure theoretical pursuits and to distinguish between these supposedly pure pursuits and more practical manual labour. But in reality, said Bergson, the human intellect is at its core a tool for making more tools. According to Bergson, an invention like the steam engine was much more important in the grand scheme of human history than any other event that we value:

> We are only now beginning to sense the depths of the shock it gave us. The revolution that it brought about in industry no less dramatically changed the relations among men. New ideas are emerging. New feelings are in the process of being born. Thousands of years from now, when the distance of the past has left nothing but the main outlines visible, our wars and our revolutions will count for very little, assuming that they are even remembered at all. But they will perhaps discuss the steam engine, along with all of the various inventions that come along with it, the way that we speak of bronze or carved stone.[8]

Our intelligence did not arise as a theoretical faculty designed for speculation. It is an evolutionary adaptation that came about to respond to pragmatic needs and enable more efficient actions. As Bergson put it, the faculty of understanding is "an extension of the faculty of action."[9] Before calling ourselves *Homo sapiens*, Bergson said, we should swallow our pride and recognise that in truth we are *Homo faber* (man the maker).

Human intelligence is a product of our evolutionary history. Over a very long period of time, our ancestors found more and more ingenious ways to assemble and fashion their environment to their advantage. Our intellect, the intellect that invents abstract and complex systems of symbols and concepts, first arose and then evolved through our attempts to understand the external world, not only to survive it but to master it. According to Bergson, throughout this evolution, our intelligence adopted the contours of the inert matter it sought to control through its tools and technology. The evolution of our theoretical tools—language, symbols, concepts, science—has followed the same trend:

> Human intellect feels at home so long as we allow it to remain among inert objects, particularly among solids, where our action finds its footing and where our industriousness finds its tools.... Our concepts have been formed in the image of solids and... our logic is, above all else the logic of solids.[10]

As a consequence, our intelligence is out of its depth as soon as it concentrates on truly mobile realities, such as life and the mind. For instance, the concepts of biology are often unable to account for the apparently incompatible features of living beings. Life tends towards unity and building individual organisms, but it also tends towards division and reproduction. In the introduction of *Creative Evolution*, Bergson wrote:

> None of the categories of our thought (unity, multiplicity, mechanical causality, intelligent finality, etc.) can be unequivocally applied to the things of life—who can say where individuality begins or ends, whether the living being is one or many, or whether the cells come together to form an organism or the organism divides up into cells? It is in vain that we force the living being into one or another of our frameworks. All of the frameworks crack. They are too narrow and, above all too rigid for what we would like to fit into them.[11]

In his 1907 book *L'Évolution créatrice* (*Creative Evolution*), Bergson had therefore formulated a paradox, one that could explain why our theories have been so bad at depicting motion, temporality, and the continual flow of existence. Bergson's paradox could explain the origin of fallacies like Zeno's negation of movement. It could explain Western philosophy's millennia-long obsession with immobility and stability. The paradox that Bergson had discovered in his study of the history of the mind was this: human intelligence has evolved in a way that makes it bad at understanding evolution.

INSTINCT, INTELLIGENCE, AND INTUITION

Bergson had been drawn to the question of the evolutionary origins of our intelligence partly because he believed this investigation would help him understand how the limitations of intelligence might be overcome. Although human intelligence alone is ill suited to understand *durée*, it is not the only evolved means of grasping reality. "Along other diverging pathways," he argued, "other forms of consciousness have developed."[12] In *Creative Evolution*, Bergson downgraded intelligence. Intelligence is not, he said, some almost miraculous instrument of pure knowledge, it is simply one among several creative solutions that organisms have evolved in order to survive and face the challenges posed by their environment.

In instinct, a different kind of strategy, the organism's behaviour and needs overlap perfectly. Instinct is life understanding life from the inside. Where intelligence adopts the contours of external matter, instinct follows the internal movements of life itself.

But neither intelligence nor instinct is a perfect adaptation. While the intellect "is characterized by a natural incomprehension of life," it allows for a sense of initiative lacking in instinct, which cannot arrive at the general viewpoint that intelligence adopts by taking a step back, classifying, and categorizing its surroundings.[13] Instinct's grasp of life may be internal and absolute, but it is also devoid of reflexivity. In Bergson's elegant summation: "There are things that the intellect alone is capable of looking for, but will never find by itself. Instinct alone could find these things, but it will never go looking for them."[14]

For Bergson, no organism is either purely instinctive or purely intelligent. Intelligence and instinct are tendencies that are represented more or less prominently along divergent lines of evolution. Though humans are predominantly intellectual, we share with other organisms the ability to tap into an internal, instinctive knowledge of life. In the words of the Bergson specialist Arnaud François, the implication of Bergson's evolutionary theory of knowledge is that "instinct in contact with intelligence could expand into intuition."[15] If the intellect can lend its self-reflexive light to instinct, then intuition—an internal knowledge of the *élan* of life itself, in other words, a philosophical knowledge of life from life's point of view that does not rely on the categories of inert matter—becomes possible.

SCIENCE AND PHILOSOPHY

Unsurprisingly, Bertrand Russell could not resist taking a jibe at what he understood of his philosophical rival's notions of instinct and intelligence:

> They are never wholly without each other, but in the main intellect is the misfortune of man, while instinct is seen at its best in ants, bees, and Bergson. The division between intellect and instinct is fundamental in his philosophy, much of which is a kind of Sandford and Merton, with instinct as the good boy and intellect as the bad boy. Instinct at its best is called intuition.[16]

This is how Bergson was often depicted: as arguing that there is no value in rationality or the intellect at all, that the findings of the intellect—and therefore of science as a whole—should be dismissed and even combatted. But this was far from the case.

Bergson's relationship to science was not the one described by his enemies. True, he did point out that our intelligence and, by extension, our science are limited when dealing with something other than inert matter. This is, for Bergson, where intuition comes in.[17] Bergson envisaged intuition as a method that would allow philosophers to shine a light on the shortcomings of the intellect, "grasp what is insufficient . . . and allow us to catch sight of the means of completing them."[18]

But contrary to what Russell suggested, Bergson was well aware of the limitations of intuition, and he did not present intuition as superior to intelligence. In fact, without intelligence, he argued, there is no intuition: "Without the intellect, intuition would have remained in the form of instinct, riveted to the specific object that interests it practically."[19] Intuition unaccompanied by intelligence would be incapable of producing any form of communicable insight.

In the same way Bergson viewed instinct and intelligence as inseparable, he also viewed science and philosophy as destined for collaboration. He argued that if philosophy is understood as complementary to science rather than subjugated to it, philosophy might come to the aid of science by making science aware of its own tendencies and limits. Progress in our understanding of reality can only come in the form of a synthesis that puts "more science into metaphysics, and more metaphysics into science."[20]

Though Bergson was smeared as an anti-rationalist, his fundamental point was actually much more straightforward: our intelligence is not the only tool at our disposal to apprehend reality, and science alone should not always get the last word. But this was one of many of Bergson's ideas that would end up misunderstood and unrecognizable after being stretched out of the initial shape he had given it. Bergson would soon come to learn that being misunderstood was one of the many burdens that came with almost cinematic levels of stardom.

CHAPTER 13

ECLIPSING DARWIN

Herbert Wildon Carr was fifty years old when he gave up his membership at the London Stock Exchange to devote his life to philosophy.[1] The sequence of events that set this decision in motion happened almost by chance. One day in 1907, he was wandering around Paris when his eye was drawn to a book positioned prominently in the window of a shop. He recognised the name on the cover. He had seen a few of the author's other books in the library of a friend who had enthusiastically praised their "striking originality." So, Carr entered the shop and bought a copy of *L'Évolution créatrice*.

Carr was already reasonably well versed in philosophy, having studied the subject in the evening classes he followed at King's College. But he had never dreamed of pursuing an academic career— that is, not until, sitting in his Parisian hotel room, he opened Bergson's latest book: "It produced the experience of a new conversion. The whole philosophical problem was transformed, irradiated with light. I found myself possessed with a new enthusiasm." Then he added: "I was not, of course, the only one to feel that Bergson had given a new direction to philosophy."[2]

Indeed, on June 13, 1907, while enjoying the mountain air of his summer home in Chocorua, New Hampshire, William James sent a postcard to F.C.S. Schiller, a friend and fellow philosopher, to thank him for the positive feedback on one of his own recent books before hastening to bring up the subject he was most eager to discuss:

> But have you read Bergson's new book? It seems to me that nothing is important in comparison with that divine apparition. All our positions, real time, a growing world, asserted magisterially, and the beast intellectualism killed absolutely dead! The whole flowed round by a style incomparable as it seems to me. Read it, and digest it if you can. Much of it I can't yet assimilate.[3]

James and Bergson had been corresponding since 1902, when James sent Bergson his comments on *Matter and Memory*. From then onwards, the American philosopher had consistently been full of praise for Bergson's philosophy, and by 1906 he was counting Bergson as a member of his own school of thought—pragmatism. But with *Creative Evolution*, James no longer saw Bergson as his equal, realising that this new book had sent the French philosopher soaring out of his philosophical league.

On the same day he wrote to Schiller, James also wrote to Bergson:

> O my Bergson, you are a magician, and your book is a marvel, a real wonder in the history of philosophy . . . a pure classic in point of form. . . . There is so much that is absolutely new that it will take a long time for your contemporaries to assimilate it.[4]

It is no exaggeration to say that, as Carr and James recognised, Bergson's book about evolution changed lives, starting with the author's own.

In many ways, Bergson's new book was seen as the culmination of his philosophy. With *Creative Evolution*, Bergson had crystallised some of his key ideas at the precise moment that the world was hungry for them. His insights into life, time, and intuition struck a chord with an entire generation. *Creative Evolution* affirmed human freedom in a language that resonated far and wide. It was what so many people, including some biologists, who felt let down by the promises of science, felt they so desperately needed.

BERGSON'S VISION

In the early twentieth century, evolution was a hot topic for debate. Though religious resistance to Darwin's ideas is well documented—and continues in some corners to this day—what is less well known is that decades after the publication of Darwin's *Origin*, many scientists remained highly sceptical regarding the theory of natural selection. The British evolutionary biologist and science populariser Julian Huxley described the period from the 1880s to the 1920s as a time of great uncertainty in evolutionary thought. Before genetics was established as a science in the 1920s, there was no robust theory of inheritance to support how selected changes could be carried down to the next generation. Another problem for proponents of natural selection was that the time required for tiny hereditary changes to transform reptiles into birds, or apes into humans, appeared to be much longer than the estimated age of the earth. While the fact of evolution was more and more widely accepted among biologists, the "methods," or mechanisms, of evolution were the source of much debate. Huxley called this period during which alternatives to Darwinism were proposed "the eclipse of Darwinism."

In *Creative Evolution*, Bergson developed a philosophical theory of evolution, his own contribution to the eclipse. In the first chapter, he criticised four of the rival scientific theories of evolution of his time, namely, Darwinian natural selection, Hugo de Vries's mutationism, Theodor Eimer's orthogenesis, and Lamarckian inheritance of acquired characters. These theories all fell short in one way or another, according to Bergson, because they expressed in different ways the mechanistic tendencies of the intellect.[5] Bergson's alternative metaphysical vision of life recast evolution as a creative force striving to liberate itself from the constraints of the deterministic limitations of inert matter.

In criticising the main four scientific theories of evolution, Bergson's aim was to underline their limits and emphasise the need for a metaphysical theory of life that could work alongside scientific theories. Such a metaphysical theory would not be subordinated to the materialistic thinking of the intellect but would attempt to study life from life's point of view. Bergson did not, however, aspire to replace the competing scientific theories of life with his own philosophical one. Instead, his theory of life would hold a mirror to their weaknesses.

After outlining the limits of each evolutionary theory, Bergson acknowledged that all of them in different ways touched upon important truths about life.[6] He wrote: "Each theory, being supported by a considerable number of facts, must be true in its own way. Each must correspond to a certain point of view on the process of evolution."[7] But these theories could only provide relative points of view, snapshots of life taken from the outside which, put together, could never exhaust life as a whole: "Each of these theories takes a partial view of a reality that must go beyond them all. And that reality is the proper object of philosophy, which, since it does not aim at any practical application, is not at all constrained by the precision of science."[8] As a philosopher, it was Bergson's job to seek a vision of life that followed the movement of life from the inside.

Though Bergson's theory of evolution was philosophical, many scientists counted among his readers. Around the time *Creative Evolution* was published, Huxley, then a young zoologist at the start of his career, was working on his first book, *The Individual in the Animal Kingdom*. He identified his essay as a work of "philosophical biology" and explicitly cited Bergson's new book as one of his main influences: "My indebtednesses are great. It will easily be seen how much I owe to M. Bergson, who, whether one agrees or no with his views, has given a stimulus (most valuable gift of all) to Biology and Philosophy alike."[9] About a decade later, Huxley published his infamous put-down of Bergson when he called him a "good poet but a bad scientist" (see Chapter 2). But Huxley's comment was not a sarcastic attempt to discredit Bergson's philosophy. While Bergson drew heavily upon the scientific research of his day, he had never claimed to be a scientist. His was a completely different *philosophical* approach. And when Huxley called Bergson a poet, he meant it quite literally. He was referring to what he saw as the philosopher's carefully crafted and masterful use of metaphorical language to put the reader on the track of an intuitive vision of the mobile nature of reality. In the very same passage in which Huxley called Bergson a "bad scientist," he lauded the philosopher's insight:

> [Bergson's] intellectual vision of evolution as a fact, as something happening, something whole, to be apprehended in a unitary way— that is unsurpassed. He seems to see it as vividly as you or I might see a hundred yards race, holding its different incidents and movements all in his mind together to form one picture.[10]

In *Creative Evolution*, Bergson used several images to suggest his "vision of evolution." He based his writing style, which so many found poetic, on the idea that fluid metaphorical language does a better job at representing the mobility of reality than does more restrictive conceptual language. Though no single image would ever be able to surmount the difficulties inherent in language, several well-thought-out metaphors might point the reader in the direction of a more intuitive vision. For instance, he compared life to a "current," or to "a shell that immediately exploded into fragments. And each of these fragments, being itself a kind of shell, in turn exploded into fragments destined to explode again, and so on for a very long time."[11] But of all these images, the *élan vital* was, according to Bergson, the one that best conveyed his philosophical vision of life.

THE *ÉLAN VITAL*

In one of Jeanne Bergson's drawings, a faceless, androgynous dancer appears to be swept away by the momentum of their own movements. As the upper half of the body sways back, the legs launch forward. In a few simple but precise strokes, the artist conveyed the initial thrust of what might turn into a leap forward, or perhaps a spin or a jump. We are invited to complete this snapshot of motion in our mind's eye.

Jeanne titled her drawing "Élan," a term that carries multiple connotations beyond the physical movement of her dancer. In French, the expression *prendre son élan* might be used to describe an athlete gathering momentum before a long jump, while *donner de l'élan* describes the movement involved in giving momentum to something.[12] In a more figurative sense, new *élan* can be breathed into a dwindling project to inject energy and a sense of direction into it. The word *élan* also ties into the language of our most intimate emotional impulses. An *élan* of love is an uncontrollable surge of warm or romantic feelings, an *élan* of generosity is a spontaneous overflowing of often collective solidarity, and an *élan* of rage might cause sudden, uncharacteristic acts of violence. All of these meanings are implicitly contained in the deceptively simple image that Jeanne's father used in his 1907 book to paint a metaphysical picture of evolution. The *élan vital* was the epitome of what Bergson called a "fluid concept."[13]

Represented as an *élan*, life takes the form of a burst of accumulated energy resulting in a forward movement. For Bergson, all of life is the continuation of the same initial impulse propelling itself along diverging lines of evolution:

> At a certain moment and at certain points in space, a clearly visible
> current was born: this current of life, passing through the bodies

that it had organized one after the other, passing from generation to generation, was divided among species and distributed to individuals without thereby losing anything of its force, and rather intensifying as it advanced.[14]

Every organism living and extinct, every attempt to survive and every failure to adapt, is a manifestation of the same *élan*: "Just like the wind that sweeps into a crossroad is divided up into diverging currents they are all still but one and the same gust of wind."[15] But unlike the wind, whose direction can be predicted in advance since its path has already been drawn out, the direction of the *élan vital* cannot be foreseen. Like the spontaneous movement of Jeanne's dancer, evolution has no predetermined goal.

The image of the *élan vital*, in addition to conjuring up visions of physical actions like a thrust, a push, or an impulsion, also related to psychological concepts, like effort, will, and freedom. Bergson conceived the *élan vital* as analogous to individual consciousness. For instance, in the same way that it is impossible to deduce a future mental state from past or present mental states, it is impossible to predict the future life-forms that will evolve from present or past life-forms. Life, wrote Bergson, "like consciousness, is creating something at every instant."[16]

Creativity requires an act of will, something like an effort by which we draw "from ourselves not only all that was there, but more than was there."[17] For a poet or an artist, a creative effort is the encounter between an unrealised inspiration and the material—the words or the canvas—with which this inspiration is expressed.[18] Similarly, the creativity of evolution results from the confrontation between the freedom and spontaneity of the *élan vital* and the inertia of matter.

For Bergson, life and inorganic matter represent two conflicting but inexorably intertwined movements, two opposite sides of the same reality.[19] Matter tends towards automatism, predictability, and repetitiveness; it "suggests the idea of a thing unmaking itself."[20] The *élan vital*, on the other hand, can be seen as "an effort to remount the incline that matter descends."[21]

The history of life presents itself "as if a vast current of consciousness had penetrated into matter" and had attempted to organise it to its advantage, to insert more "indetermination and freedom" into the world.[22] Each one of the myriad of directions life has taken over the course of its evolution represents a new attempt at liberation, each one bolder than the last. But, for all its creativity and freedom, the *élan vital* is limited; it is, wrote Bergson, "finite and was given once and for all." In other words, there is no guarantee that life will always prevail.[23]

For the most part, over the course of evolution, the repetitive tendencies of inert matter had won and the efforts of the *élan vital* had turned short with "regressions, halts, and accidents of all sorts."[24] Instead of pushing for more freedom, life has often become stuck or has settled for the automatous ways of the matter it inhabits. But with the advent of humankind, evolution had taken a veritable leap: "In man, and in man alone, consciousness liberates itself. The entire history of life up until then had been the history of an effort by consciousness to lift up matter, and of consciousness being more or less completely crushed by the matter that fell back on it."[25]

The range of human action and choice is unprecedented. Human language and, more generally, human culture and societies allow for the conservation of the past efforts of humankind, the anticipation of an infinity of problems, and the creation of an infinity of solutions. Nothing predestined the emergence of humankind, but humankind realises to the highest degree the main tendencies of the *élan vital*: creativity and freedom.

Bergson's definition of life in terms of striving, effort, and creativity satisfied those who viewed other evolutionary explanations, in particular Darwin's, as presenting the history of life as a cold mechanical process. *Creative Evolution* ended up speaking to a wide audience because it gave human life meaning at a time when so many felt that meaning in life was lacking.

MECHANISM VS. VITALISM

Evolution was not the only debate shaking up early twentieth-century biology. In the second half of the previous century, new methods and discoveries in physiology, bacteriology, and biochemistry had fuelled the hope that biological phenomena might one day be entirely explained with the laws of physics. In such mechanistic conceptions of life, organisms were reduced to the sum of their physical parts. But mechanistic biology was now facing serious criticism. Many biologists argued that there were phenomena, like reproduction, reactivity, and evolution, that were specific to life and could not be entirely explained in terms of physics or chemistry.

On the extreme opposite side of the debate, there was a school of thought called vitalism. Crudely put, vitalism posits the existence of a vital force that is independent from the laws of physics and that accounts for organic phenomena. Like mechanism, vitalism also faced criticism from biologists in the early twentieth century, mainly because it resorted to something akin to a supernatural force to explain life. The most prominent vitalist at the time was a German embryologist called Hans Driesch whose experiments on sea urchins had led him to believe that certain biological phenomena, like the development of the embryo, could only be explained by invoking an immaterial vital principle which he called the "entelechy."[26]

Superficial readings of *Creative Evolution* have led commentators to conflate Bergson's *élan vital* and Driesch's entelechy. In 1908, Driesch himself reinforced this association by publishing a mostly positive review of the book in a biology journal.[27] But, while Bergson was sympathetic towards Driesch's dismissal of mechanistic biology, he was also critical of this kind of vitalism because it resorted to "finalism," meaning that it portrayed life as following a prewritten plan.[28] Contrary to the entelechy, the *élan vital* was completely open-ended and unpredictable. Bergson did not think of the *élan vital* as a "vital force" that is completely independent or different from matter. As the philosopher Mathilde Tahar notes, the image of the *élan vital* "points to a reality that is more than matter, but only exists through matter, which is both its other and its necessary complement, the cause of its detours as well as the origin of its inventiveness."[29]

Driesch's positive review of Bergson's book nevertheless cemented in many minds the association of Bergson's philosophy of life with a school of thought deemed pseudoscientific and already bound for obsolescence in the early twentieth century. This did nothing to help Bergson's reputation as being anti-science.

Most biologists at this time occupied a middle-ground position between vitalism and mechanism. In their view, biological phenomena cannot be entirely explained in terms of physicochemical laws, but at the same time they conceded that there is nothing like a supernatural vital force. Despite the (exaggerated) assimilation between Driesch's vitalistic biology and Bergson's philosophical vision of life, many of these middle-ground biologists nevertheless turned to *Creative Evolution* for ammunition in the fight against mechanism.

The British geneticist Arthur Darbishire counted among them. He was deeply impressed by Bergson's idea that human intelligence has evolved in such a way that it is bad at understanding evolution. He believed that Bergson's insights into the limitations of scientific knowledge could be used to give biology entirely new foundations: "The biologist, if he is to succeed in giving an approximately correct interpretation of life, must, to a large extent, begin over again and follow up the clues given by ... Henri Bergson."[30] Darbishire arrived at a surprising conclusion (one that Bergson himself did not express): if biologists are naturally disposed to overlook what is mobile and versatile about life because they are drawn to mechanical simplifications, then the fact that they find a theory appealing should alert them to the possibility that this theory is far from the true nature of things. In other words, Darbishire proposed to use

Bergson's theory of the origin of human intelligence as a principle to discriminate between good and bad theories.[31]

Bergson's idea that, from individual organisms to evolution as a whole, vital phenomena are above all temporal also resonated with many early twentieth-century biologists. In *Creative Evolution*, Bergson wrote: "An organism that lives is a thing that endures. Its past, as a whole, is prolonged into its present, and remains present and active there.... *Wherever something is living, there is a register, open somewhere, in which time is being inscribed.*"[32] In short, for Bergson, the main difference between organisms and inert matter was *durée*.[33]

A few years after Bergson published *Creative Evolution*, the Scottish zoologist E. S. Russell wrote to his friend the biologist and mathematician D'Arcy Thompson: "I don't hold with vitalism in Driesch's sense, but I should like to work out a biology on Bergsonian lines—if it can be done."[34] Following Bergson, Russell believed that the temporality of organisms made them different from physical phenomena and that, for this reason, biology would never be a mere subdiscipline of physics:

An organism is above all a historical being because its structure and its activities are determined by its individual experience and by its heredity, in other words, the experience accumulated by the race. In order to understand the current activities of an organism, it is imperative to know its past experience, its genetic history. This fundamental fact alone is enough to absolutely distinguish between the biological and the physical sciences. In organisms, the past is always interwoven to a certain extent with the present; we could say, borrowing Bergson's expression, "the past is extended into the present." Therefore, living beings must be explained by their history.[35]

Bergson's philosophy of life, in which organisms are inherently temporal and life spontaneous and creative, provided valuable arguments to those who opposed the mechanisation of biology. But the impact of *Creative Evolution* extended far beyond the life sciences.

When it was first published in 1907, *Creative Evolution* did not initially sell many copies. "This," wrote the critic, poet, and translator of Bergson's "Introduction to Metaphysics," T. E. Hulme, "is as it should be. A book on pure philosophy has no business to sell in large numbers."[36] But soon enough it started flying off shelves. In a review of the book, the American psychologist George T. W. Patrick summed up what made it so appealing to an early twentieth-century audience:

In Bergson's philosophy we have the metaphysical first fruits of the biological age in which we of the twentieth century are living. We have here a reaction against all the last century philosophies which treat the physical sciences as if they represent the last word of truth and either like Spencer build their systems upon these sciences, or else like Comte doubt whether it is possible to transcend them. Now we have a philosophy of *life*, in which life is loosed from all its physico-chemical limitations and shown to be reality itself. It is only that which *endures*, which flows, which creates, that is *real*. Such is life, or, going still deeper, consciousness, a self-creative, unforeknowable stream.[37]

In the months and years following the publication of *Creative Evolution*, Bergson's Collège de France lectures attracted crowds of unprecedented size. "Now," complained Hulme in 1911, "it is impossible to get a seat without sitting through the hour before and listening to that intolerable bore, Leroy-Beaulieu."[38]

To use one of Bergson's own images for evolution, his popularity and the various appropriations of his ideas by his admirers can be likened to "a shell that immediately exploded into fragments. And each of these fragments, being itself a kind of shell, in turn exploded into fragments destined to explode again, and so on for a very long time."[39] In other words, much like Bergsonian evolution, the trajectory of Bergson's immense cultural impact is difficult to chart because it followed many divergent directions and took on often unpredictable lives of its own, in a self-perpetuating, self-creating movement in which Bergson rapidly found himself engulfed and overwhelmed.

CHAPTER 14

DELUGED

Ever since it was placed on a pillar of the Alma bridge in the mid-nineteenth century, the Zouave statue has provided Parisians with an unofficial marker of the level of the Seine: when the soldier's stone boots are submerged, it is a sure sign of flooding.

On January 21, 1910, after months of unusually heavy rain, the evening newspaper *Le Petit Parisien* warned: "The Seine is rising alarmingly."[1] That night the water reached the statue's knees and the river overflowed. A week later, when only the Zouave's head was visible above the murky waters, the headlines announced, "AN UNPRECEDENTED DISASTER."[2] In the suburbs, fifteen thousand lost their homes. The deep tunnels under construction for future metro lines became "invisible rivers" beneath the surface of Paris and threatened to collapse the roads above. Public transport had ceased, canoes were deployed, streetlamps went dark, and telephones and telegraphs were cut off. The city had come to an almost complete standstill, and the water was still rising. On February 19, it rose at the rate of a centimetre an hour, turning the boulevard Haussmann below Marcel Proust's apartment into a torrent.[3]

In the early days of the flood, information circulated slowly. Bergson had arranged to meet his friend the philosopher Isaak Benrubi at the Institut de France, but the entrance on rue de l'Ancienne Comédie had been transformed into a small lake. The main courtyard could now be accessed only by boat. So the two men crossed the Pont des Arts and spent the next couple of hours walking along the few quays that were not yet submerged or barricaded and then through the Tuileries Garden. Naturally, the flood dominated the first part of their discussion, but soon their attention drifted to another topic that was just as pressing—Bergson's growing influence.

Just three years earlier, the first printing of *Creative Evolution* had completely sold out within a few weeks of being published.[4] By the time the Seine had risen over its banks, the book was set to become an international bestseller, with translations in English, Spanish, German, and Swedish in preparation. The historian Georges Batault called the book "a philosophical monument which can be said without exaggeration to be the most important manifestation of critical thought since Kant."[5] In a lengthy review of the book in the *Revue de métaphysique et de morale*, the philosopher Louis Weber presented Bergson as a better alternative to Spencer, who had previously enjoyed considerable fame in France, and the British geneticist Arthur Darbishire called the publication of the book "the greatest event, so far, in the history of thought in the twentieth century."[6]

Bergson's notoriety rapidly swelled and spread well beyond university settings. After a trip to France around this time, Huntly Carter, the art critic for the British literary magazine *The New Age*, wrote:

> The intuitional philosophy of Bergson ... has so taken possession of Paris that the spirit of it seems to fill every place. I have heard it discussed, when seated at the long glittering café that shoulders

the perpetual mass of the magnificent Renaissance Opera House breasting the broad boulevards that flow away in leagues of rhythmical lustre.[7]

Bergson's friend Gilbert Maire later recalled: "It became fashionable to proclaim oneself a Bergsonian. Every salon became Bergsonian. Every society woman became a Bergsonian."[8] As his ideas were seeping into every aspect of cultural life, Bergson himself was about to be swept away in the tsunami of obligations, misunderstandings, and miseries that came with notoriety.

A "WHIRLWIND OF OCCUPATIONS"

In the summer of 1907, Bergson's health deteriorated. He wrote to Raffalovich:

I was very unwell during the holidays so, on my return to Paris, I had to be seen by a doctor. I was diagnosed with a serious case of enteritis! As a result, I was condemned not only to a very strict diet but also (and this was infinitely more annoying) to eat my meals in bed and to remain there for an hour afterwards.[9]

The treatment did not entirely alleviate the symptoms, and Bergson became convinced that his illness was a bad case of nerves and had nothing to do with his diet. With a bestseller on his hands, Bergson was soon inundated with obligations and deluged with requests. The intense fatigue, headaches, and insomnia Bergson had started experiencing in the early 1900s intensified. In letters to close acquaintances, Bergson repeatedly complained of feeling overworked and overburdened by a "whirlwind of occupations" from which he could not escape.[10] His health forced him to put in place increasingly strict restrictions on his social life. He received more invitations to dinners and other social events than he could honour and was plunged into impossible dilemmas in trying to manage them. One of Bergson's worst fears was to unintentionally offend a countess, a professor, or a politician, and to become the object of some secret vexation he could not assuage. He started refusing all invitations, assuring his closer friends that this was a necessary precaution to maintain fairness in how he distributed himself, but those who knew him well guessed that this blanket response to invitations was merely another way of mitigating the noise and the exhaustion. Bergson still happily met people on terms that were agreeable to him: one on one, in his home, in the afternoon, for quiet discussions of philosophical matters.

A few years before Paris flooded, Bergson had started drowning in correspondence. He noticed that the letters were arriving from further and further away. People from all over the world contacted him to enquire about certain details of his doctrine, or to ask for his views on works of their own. Bergson did his best to respond to them all, though this task used up a lot of his time, sometimes whole afternoons, as he replied to each letter by hand, having never owned a typewriter.[11] In 1914, his friend Isaak Benrubi wrote in his journal:

> Bergson told me that he received an average of thirty letters a day and that he did not know how to both answer them and complete all the work with which he was overloaded. He longed to leave Paris and settle somewhere else. I asked him: "Why don't you get a secretary?" He replied that it wouldn't do him much good, because he'd still have to do everything himself.[12]

As the correspondence piled up, so too did a mountain of new tasks, obligations, and invitations to give talks, write articles, or offer career advice. In 1911, he wrote to Reinach: "I haven't taken a single day—I'd almost say not a single hour—off this year, and I'm afraid I probably won't next year either."[13]

BERGSON-MANIA

Around the time of the publication of *Creative Evolution*, Bergson's lectures had seen a massive increase in attendance. As numbers in the lecture theatre went up, so did the social standing of the audience members. Bergson admirer Gilbert Maire remembered watching elegant men and women crowding "into the narrow lecture hall" and their "luxurious cars" lining the rue Saint-Jacques and the rue des Écoles. He remembered hearing the corridors of the Collège de France echoing "with perfumed cackles and languorous exclamations, such as one might hear after an enthralling play."[14] These denizens of high society may have attracted the most attention from the press, but in fact Bergson's audience represented a heterogeneous sample of early twentieth-century society. Observing the scene in the lecture theatre one day, Bergson's disciple Charles Péguy wrote:

> I saw elderly men, women, young girls, young men, many young men, Frenchmen, Russians, foreigners, mathematicians, naturalists, I saw there students in letters, students in science, medical students, I saw there engineers, economists, lawyers, laymen and priests ... I saw there poets, artists ... they come from the Sorbonne and I think the Ecole Normale; I saw there well known bourgeois types, socialists, anarchists.[15]

Every Friday, this eclectic group gathered to hear Bergson speak. Perhaps some of them had merely come to be able to say they had *been there*, but even the socialites found themselves entranced by the professor's lecturing style. Bergson never wrote a script for his lectures; he prepared only a loose outline to serve as the thread upon which his thoughts could crystallise. T. E. Hulme described the effortless flow of Bergson's thought process materialising into speech in real time:

> His eyes seemed always to be half-closed, and he gave you all the time the impression of a man describing with great difficulty the shape of something which he just saw. There was a curious pause and a gesture of the thumb and forefinger which looked as if he were pulling a fine thread out of a tangled mass. It carried over to one an extraordinary

feeling of conviction. It appeared as if in the confused flux of things he was able by great attention to just see a certain curve, and that he was carefully choosing his words and picking out metaphors and illustrations in order to make sure he was conveying over to one just the exact shape of the curve he saw and no other. It is perhaps the most pleasing form of delivery possible, because in a subtle way it gives one continually the feeling that one is helping the lecturer to discover something.[16]

In the 1910s, the crowds that met Bergson every Friday in room 8 of the Collège de France were becoming more and more unmanageable. Every week at least 700 men and women attempted to squeeze into a space that could hold only 370. To make things worse, the wealthiest members of the audience had started sending their valets to reserve seats for them.

In January 1914, a group of students addressed a petition to the administrator of the Collège de France. They demanded reserved access to Bergson's lectures. In their letter, the students complained that, unlike the more privileged members of Bergson's audience, they did not have the leisure to arrive two hours in advance to secure a spot. But when measures were taken to ensure that the students got first pick of the seats, Bergson received complaints that they were taking advantage of the privilege by occupying seats that were not reserved for them. Bergson also received reports of violence in the corridors, and it was pointed out to him that, in the event of panic, the consequences could be terrible. "So what should be done?" Bergson wrote to the administrator. "The problem is truly insoluble."[17] Someone suggested that the lectures be moved to the grand amphitheatre of the Sorbonne, or even the Garnier opera house, but in the end Bergson managed to obtain permission to leave the windows open so that people outside the room could listen in.

During these tumultuous years, Bergson often complained to Raffalovich about "struggling against" a "rising tide of occupations," noise, and general chaos that threatened to "submerge" him, just as the Seine had done to his home city.[18]

It took Paris and its surrounding areas months to recover from the flood of 1910. For Bergson, from the publication of *Creative Evolution* in 1907 until the start of World War I in 1914, the tide seemed to never stop rising. Day after day, the obligations kept piling up, and the disturbances and commotion only got louder. And unlike the city of Paris, Bergson would never recover.

CHAPTER 15

THE BERGSON BOOM

In the late months of 1911, T. E. Hulme wrote in the *Saturday Westminster Gazette*:

There have been stirring times lately for those peculiar people amongst us who take an interest in metaphysics. We have not been able to buy even a sporting evening paper without finding in it an account of a certain famous philosopher. All of us in the craft have been shining with a certain amount of this reflected radiance. No less than five times recently wonderful young men have dashed up to my house in taxis, rung the bell furiously, and on being admitted have announced breathlessly: "I am the representative of the Daily ——. Can you give me Bergson's private address, as my paper wants to print a little talk with him." In the course of its varied history, philosophy has been many things, but never before has it attained the dignity of being "news," and news which was so pressing that it had to be got out before a certain edition. One began to imagine that one would someday see the newsboys running along the street with the flaring placards, "Secret of the cosmos discovered: special interview."[1]

PHILOSOPHER OF THE HOUR

By this time, Bergson's popularity was close to its peak. Since the publication of *Creative Evolution* in 1907, his notoriety had spread beyond the walls of the Collège de France, beyond Parisian academic circles, and beyond France. Bergson's new book was rapidly translated into several languages, including English, Swedish, Spanish, Polish, and German. Beyond Europe, Bergson would have a profound impact on Chinese aesthetics and artistic creation, the Kyoto School of Japanese thinkers, and South American literature, to cite only a few.[2]

In Britain alone, over two hundred articles and books about Bergson and his theory of life were published between 1909 and 1911.[3] It seemed that not a day went by without his name being mentioned in anglophone journals and newspapers. An article in *Nature* described him as "the most discussed and the most interesting philosopher in Europe at the present time."[4] A reporter for the *Aberdeen Daily Journal* remarked: "Perhaps there is no living writer who is commanding so much attention today in the world of philosophy as Bergson."[5] And the *New York Times* declared:

> Bergson is the popular philosopher of the day. He is the pet of the Intellectuals. Being the newest philosophic fad—the latest drawing room attraction—we must—every one of us—know something about him. Else, how shall we move in the highest intellectual circles?[6]

In the United Kingdom, one article attracted a lot of attention. Former prime minister Arthur Balfour published a lengthy review of *Creative Evolution* in the *Hibbert Journal*. Despite being critical of certain aspects of Bergson's philosophy (in particular relating to the *élan vital*), Balfour concluded that Bergson's "admirable criticisms, his psychological insight, his charms of style" granted "permanent value in his theories."[7] Hulme, who had been supporting Bergson since before he was famous, rolled his eyes: "Paris is only seven hours' journey from here, and there must have been quite a considerable number of people who for several years have known that Bergson was an important person, but it was necessary for Mr. Balfour to write an article, for him to become famous."[8]

Before Balfour's piece, the idea that France had produced a radically original philosopher had been floating in the anglophone ether for a few years, planted there by a handful of notable figures. In 1908, the recently excommunicated Jesuit priest George Tyrrell informed the readers of the *Hibbert Journal* that the ideas developed in *Matter and Memory* were "surely revolutionary enough and serious enough to have deserved more attention than it has roused on this side of the Channel!" Bergson had, according to Tyrrell, "suggested a new method and almost invented a new mind," and his theories about life, if they proved to be true, "must bring all the philosophical structures of the past in ruins."[9]

If Tyrrell's pronouncements had been sure to intrigue English-speaking readers, what William James declared in a lecture the same year, on "Bergson's Critique of Intellectualism," certainly contributed to heightening curiosity about the French thinker in the United States:

> I have to confess that Bergson's originality is so profuse that many of his ideas baffle me entirely. I doubt whether anyone understands him all over, so to speak.... Bergson's resources in the way of erudition are remarkable, and in the way of expression they are simply phenomenal. This is why in France, where *l'art de bien dire* counts for so much and is so sure of appreciation, he has immediately taken so eminent a place in public esteem. Old-fashioned professors, whom

his ideas quite fail to satisfy, nevertheless speak of his talent almost with bated breath, while the youngsters flock to him as to a master.[10]

But alongside the words of praise from eminent figures in the anglophone world, backlash was already looming.

BERGSON IN BRITAIN

As early as 1908, Bergson had been in discussions with publishers interested in producing an English translation of *L'Évolution créatrice*. Of all his books, this one had been in high demand from the anglophone audience.[11] Bergson had been pessimistic about the reception of the German translations of his works, as he was certain that the dominant philosophical trends in German philosophy were not conducive to a positive reception of his ideas. But he had much higher hopes for the English-speaking world and had carefully overseen the English translation of the book. Bergson was well aware of the challenges his translator would face. In 1908 he wrote to the Macmillan publishing house: "I must admit that the translation of my book presents exceptional difficulty. It would require a translator who is very competent in terms of philosophy and who is capable at the same time of giving an artistic form to their work."[12]

After rejecting a first attempt by the translator of *Laughter*, Frederic Rothwell, because it did not "sufficiently penetrate the spirit of the text," nor did it "capture the nuances," Bergson finally settled for the work of Arthur Mitchell, a Harvard doctoral student who was working on a thesis about Bergson's notions of freedom and intuition and who had taken it upon himself to translate the book, partially supervised by James.[13]

By 1911, all of Bergson's most important works had become available in English and Bergsonism exploded. The *New York Times* announced:

Henri Bergson, a man of 53, a quiet French gentleman of kindly manners and charming personality, has just been introduced to the

English-speaking world. . . . The chief works of the foremost thinker of Europe are now available to students in this country who are not able to read the original French. It formally presents to America the man who is rapidly coming to be perhaps the most potent force in the Old World to-day.[14]

It was also in 1911 that Bergson abandoned his responsibilities as *professeur* at the Collège de France to deliver his much-anticipated and first-ever public lectures on British soil. On May 26 and 27, 1911, he delivered two lectures in French at the University of Oxford before crowds of about three hundred people titled "La Perception du Changement" ("The Perception of Change"). In these lectures, Bergson outlined his philosophical project. Since Plato, he said, philosophy has been suspicious of the unreliable human senses and thus has taken refuge in conceptual thought. He argued that a more intuitive, nonsystematic philosophy is possible, one that would echo the way in which artists like Turner embraced and transcended the senses by making visible certain aspects of reality that would otherwise have gone unnoticed. In his second lecture, Bergson described in detail his key notion of *durée*. There are, said Bergson, "changes, but there is no thing that changes: change doesn't need anything to stand upon. There are movements, but there aren't necessarily invariable objects that move; mobility does not presuppose something that moves."[15]

Two days later, on May 29, he was at the University of Birmingham giving the seventh (Thomas Henry) Huxley lecture. Speaking in English this time, he addressed "Life and Consciousness." Bergson's invitation to lecture in Birmingham was most probably instigated by the physicist Oliver Lodge, who was one of Bergson's many admirers and at the time was serving as principal of the university. Bergson's audience had been prepared for the event by a series of lectures delivered the week before by the British philosopher John Henry Muirhead on the "Main Ideas and Present Influence of Professor Bergson." Bergson attempted to address "the question of consciousness in general—of its relation with nature and life." In this talk, Bergson condensed some of the main ideas of *Creative Evolution*, in particular the idea that "consciousness," understood as recollection of the past and anticipation of the future, "is in principle present in all living matter but that it is dormant or atrophied wherever such matter renounces spontaneous activity, and on the contrary, that it becomes more intense, more complex, more complete, just where living matter trends most in the direction of activity and movement."[16] With a version of "Life and Consciousness" published the same year in the *Hibbert Journal*, and in the same issue as Balfour's piece, the public gained a condensed, more digestible version of Bergson's book.

In October, after a pause of a few months, a reporter for *The Citizen* wrote:

> The intellectual world here is very much fluttered to learn that Bergson is coming to London to lecture this month. Professor Bergson . . . is emphatically the philosopher of the hour, having dislodged the late William James from the place of favour amongst the young philosophical bloods at the Universities, and having by his unusual common sense and wonderfully brilliant style, secured a big audience among non-specialists.[17]

Bergson gave four lectures at University College London on "The Nature of the Soul" to "a very large audience." His third lecture filled the theatre "to its utmost capacity," and he was greeted to the sound of "loud cheers."[18]

When Hulme asked Bergson what he made of the "tremendous *réclame*" he had received during these visits, Bergson replied that it both amused and exasperated him, mainly because he found that it predisposed other philosophers to be suspicious of him.[19] In Britain, despite the success of Bergson's lectures, he was also subjected to severe critiques from some of his anglophone peers who were expressing concerns about what they perceived as the lack of rigour and clarity at the heart of Bergson's philosophy. In 1911, the philosopher Mary Gilliland Husband wrote:

> M. Bergson's brilliant pictorial style with wave after wave of metaphor, carries forward his reader, with an extraordinary sense of exhilaration, and almost convinces him for the time being that all difficulties are resolved and all antinomies reconciled. When one closes the book and reflects upon it all, that perilous and materialistic process, there emerges a stubborn discontent which had so often been overleaped or shoved aside, and one feels the need, the crying need, for more closely direct logical argument.[20]

But no one was more suspicious of Bergson than Bertrand Russell.

RUSSELL'S RANCOUR

Lady Ottoline Morrell liked to surround herself with creative minds. In her London townhouse and her Oxfordshire manor, she gathered talented writers—among them, Henry James, D. H. Lawrence, Aldous Huxley, T. S. Eliot, W. B. Yeats, Virginia Woolf, and G. E. Moore—and provided them with a space to meet and share ideas. In the spring of 1911, after one of her famous dinners, she had found herself alone with Bertrand Russell, whom she knew to be an unhappily married Cambridge logician and whose intelligence she greatly admired. When they had first met a few years earlier, she had described the philosopher as "attractive, but very alarming, so quick and clear-sighted, and supremely intellectual—cutting false and real asunder."[21]

Soon after Lady Morrell and Russell started an affair, Russell travelled to Paris to deliver lectures at the Sorbonne, the French Mathematical Society, and the French Philosophical Society about his theoretical obsessions of the moment. But he found it impossible to concentrate on anything else but his budding passion. Wandering around the world's most romantic city, thinking about his new mistress, he had entered a bookshop and chanced upon a copy of *L'Évolution créatrice*, a title that everyone seemed to be talking about. That night, sitting alone in his hotel room, he flipped distractedly through the best-selling book. But he could not concentrate for more than a few sentences at a time, his mind swaying hopelessly back to his mistress. He later confessed to her that, at the time, "the *élan vital* had hold on me too much for me to wish to read about it."[22]

Russell did not pay serious attention to Bergson until the autumn of 1911. It was not that he had particularly cooled down—his extramarital life was still as scandalous as ever—but he now found himself animated by a sentiment almost as strong as romantic infatuation: professional spite. Over the summer he had been elected president of the Aristotelian Society and was due to deliver an address that took place every year, like clockwork, on the first Monday of November. But this plan did not account for Bergson's return to Britain, scheduled for the end of October. All the French philosopher had to do was express his wish to attend that year's presidential lecture for something as seemingly immutable as the Aristotelian Society's schedule to be modified. Russell was highly irritated by the minor inconvenience of having his talk moved to an earlier date, and he promptly complained to his mistress.[23] At the time, Russell was a well-regarded Cambridge philosopher, but he was nowhere near as famous as Bergson. In his correspondence, Russell's jealousy was palpable. In a letter to his friend Lucy Donnelly, he struggled to contain his irritation: "all England has gone mad about him for some reason."[24] Russell was very ambitious, and in many ways Bergson represented what he had not yet managed to achieve. Before having ever properly engaged with Bergson's ideas, Russell therefore viewed his French colleague as a direct competitor, as a rival to be surpassed and put down.

Russell's combative mood intensified when less than a month before he was due to give his presidential address he received a letter from Bergson himself. Bergson wrote that he was looking forward to Russell's lecture, though he suspected there would be a lot for them to disagree about. Bergson had no doubt intended these words as a way of establishing a friendly, perhaps even playful rapport with someone whose work and outlook he knew would otherwise make them intellectual adversaries. But Russell took Bergson's letter as a declaration of war.

It was in this mindset of jealousy and keen professional ambition that Russell decided to take a more serious look at Bergson's ideas. Alongside the preparations for his Aristotelian Society presidential address, he began obsessively dissecting Bergson's ideas, finding, as Bergson had predicted, that there was virtually nothing they agreed upon. At the end of September, he wrote to Ottoline: "His view is that the raw material is a continuous flux to which no concepts are exactly applicable. I might suggest that the continuous flux is a philosophic construction, not 'raw' at all." A few days later he wrote to her again: "He is the antithesis to me; he universalizes the particular soul under the name of *élan vital* and loves instinct. Ugh!"[25]

Russell now found himself in possession of so much anti-Bergsonian material that he started working on a second, entirely different talk, which he ended up delivering several months later at the famous Heretics Club.[26] He came to view himself as something of a heroic figure defending rationality from the repeated attacks of an increasingly powerful foe and represented Bergson as a danger to reason and clear discourse.

This impression was soon confirmed for Russell when Bergson arrived in London. Most members of the Aristotelian Society had been aching to meet the French philosopher in the flesh.[27] The night of the dinner given by the society, Russell was seated at a large table next to Bergson. Like most people, Russell found Bergson to be quite charming, "urbane and gentle." But he left the dinner feeling even more convinced of his own philosophical superiority. He wrote to Lucy Donnelly that, as a philosopher, Bergson "never thinks about fundamentals, but just invents pretty fairy-tales."[28] Russell felt that at this event he had belonged to the minority of sensible thinkers who still valued the scientific dogmas of the past.[29]

Then came the day of Russell's presidential address. The philosopher had prepared an enquiry "On the Relations of Universals and Particulars." No record of the ensuing discussion survives, but according to existing testimony, an animated debate pitted Russell against his greatest philosophical enemy, Bergson. Many years later, Bergson confided to his friend Jacques Chevalier that he was convinced he had completely refuted Russell's argument, thus publicly humiliating the society's president. Bergson believed that Russell had never entirely forgiven him, and that this explained why the British philosopher had continually lashed out at him over the years. It is hard to be sure exactly what happened, but it seems likely that Russell left the meeting furious. After that, taking down Bergson at the Heretics Club became his number-one priority.

In the weeks leading up to his talk, Russell wrote to Ottoline that he was feeling "venomous" about Bergson, and he joked: "If I could love Bergson I should have achieved a really Christian spirit—but I am miles away from it as yet."[30] Whether from jealousy or lingering resentment after the debacle of the presidential address, Russell admitted that he could not read Bergson without first having to overcome, with great difficulty, "the instinctive hostility." He added, "Speaking seriously, I don't hate Bergson. If I didn't have to read him I shouldn't be tempted to; when I met him I liked him. But I think he is a man of low ideals, action without contemplation. And I hate his dogmatic pontifical style."[31]

Russell's relentless attacks are partly to blame for Bergson's eventual descent into a period of oblivion in the English-speaking world. Even after Bergson's death, when the power of the French philosopher's name had faded, Russell wrote in his best-selling *History of Western Philosophy*: "One of the bad effects of an anti-intellectual philosophy, such as that of Bergson, is that it thrives upon the errors and confusions of the intellect."[32] It seems that, beyond his many theoretical objections, Russell was most annoyed by Bergson's reach, which extended beyond anything any living philosopher had ever experienced.

The hysteria associated with Bergson-mania was frequently the subject of ridicule. In 1912, a reporter for *Le Temps* joked that the frenzy of the crowd attempting to make their way into the already overcrowded lecture theatre was an illustration of Darwin's struggle for life.[33] There was a growing view among commentators that the lack of seriousness displayed by Bergson's audience reflected badly on Bergson's philosophy and on Bergson himself. Yet Bergson remained fascinating to the press, and as his influence grew the backlash against him only worsened. But as the historian Henry F. May noted: "These attacks, of course, increased Bergson's popularity among the liberated; all he had needed was to be made just a little less respectable."[34]

CHAPTER 16

A PHILOSOPHER FOR WOMEN

In the 1910s, as Bergson became the most talked-about thinker in the world, journalists and commentators were fascinated with a remarkable feature of his audience: it consisted mostly of women.[1] The trend was not confined to Paris. When Bergson lectured in London, tickets were near-impossible to obtain. A reporter, one of the lucky few who managed to secure a seat, was met with an unexpected sight:

> The approaches to the lectures seemed to be as well guarded as those to a harem. . . . I look round and find that my speculations about the harem have at least this basis of fact—nine people out of ten present here are women, most of them with their heads lifted up in the kind of "Eager Heart" attitude, which resembles nothing so much as the attitude of my kitten when gently waking up from sleep.[2]

Accounts of Bergson's talks often skimmed over their philosophical content and concentrated on the more practical problems
that came with a female crowd. *Le Temps* reported that on one
occasion the heat in the lecture theatre became so unbearable that
"several young women were indisposed and had to be escorted
outside."[3] A writer for the British literary magazine *The New Age*
scoffed that Bergson's lectures were characterised by "the unbearable odours of perfume," "the crush of fashion," and "the rude-
ness" of the audience.[4] Tancrède de Visan conjectured that these
women wearing their "disdainful opera glasses," "silk skirts," and
"theatre hats" were not at Bergson's lecture to listen but to be
seen.[5]

Journalists frequently contrasted the perceived frivolity of
women and the solemnity of a philosophy lecture. Their reports seldom considered the philosophical motivations of these women, nor
did they celebrate their intellectual achievements. The presence of
women in a traditionally masculine space was regarded at best as a
source of ridicule, and at worst as a nuisance.

Comments about perfumed, fainting, fashionable, chatter-
ing women became a common comical device that added to the
frenzy surrounding Bergson's fame. In France, Bergson's female
followers were given derogatory nicknames such as *caillettes*[6]—
which designated a type of *pâté*, a kind of small bird, and, in this
context, a frivolous babbling woman—and *snobinettes*,[7] which
conveyed the common assumption that these women were igno-
rant socialites more interested in being seen at a fashionable event
than in learning about philosophy. To the men writing these articles, the women in attendance at Bergson's lectures were nothing more than a crowd of posers, too shallow to be motivated by
true philosophical curiosity. It was not long before this misogyny
was turned against Bergson himself. The idea arose that perhaps
women were drawn to him because Bergsonism was a philosophy
of the irrational.

RIDICULED *PRÉCIEUSES*

These prejudices were embedded in a long tradition of French satire at the expense of learned women. In the seventeenth century, the word *précieuse* was used to ridicule women's intellectual curiosity and minimise their scholarly accomplishments. Many such women were wealthy and highly educated. They would meet regularly in sumptuous Parisian apartments to talk about literature, debate the codes of moral and linguistic refinement, and showcase their eloquence and quick wit by competing in complicated word games.

In 1659, France's most celebrated playwright, Molière, famously cemented the association between the *précieuses* and pseudo-intellectualism. In *Les Précieuses ridicules*, two naive young women arrive in Paris hoping to join fashionable literary salons and meet the most intelligent women of the century. Their downfall comes after they reject the advances of two eligible bachelors they deem unrefined and therefore unworthy. As punishment, the men plot to humiliate the women by training their valets in the ways, jargon, and literary interests of the *précieuses* in order to seduce them. After it is revealed that the women were wooed by a pair of common servants, they are exposed as shallow impostors and forced to return to their provincial homes, where they are greeted with further mockery.

Molière assured the women of his time that they should not be offended. Comedy, he said, required "vicious imitations of what is most perfect." But his portrayal of the *précieuses* was in line with the pervasive idea that the women who attended the salons were superficial socialites, that their language was affected, and that their attempts to produce intellectual content were laughable. This belief was so widespread that it found its way into the first monolingual French dictionary, published in 1680 by the grammarian Pierre Richelet. Using his authority as general gatekeeper of the French language, he defined the *précieuse* as "she who deserves to be mocked for the way she acts and speaks."

One of the most famous seventeenth-century salons was held by the prolific novelist and philosopher Madeleine de Scudéry. In her writings—which she mostly published under her brother's name— she told women that they should aim to be more than voiceless, decorative muses and to write their own stories: "You must overcome the doubt concerning yourself that is planted in your soul. It is this false modesty which prevents you from employing your mind to achieve all that it is capable of attempting."[8]

Did the men who scorned the *précieuses* feel threatened by their calls for female autonomy, or by the fact that many of them, including Madeleine de Scudéry, refused marriage? Their repeated attacks were at least implicitly used to justify the exclusion of women from traditional academic spaces. The French Academy, a council of forty members (nicknamed "the immortals") elected to serve as the absolute authorities on matters pertaining to the French language, was founded in 1635. Madeleine de Scudéry was briefly considered for membership but was never elected, nor were any of the brilliant and eloquent women of letters of the time.

When, in 1914, Bergson himself was elected to the French Academy and became an immortal, little had changed. Women were still derided for their attempts to educate themselves, and the idea that they were unworthy posers continued to be used to justify keeping them out of prestigious institutions like the French Academy. It was not until 1980 that the first woman, the novelist Marguerite Yourcenar, was elected to the "immortals."

In the 1910s, as more and more women flocked to Bergson's lectures, the press nicknamed them Philaminte and Cathos, after two of Molière's fictional *précieuses*.

A FEMININE PHILOSOPHY

For Bergson's opponents, the fact that so many women were drawn to his philosophy not only represented a hilarious oddity but was also the sign of something more serious. They argued that the reason the most irrational beings of all, women, were so enthusiastic about Bergson's ideas was because he was a philosopher of the irrational. Traits stereotypically associated with femininity, such as irrationality and sentimentality, clashed with the traditionally masculine qualities deemed necessary to be a good philosopher.

Some saw signs of a lack of rigour in Bergson's style, which, both spoken and written, was highly evocative and metaphorical. His critics used as evidence his argument that the symbols and concepts of science and logic are limited in what they can say about the world. Bergson's philosophy, they said, lacked clarity and should be combatted, because it was grounded in an unreliable and obscure mysticism that was "feminine" in nature. In 1913, a writer for *The New Age* expressed this idea succinctly and scathingly: "True, Bergson was nearly suffocated by scent when women attended his lectures; but had Bergson really been a philosopher, no woman would have listened to him."[9]

The associations between femininity, irrationality, and Bergson's philosophy often overlapped with anti-Semitic attacks against the philosopher. In France, these attacks were coordinated by the right-wing, overtly anti-Semitic political movement Action Française. Between 1910 and 1911, Pierre Lasserre, the main literary critic for the movement's newspaper (also called *Action Française*), published a series of anti-Bergsonian articles. He painted Bergson's philosophy as sentimental and vague, and in his final article he claimed that Bergson would never reach the level of an Aristotle or a Leibniz because he was Jewish.[10] Such ideas were in line with the theories of the intellectual leader of Action Française, Charles Maurras, who frequently warned that French civilisation was declining because of the influences of "barbarian" and "feminine" ideologies. According to Maurras, Bergson, as the "Master of Jewish France" and a defender of "feminine romanticism," embodied both threats.[11]

It is difficult to overestimate the influence of the toxic ideologues of Action Française, whose reach extended far beyond French politics. For instance, around the time he wrote his famous "Love Song of J. Alfred Prufrock" (between 1910 and 1915), T. S. Eliot had been reading Lasserre's and Maurras's accounts of what they viewed as the decline of French culture.[12] It is therefore difficult not to read Maurras's warning about the dangers of a feminised culture in Eliot's twice-repeated lines:

> In the room the women come and go
> Talking of Michelangelo[13]

In an interesting twist, Eliot later claimed that he had been undergoing "a temporary conversion to Bergsonism" when he wrote the poem.[14] Bergson and Maurras were as opposed as two thinkers could be, but Eliot had digested elements from their respective messages. It is a testimony to the complexity of the cultural politics of the time that one of the seminal pieces of literary modernism could be influenced by Maurrassian ideology while being structured around literary symbolism and stream-of-consciousness techniques inspired by Maurras's enemy, Bergson.

IRRATIONAL WOMEN

Attacks against the supposed femininity of Bergsonism were eventually redirected, in a circular movement, against the *Bergsoniennes*. Bergson rose to fame at a time when women's right to vote was being debated. The intellectual abilities of potential female voters therefore were coming under close scrutiny.

The fact that so many women seemed naturally drawn to a philosophy as "unrigorous" as Bergson's constituted, according to some male commentators, incontestable proof that women could not be trusted with intellectual matters. The Bergson critic and writer Jules Lermina denounced "Bergson's sentimentalist propaganda," which, he said, women used to justify their irrational beliefs, like the possibility of life after death.[15] A writer for the British magazine *The Bystander* invited his readers to imagine a future in which women would occupy positions in all areas of society. Women's "devastating affability" would render them incapable of maintaining the seriousness required for the effective operation of "civic life," he suggested. The effect on the literary world would be devastating: "Whole shelves emptied of deeply theological and scientific works" would be replenished with more frivolous feminine topics. And, he added,

> as far as my affrighted intelligence can judge, the position of affairs will, at least, be a gigantic test of Bergson's theories. Everything will, of course be done by intuition. Trains will be driven, arrive, and depart as Woman's sub-sub-conscious mind directs. There will be no such thing as scheduled time, only Time—if that.[16]

But nothing the anti-feminists said could undo the spread of the growing movements around the world, which had been challenging the status quo for decades. In France, energised by the British and American suffragette movements, the French Union for Women's Suffrage was formed in 1909.

The group's various actions forced French lawmakers to pay closer attention to the issue. In 1913, Hélène Miropolsky, the first woman barrister to practice in France, attended sessions in which senators debated the question of women's vote. One of the main arguments mobilised against female suffrage rested upon the idea that such a radical change might undermine the recently implemented separation between church and state. Women were deemed highly suggestible, and it was feared that priests would be able to find their way back into the political sphere by manipulating the political opinions of their female parishioners.[17] As a result, while many of the senators were favourable to the idea "in theory," the time was not ripe, they thought, for the female vote. One senator, Eugène Lintilhac, argued that it would be the duty of the state to provide women with a secular education, which might in time provide them with the intellectual tools to make rationally informed decisions. He explained, Miropolsky reported, that such measures would protect women against "their innate mysticism [and] against the immoderate impulses of their sensitivity, which is more intuitive than rational." "Admittedly," he added, "intuition—according to Bergson—is an instrument of knowledge, but it is not an instrument of democratic order."[18]

THINKERS IN THEIR OWN RIGHT

In 1913, the American author and feminist Marian Cox (born Mabel Marian Metcalfe) published an article titled "Bergson's Message to Feminism." She argued that humanity's quest for a better understanding of the universe, both scientific and theological, had so far been entirely based on male, materialistically driven methods. Instinct and intuition, on the other hand, were in tune with the creativity of life and with the female mind. By placing instinct and intuition at the centre of his philosophical method, Bergson's outlook was therefore "an exposition and a plea for this female-method in the future quest of knowledge."[19] Ultimately, said Cox, Bergson's philosophy would aid the liberation of women. Therefore, at a time when Bergsonism was characterised as inherently feminine in order to diminish Bergson's authority as a philosopher, Cox argued that it was because Bergson's philosophy was feminine in nature that it should be taken seriously.

The same year, Bergson was asked about his views on the "feministic movement in Europe and America." He made a point of stating that he had "not found any difference in level between the male and female mind," and that in the days when he taught both young men and women he would have been incapable of distinguishing between the essays written by female students and those written by male students.[20] In another interview, Bergson stressed that it was a mistake to think that "women are not capable of understanding philosophical speculation."[21] But he nevertheless expressed some reservations about giving the vote to all women, all at once: "When you ask me about the woman's movement, I say I am for experimenting, but I must add that it is a dangerous experiment; since half of the people would suddenly get votes. I think it should be done gradually. Women have thus far not had the interest in politics and could not be expected to have the aptitude for it." He concluded, "I certainly do not approve of the militant methods of the suffragettes. I know that wherever there is enthusiasm there is violence, but the women are injuring their own cause."[22] This type of argument, as well as those advanced by senators like Lintilhac, evidently made quite an impact, as French lawmakers consistently voted against female suffrage. French women would have to wait until 1944 to be eligible to vote.

A combination of factors, including the public nature of his lectures and the clarity of his lecturing style, no doubt contributed to Bergson's popularity among women. Women would have benefitted from the fact that Bergson's lectures, which were held outside the rigid confines of the exclusive Sorbonne, presented complex and subtle ideas in a way that was accessible to those who had not been given access to a formal philosophical education. More importantly, Bergson's philosophy was a philosophy of change, creativity, and freedom, which, in the years leading up to World War I, many used as a way of channelling their own political hopes. Perhaps Bergson's philosophy appealed to the women of the late Belle Epoque because it centred on radical change at a time when women were redefining their place in society. Perhaps they were so drawn to Bergson because his philosophy was then a rallying point for those who believed change was possible—much as their descendants would be drawn to the philosophy of Jean-Paul Sartre and Simone de Beauvoir in the late 1940s.

In newspapers, the *Bergsoniennes* remained faceless "crowds of fair damsels" who were criticised for their appearance (one reporter was shocked by the presence of "Polish and Russian female students with messy hair and bare arms") or described sarcastically as the elite of French feminism.[23] Only high-status women were mentioned by name and the Romanian-born countess Anna de Noailles was among them. Noailles was an outspoken feminist and a celebrated poetess. Like the *précieuses* of Molière's time, she held literary salons in her lavish Parisian apartment that were attended by famous writers and artists like André Gide, Jean Cocteau, Colette, and Edmond Rostand. Henri Massis remembered the first time Noailles attended one of Bergson's lectures:

> Tiny and tightly wound, barely seated in the middle of the group of Normaliens, she contemplated with eyes like those of a royal bird the marvellous artist for whom metaphysics was nothing more than a reflection on art and art itself nothing more than a figurative metaphysics. When we left, and before going through the gates of the Collège de France to take her back to her car, we dared to ask her what she thought of what she had just heard. She cried: "But I've known all this since I was born!"[24]

When, in 1931, she became the first woman to be awarded the Légion d'honneur (the highest French order of merit), she asked Bergson to present it to her. But to many male commentators, her main accomplishments were her good looks and her scandalous love life. Another of Bergson's friends and another countess, Thérèse Murat, was also frequently name-checked in the tabloids reporting on Bergson-mania. For years Bergson and the countess had met regularly to discuss philosophy, art, music, and literature. Despite the fact that she was an accomplished writer and musician, the language used to describe her was anything but empowering. In the eyes of the press, she was a mere "socialite," a "diligent" and "well-behaved schoolgirl" taking notes as though she were "preparing for an exam."[25] These accounts ignored the fact that these women were thinkers in their own right.

At least one reporter, writing for the French newspaper *Excelsior*, recognised that he had underestimated the women in Bergson's audience. He confessed that he had attended a lecture expecting to encounter sleepy socialites. At the start of the lecture, he had fixed his attention on "an elegant young woman" sitting near "an old professor with glasses and a white beard." He believed that these two contrasting figures would confirm his preconceptions and "was already inwardly mocking this pretty woman." But what he actually witnessed was a fully focused woman jotting down the professor's every word and an old male professor "fast asleep, his glasses on his beard and his beard on his waistcoat."[26]

CHAPTER 17

BLOCKING BROADWAY

In 1913, the streets of New York bustled with the same palpable energy as they do today. One notable difference, however, was that pedestrians had a lot more legroom. The sidewalks were twice as wide as they are now, but even so, it was common to see people walking in the middle of the road, forcing the automobiles driving through the city to cede passage to the people on foot.

But then, one afternoon in February, the New Yorkers who happened to stroll along Broadway found themselves struggling to make their way through. An endless row of large automobiles, joyfully clanking and honking, had clogged up the road.[1] It is hard to imagine today that, back then, most New Yorkers had never seen a proper traffic jam. Ford had just started putting his moving assembly line in motion, and the mass production of automobiles was a capitalist fever dream on the cusp of being realised.

Inside the vehicles sat a well-to-do and fashionable crowd dressed up as though on their way to the opening night of the newest theatre craze. But that day the passengers in the cars on Broadway had not been queuing for a show; instead, they were on their way to a philosophy lecture. Around the corner, at Columbia University, hundreds of people were hurrying towards the main entrance. In the crush of the commotion, a woman fainted on the steps. Professor Bergson was about to speak.

THE TIMELINESS OF BERGSON

The president of Columbia University, Nicholas Murray Butler, had invited Bergson to deliver a series of lectures as part of a professorial exchange programme between his institution and the Université de Paris.[2] For Bergson, the trip was not only an academic activity but a diplomatic one as well: his lecture series would be an occasion to present the French university model in a positive light in the new world. Bergson prepared for his American sojourn for almost a year. In the weeks leading up to his trip he complained to the Comtesse Murat that he had been "crushed with work." Two days after Christmas 1912, he told her: "Preparing for the courses I have to do there has taken me much longer than I expected; and I have not been able to think and work for myself as much as I would have liked."[3]

As Bergson was preparing to leave, a writer for the magazine *La vie Parisienne*—known for its literary critiques, erotic illustrations, and satirical takes on art, culture, politics, and the indiscretions of the Parisian elite—scoffed: "How will our snobinettes quench their thirst for metaphysics?" Which professor would these "anxious women" choose to replace Bergson while he was abroad? Surely, predicted the reporter, their decision would be based on the convenience of the time slot of the lectures rather than their content.[4]

In January 1913, less than a year after the *Titanic* sank into the icy depths of the Atlantic, Bergson travelled to Liverpool and boarded the *Carmania*. Seven years earlier, in 1906, when the science fiction writer H. G. Wells had made the voyage to New York on the same ship, he marvelled at its scale and meditated on the vertiginous new heights reached by technological progress:

> We're a city rather than a ship, our funnels go up over the height of any reasonable church spire, and you need walk the main-deck from end to end and back only four times to do a mile.... We have our daily paper, too, printed aboard, and all the latest news by marconigram.... Anyone who has been to London and seen Trafalgar Square will get our dimensions perfectly, when he realizes that we should only squeeze into that finest site in Europe, diagonally, dwarfing the National Gallery, St. Martin's Church, hotels and every other building there out of existence, our funnels towering five feet higher than Nelson on his column....
>
> Never was anything of this sort before, never.... The scale of size, the scale of power, the speed and dimensions of things about us alter remorselessly—to some limit we cannot at present descry.[5]

Wells was both impressed by the magnitude of this human accomplishment and wary of the implications of such rapid progress. The idea of a "natural and necessary" progress "carrying us on quite independently of us" was a "delusion," and the industrial prowess and scientific advances many took as cause for unlimited optimism were "only a sudden universal jolting forward in history, an affair of two centuries at most, a process for the continuance of which we have no sort of guarantee."[6] This delusion, he said, was particularly strong among the American people, towards whom Bergson was about to hurtle aboard the same ship.

During the voyage, Bergson experienced such severe seasickness that he remained confined to his room and was unable to much appreciate the grandeur of the vessel. As he embarked on this unpleasant journey, anticipation on the other side of the Atlantic mounted.

In the United States, Bergson was met with tremendous enthusiasm and bustling energy. In a way, Americans were even more welcoming to him than the British had been. In the United Kingdom, some Cambridge philosophers had given Bergson a somewhat colder reception than the rest of the British public. By contrast, US philosophy had not yet adopted the Russellian logical positivism that was so allergic to *durée* and intuition. The fulsome praise of William James, one of the leading figures of the American school of pragmatism, had also contributed to Americans' enthusiasm as they prepared for his visit.

In the years leading up to World War I, Bergson's philosophy became extraordinarily appealing to a wide and heterogenous mix of intellectual and ideological milieux. The journalist Edwin Emery Slosson noted that Bergson's "philosophy ... appears to some people reactionary in tendency and to others far in advance of anything hitherto formulated. But to all it appears important."[7] Figures as different as the twenty-sixth US president Theodore Roosevelt, the naturalist John Burroughs, and the theologian Lyman Abbott praised Bergson "as a restorer of spirituality."[8] Bergson was reviewed and discussed in serious journals and newspapers as well as in less serious magazines. As noted by the historian Henry F. May, "More surprisingly, [Bergson was] admired by the new organs of the rebellious younger generation," from *The New Republic* (originally a progressive and liberal publication) to one of the leading publications of the literary avant-garde, *The Little Review*.[9]

For many young Americans, the idea of progress was not linked to the dull clanking of machines but to the liberation of life from matter. In the years before World War I dragged them violently back to earth, Bergson fascinated the young minds who were part of a miscellaneous movement characterised by a general "mood or a manner" that Slosson called "the reanimation of the universe."[10] Creativity, hope, and freedom was the credo, and so Bergson's arrival in New York was timely.

BERGSON IN NEW YORK

Bergson's trip had been meticulously planned, and he found he barely had a minute to take in his new surroundings. Throughout the month of February, New York City enjoyed glorious sunshine, although as the city's inhabitants would discover in time, the worst of the winter was not yet behind them. But for a few pleasant weeks, a generous, unwavering brightness enveloped the city in the illusion of spring. Bergson, who had been warned that the weather would be unbearably cold, was delighted to discover a "radiant sun which insisted on remaining radiant." He basked in "a wonderful light" that reminded him of the south of France, or even Italy.[11] Watching the sun set behind the gigantic buildings, he was transported back to one of his trips to Rome, where, from the top of one of the seven hills, he had watched the sun disappear behind the dome of Saint Peter's.[12]

The day after his arrival, Bergson delivered the first of his six Columbia lectures. Used to the disruption that his presence could cause and the size of the crowds he attracted, Bergson had anticipated being booked into a large venue by the organisers. Before arriving, he had asked them to schedule the lectures in a smaller room, so that he could avoid straining his voice. He wrote to Butler: "It is impossible for me to obtain clarity of articulation if I'm obliged to make an effort with my voice."[13] But in the end he was given a five-hundred-seat theatre. From the first talk, the room was full, with hundreds outside trying to get in. *The Sun* reported:

Five hundred women and men, the women outnumbering the men about ten to one, who went yesterday afternoon ... to Columbia University, heard the first of six lectures in French by the philosopher Prof. Henri Bergson. Hundreds more could not get into the lecture hall. There were all sorts in the audience—distinguished professors and editors, well dressed women, and overdressed women. The audience was apparently intensely interested in what the French philosopher had to say and in the manner in which he said it. The frail, thin, small sized man with sunken cheeks was somewhat nervous as he faced his first American audience. Perhaps he was not sufficiently rested from his voyage across the Atlantic.

But as he proceeded with his lecture on "Spirituality and Liberty" he grew eloquent, aroused his audience and made a profound impression.[14]

By the second lecture, two thousand people were requesting a ticket, and many of the unsuccessful had apparently convened anyway, in automobiles and on foot, hoping to get in.[15] Bergson had insisted on delivering his talks in French despite protests from Butler. Though he was fluent in English, he found that speaking in his Yorkshire-born mother's native tongue required a greater effort. His ideas did not flow as readily in English as they did in French.

On February 12, Bergson spoke at Princeton University on "Philosophy and Common Sense." A week later, he drew an even larger crowd at the City College of New York, where he spoke on the role of universities in democracy:

> The two thousand students, all of them New York boys and young men, greeted the distinguished visitor with two or three striking forms of the characteristic American "college yell," a kind of greeting which the guest of the occasion seemed to understand and to appreciate. Indeed understanding and appreciation were mutual, for the great portion of the assembled students of the College, which justly prides itself on maintaining a highly developed and largely attended department of French, clearly understood Mr. Bergson's address, as was indicated by their applause and other marks of appreciation and approval of the points which he successively made.[16]

One of the biggest crowds Bergson attracted was not for a talk at all, but for a tea hosted by the wives of Columbia faculty. According to the *New York Times*, over one thousand were in attendance.[17] The mild-mannered Bergson had become the most famous philosopher in the world.

BERGSON VS. BERGSONISM

In 1912, *The Sun* had published a lengthy interview with the philosopher from his Parisian home. The interviewer was Herman Bernstein, a Jewish journalist, poet, diplomat, and activist who, over the course of his career, also interviewed Tolstoy, Trotsky, Einstein, and US president Woodrow Wilson, to name a few. It had become rare for Bergson to accept interview requests, but he saw this conversation with a reputable interviewer as an opportunity to prepare the American public for his arrival. Indeed, "in his home in Villa Montmorency, in Auteuil, Paris [Bergson] spoke with enthusiasm about America and American thinkers and never tired of expressing his admiration for the late William James," who had died two years earlier.[18]

Asked what he was currently working on, Bergson told Bernstein that he had a "special," "anarchistic way of working" in which he explored "several avenues," many of which ended up leading nowhere. For this reason, it was difficult for him to indicate the form his future study would take, but he envisioned it dealing "with ethics and aesthetics, with the principles of morals and the principle of art."[19] Bernstein then asked Bergson if he was "interested in any of the new movements in art and in literature." Bergson replied: "Any school is interesting if it shows talent. I do not believe in any special schools of art, in any special methods. In literature and in art schools, methods are nothing. Genius is everything."[20]

Artistic genius, for Bergson, transcends the materials, the techniques, and the theories of the artist. What genius adds, in the words of the Bergson expert Mark Sinclair, is "a better, a truer apprehension of reality than the one that conventional conceptual experience can grasp."[21] In art, as in philosophy, Bergson believed that the final product should not result from the application of a predefined method or system, but rather that it should strive to tap into the creative process itself. New rules and methods, said Bergson, should emerge from creative genius, not the other way around. For this reason, Bergson was not especially moved by the new artistic movements, whose innovation, it seemed to him, resided mainly in their manifestos, not in their creations. But while Bergson showed no interest in keeping up with modern trends, the members of the avant-garde were paying close attention to Bergson.

Bergsonian themes were omnipresent in the theories associated with the artistic movements emerging in the 1910s. The novelist, poet, and art collector Gertrude Stein recalled that Bergson's *élan vital* was often discussed in her salon, which was frequented by the literary and artistic innovators of her day, including Ernest Hemingway, Pablo Picasso, Ezra Pound, and Henri Matisse.[22] In the Futurist manifesto, Filippo Tommaso Marinetti exalted the power of motion and dynamism. To "sceptical and pessimistic determinism" the Futurists opposed "the cult of creative intuition," and to "the concept of the imperishable and the immortal" they opposed "the becoming, the perishable, the transitory and the ephemeral."[23] In their wish to transform painting into a temporal experience, they rejected, in a Bergsonian fashion, artificial divisions between objects. Marinetti wrote: "Our bodies enter the sofas we sit on, and the sofas enter us. The bus rushes into the houses it passes, and in turn the houses rush into the bus and merge with it."[24] The Cubists too, were enamoured with a Bergsonian vision of instability and change. In their paintings, they "cleverly instituted confusion between succession and simultaneity." Their subjects were never shown from a fixed point of view; instead, multiple, sometimes contradictory, points of view were melded into one. Here too dynamism was central, and it became commonplace to hear that Cubism was the painting of *durée*.[25]

When asked about the associations between his theories and these movements, Bergson was embarrassed. To one reporter he simply replied, "I regret never having seen the works of these painters."[26] To Bernstein he said of the Cubists and Futurists that he preferred "genius" over manifestos. Despite his reputation as the philosophical leader of the avant-garde, Bergson was quite traditional in his tastes. The art of his day did not move him and he much preferred a Rembrandt to a Delaunay.[27]

Bergson's reputation as a pioneer, a trailblazer, and a trendsetter had been made without him, and he rarely recognised himself in the feats that were being attributed to him. One minute he was said to have fathered new artistic movements he did not understand, and the next he was being heralded as a voice for revolutionary syndicalism.

In 1907, *Le Figaro*'s literary critic, André Beaunier, joked that the syndicalists trying to reduce the workday to eight hours were evidently not in desperate need of more leisure since they found the time to read Bergson.[28] Slosson noted that the syndicalists "seized upon one side of Bergson's doctrine and declared the *élan ouvrier* brother to the *élan vital*, or a part of it."[29] In his controversial *Reflections on Violence*, the renowned philosopher and sociologist Georges Sorel invoked Bergsonian intuition in his defence of general strikes.[30] A week before Bergson arrived in America, the *New York Times* published an article on the relationship between Bergson's philosophy and Sorel's revolutionary syndicalism:

> Many speak and write as if syndicalism were the sociological application of Bergsonian philosophy and Prof. Bergson's metaphysics the theoretical basis of the syndicalist movement. The idea has been so often put forth in books and articles by people who were supposed to know both that it has become firmly lodged in the minds of those interested in the subject.[31]

But the author also noted that the use of Bergsonism by the syndicalists was overall quite superficial: "They have simply made use of Bergsonian terms to describe and analyse the syndicalist ideas which had already been formulated."[32]

Surprised to discover that the far left was affiliating itself with his philosophy, Bergson told one of his friends: "There is undoubtedly some degree of convergence between my conception of movement and that of Georges Sorel, the leading theoretician of trade unionism. I also sympathise with Sorel's anti-intellectualism. But on the other hand, I see no connection between my metaphysics and syndicalism."[33]

Bergson had started noticing a common theme in the reception of his ideas: he was the most influential thinker in the world, but he did not always feel like he was the one doing the influencing. His own ideas seemed to be escaping him and taking on a life of their own. In 1914, a writer for the British literary magazine *The New Age* asked: "What is your opinion of Bergson? I would rather give you my opinion of Bergsonism, for by this time his doctrine has ceased to be under his control, though it still carries his name on its collar."[34]

Nothing better embodied this impression than Bergson's encounter with the Irish playwright George Bernard Shaw at a dinner that took place during Bergson's tour of Britain. According to Bertrand Russell's account of the evening, after a few glasses of wine, Shaw launched into an improvised presentation of Bergson's main ideas. Bergson politely expressed some reservations, but this did not discourage Shaw, who cheerfully retorted: "Oh, my dear fellow, I understand your philosophy much better than you do."[35]

In the headlines of reporters, in secondhand accounts of his lectures written for the general audience, in dinner party conversations, and in the noisy chatter of tearooms, Bergson's complex developments were reduced to catchphrases and stripped of their context and intended meaning. There was no one school of Bergsonism, but rather multiple Bergsonisms representing diverse, often contradictory movements. As the historian Donna Jones wrote: "The diversity of uses to which this Bergsonian vision was put—anarchosyndicalism, mysticism and occultism, aesthetic modernism, fascism, pacifism, literary subjectivism, environmentalism, scientism and antiscientism, etc.—astounds."[36] A reporter for the *New York Times* attributed the multitude of interpretations and appropriations of Bergson's thought to the fluidity of the thought itself: "His is a method of thinking, not a set creed, and it therefore lends itself to many different points of view."[37]

In 1914, Péguy wrote: "M. Bergson's philosophy is almost equally misunderstood by his opponents and his supporters."[38] That a multitude of artistic, political, and philosophical movements claimed Bergson as one of their own meant that more often than not Bergson's original intentions were misread. Bergson was known as the philosopher of "intuition," but the special meaning he gave to the word was most often ignored or misrepresented. His other emblematic notions, like *durée* and the *élan vital*, took on different definitions depending on whether it was a revolutionary syndicalist or a Catholic modernist who was using them.

IN THE AIR

Many attempted but few succeeded in explaining Bergson's almost ubiquitous appeal. Why was Bergsonism—or rather, various interpretations of what Bergsonism represented—so popular?

It is tempting to retrospectively read Bergson's incredible success as a measure of his extraordinary originality as a thinker in the final decade of the Belle Epoque. Some of Bergson's readers from the period saw the same creative power in Bergson's philosophy that Bergson attributed to his notion of creative evolution. Many of Bergson's contemporaries, however, recognised the philosopher's originality while at the same time placing his ideas within the wider culture of the day. In 1912, at the height of Bergson's fame, an article titled "The Return of the Gods" situated the origins of Bergson's "intuitive" method in works such as Edgar Allan Poe's 1848 "prose poem" "Eureka," in which Poe proposed his intuitive vision of the universe.[39] Bergson was portrayed as belonging to a lineage of philosophers which included Heraclitus, Schelling, and Nietzsche: "As Lamarck, St. Hilaire, Goethe, the elder Darwin, and Tennyson put forth Darwinian ideas before the theory was formulated, so Bergsonism has been in the air for a long time."[40]

A decade later, in March 1924, the French author André Gide opened his journal and jotted down a few thoughts about Bergson's success earlier in the century. Gide too wrote that "Bergsonism" had been "in the air" long before Bergson, and he predicted that, because Bergson was so representative of his own time period, future historians would exaggerate the influence he had on his contemporaries.[41] According to Gide, Bergson's philosophy was a symptom of the intellectual climate of the time, rather than one of its causes.

Bergson himself did not mention originality as the reason for his popularity. At the peak of his fame, he ascribed much of his success merely to his lecturing style:

> I attribute a good part of the effect of my lectures to their being spoken lectures. . . . During the lectures that I gave recently in London, I had articulated distinctly enough to be able to be followed even by those who had only a very superficial familiarity with French.[42]

But though Bergson was very much a product of his time, and his success a symptom of a general rebellion against mechanism, his importance during this period must not be underplayed. If he was perhaps not as astoundingly original as his followers sometimes made him out to be, something about the manner in which Bergson presented his ideas, in his lectures and in *Creative Evolution*, allowed him to become a rallying point around which those who were dissatisfied with mechanical explanations of nature could assemble. More importantly, Bergson's philosophy, as a philosophy of change, creativity, and freedom, gave many in the years leading up to World War I ways of channelling their own artistic, ideological, and political hopes. It was as though all the anxieties of the time—the unease surrounding the disenchantment and mechanisation of the universe, the fear of not seeing various hopes realised, the feelings of emptiness left by shifting values, and the space taken up by science in public discourse—and all the enthusiasms and aspirations of the age converged in Bergson's philosophical imagery.

Like an artist who is able to show us what we have not yet been able to perceive, Bergson was able to give form to the confused and all-consuming feelings of a generation.

CHAPTER 18

"THE MOST DANGEROUS MAN IN THE WORLD"

In February 1914, the daily newspaper *Excelsior* printed a photo-graph taken outside Bergson's lecture theatre. Dozens of men and women can be seen spilling out of the Collège de France and into the courtyard. Two men have apparently used a nearby ladder to climb up on the ledge of a window. The photo is captioned "People listen to Bergson's lectures through the windows."[1]

That day the crowd was even larger and more enthusiastic than usual. Bergson had just been elected to one of the forty seats of the Académie française. This represented an honour beyond all others, for to be elected was to be inscribed into French history. Following in the footsteps of giants of French literature like Voltaire and Victor Hugo, Bergson became an "immortal" whose duty was to guard and promote the French language.

Bergson was to occupy the seat that had previously belonged to Émile Ollivier, the prime minister in office when France entered the war with Prussia in 1870. Soon after Ollivier died in the summer of 1913, Bergson had started campaigning for his seat. As with his election to the Collège de France, Bergson had waited for the opportune moment to apply, and he had mobilised the right contacts to put in a good word for him among the living "immortals." Even though Bergson had complained for years that the noise surrounding him had become too loud, he must have known that joining the most distinguished French institution would draw even more public scrutiny. But this step was consistent with the path of pursuing French institutional excellence that Bergson had been following all his life.

The day his election was announced, Bergson entered the lecture theatre and found his entire desk covered in flowers. Not everyone, however, was celebrating.

BACKLASH

A few streets away, one of Bergson's old École normale supérieure classmates, Émile Durkheim, ruled over the Sorbonne. Durkheim, one of the fathers of modern social sciences, was known for his idea that social phenomena can be studied objectively, "from the outside, as external things."[2] His thinking was representative of the Sorbonne's dominant rationalist trend, which was at odds with the idea of intuition, the possibility of knowledge beyond the confines of human reason. Around the time Bergson announced his candidacy for the Académie française, Durkheim concluded a lecture stating his concern about what he viewed as the nefarious influence of new philosophical trends that were fanning the flames of anti-rationalist sentiments. He warned that "a total negation of rationalism would ... be dangerous: it would turn our entire national culture upside down."[3]

There were many others in France who, like Durkheim, saw Bergson's influence as a threat. Bergson's adversaries resented and feared his cultural ubiquity. How could they defeat Bergsonism, a cultural disorder so fluid it took on innumerable unpredictable forms and seemed to permeate all aspects of early twentieth-century life? Even worse, Bergson was not some fringe figure. He somehow managed to combine an image of disruptiveness with immaculate institutional credentials. A month before he was elected to the Académie française, Bergson had become president of another venerable French learned society, the Académie des sciences morales et politiques. The more Bergson's institutional authority grew, the more dangerous he was perceived to be and the more vicious his opponents' attacks became.

When it became public knowledge that Bergson was being considered for a seat at the Académie française, the right-wing, anti-Semitic press immediately rallied against the Jewish philosopher. The members of Action Française had been warning of the Bergsonian "threat" for years. The movement's ideological leader, Charles Maurras, repeatedly claimed that Bergson should not be considered French, neither in race nor in tradition of thought. France was the country of Cartesian rationalism, and Bergson, the philosopher of intuition, was a "barbarian." Maurras found it intolerable that Bergson, the "Master of Jewish France," could be considered for election to the Académie française, one of the oldest bastions of French culture.[4] A few days before Bergson's election, Maurras alleged that a "Jewish plot to get Mr. Bergson into the Académie" was taking place.[5] Another member of Action Française, Léon Daudet, painted Bergson as a "militant Jew . . . as dangerous as he is cunning."[6] Like Maurras, Daudet imagined that Bergson was at the forefront of a "cleverly hatched intrigue" that "through the Jewish control of the press is exploiting the weakness of everyone's character."[7] He predicted that certain key members of the French Academy would be conveniently absent on the day of the vote to favour Bergson's election. Bergson did not dignify these accusations with a response.

Bergson also found enemies on the other side of the political spectrum. The Jewish writer Julien Benda, who has been characterised as a "left-wing reactionary," made a career out of lambasting Bergson. Benda had once collaborated with Bergson's friend and supporter, Charles Péguy, and admitted that he had briefly found himself under a Bergsonian "enchantment," after reading *Creative Evolution* in 1907, before regaining his senses.[8] By 1914, he had published several anti-Bergsonian pamphlets accusing Bergson of perpetuating a "feminine," sentimental style of thinking, which he opposed to more rational and "virile" reasoning based on conceptual "firmness."[9] Benda deplored the loss of Cartesian ideals of rationality and stability in a world that preferred vagueness and mobility: "Philosophy, which once taught us to feel that we exist because we think, to say: 'I think, therefore I am,' now teaches us to say: 'I act, therefore I am,' 'I think, therefore I am not.'"[10]

As a defender of logic, reason, and rationality, Benda mainly took issue with Bergson's idea of intuition, which he thought was in reality merely "our self-awareness at its most common most typical instant . . . it is nothing else than the act by which the mind has an idea."[11] For Benda, Bergson's philosophy was a kind of prestidigitation which duped the audience into thinking that the "commonest act on earth" was in fact enigmatic and special.[12] According to Benda, Bergson's audience—"the princes of the oblique, the clerics of [mental] pirouettes," the "confused doctors, bogged-down bards," and "unstable poetesses"—had "flocked to a philosophy that elevates their anxiety into an aesthetic summit," and Bergson, a philosophical demagogue, had knowingly catered to these bourgeois concerns.[13] Gabriel Reuillard, a pacifist and later a Communist journalist, similarly argued that Bergson's popularity boiled down to his placement of intuition above reason:

This is flattering to an idle and worldly audience; to an audience composed for the most part of women who belong to the lower or upper middle class; to an audience to whom study and effort is instinctively repugnant; to an audience which is horrified by the peril of assuming a definite attitude. . . . These aphorisms expressed by an eminent man, wearing all sorts of decorations and heavy with honours, pronounced at the Collège de France, have the effect of attracting a naturally lazy and mediocre audience.[14]

Benda wrote that he wished Bergsonism had been nothing more than a passing fad, because this would have made the movement surrounding his philosophy easier to dismantle and destroy. But "how can we call 'fashion' a movement that has been going on for over ten years," Benda lamented, "encompassing all areas of the spirit . . . religion, literature, morality, painting, music, etc.?"[15] At his most spiteful, Benda "went so far as to say that he would joyfully have killed Bergson if in that way his influence could have been stopped."[16]

Many of Benda's polemical takes distorted Bergson's views. His representation of Bergson as completely opposed to all products of rationality and as favouring a form of blind instinct over intelligence was caricatured, to say the least. But Benda's vehemence was representative of a worry among those who valued rationality at a time when they felt the world was descending into anarchic, romantic, sentimental chaos. Though Benda and Maurras were ideologically opposed, they were united in seeing Bergson as a threat to the kinds of society that they wanted. For them, Bergson represented "both symptom and cause of everything that threatens to erode modern society."[17]

But even within the ranks of Action Française, Bergson also counted some admirers—for example, Gilbert Maire, the son of Albert Maire, the Clermont-Ferrand librarian whose salon Bergson had frequented decades earlier when he was still coming up with his theory of durée (see Chapter 4). Albert had asked Bergson to mentor his son, who was struggling academically, and for the rest of his life Gilbert would revere Bergson as a master. Thus, Gilbert Maire had to find ways of reconciling the apparently irreconcilable: his devotion both to Bergson and to those who were relentlessly and viciously attacking Bergson. Eventually, in early 1914, Maire found that the attacks against Bergson from his own camp had become too violent, and he broke ties with Action Française. Bergson held no grudges against Maire for his affiliation with his tormentors, confessing to his old mentee that he did not have time to think much about politics.[18] Bergson even wrote to Maire: "I'm a bit embarrassed to think that it was because of an article about me that you decided to part company with your friends."[19]

In the midst of all the noise created by the various appropriations, condemnations, and mishandlings of his ideas, as well as by the increasingly vicious attacks against him, Bergson remained disconcertingly silent.

BERGSON'S SILENCE

Bergson never responded publicly to the attacks of Action Française. He did, however, closely monitor what his enemies were saying about him. When, in 1911, Pierre Lasserre gave a series of lectures arguing against Bergson's philosophy, Bergson asked his friend Isaak Benrubi to attend and report back. "He was outraged," wrote Benrubi, "as I was, by Lasserre's hateful and absurd interpretation of his doctrine."[20] But they kept their outrage to themselves. When Gilbert Maire found out that Bergson's friend was in attendance, he invited Benrubi to participate in the discussion. This invitation caused Bergson to promptly put an end to the surveillance mission, since participating, even indirectly, was the last thing he wanted. He had elected to not respond to Lasserre's attacks, and he did not want to draw even more attention to himself. Bergson discouraged his friends not only from defending him against his enemies but also from associating their own ideas with his, as he knew that in the hands of most readers all nuances would be lost and his friends' words and his own would be melded into one, leading to further confusion.[21]

In 1914, one of Bergson's most committed defenders, Charles Péguy, published a "Note on M. Bergson" that served as a rebuttal to all of Bergson's detractors, left, right, and centre (see Chapter 8). Whatever their agenda, they all seemed to rally around the idea that

Bergson's philosophy rejected rationality as a faculty and as a concept. But as Péguy wrote, Bergson was widely misunderstood. Bergson had never attempted, said Péguy, to "displace" rationality but rather to "renovate," "excavate," and "restore" it:[22]

> Bergsonism was never either irrationalism or anti-rationalism. It was a new rationalism, and it was the crude metaphysics that Bergsonism untied (materialist metaphysics, forensic metaphysics, neuro-physiological metaphysics, sociological metaphysics and so many others) which, being hardened, sclerosed, stiffened, ankylosed, were quite literally the damping of reason.[23]

Walter Lippmann echoed this idea in an article published in the *New York Times* titled "Bergson's Philosophy: It Is Necessary for One to Become a Bergsonian Before One Can Thoroughly Understand Bergson":

> Far from being a haphazard and moody impressionist, Bergson is a thinker so extraordinarily systematic that his published books, extending from "Time and Free Will" in 1888 [*sic*] to "Creative Evolution" in 1907, seem almost architectural in their design. They rest upon the closest kind of contact with psychology, mathematics, and biology, the problems they deal with are suggested by scientific difficulties, the treatment is enriched by intimacy with the history of speculation, and the conclusions are put forth in the interest of a science and a philosophy that shall fertilize each other. Nothing is more unjust than to group Bergson with the romantic irrationalists.[24]

Péguy, who deployed so much of his energy defending his master, resented that Bergson did not do anything to set the record straight himself. In a letter to one of his friends, Péguy decried Bergson's cautious attitude as cowardice: "Bergson does not want to be called a poet. He wants to show that his philosophy is indeed philosophy, and even the philosophy of a philosophy professor. How petty! Deep down, he has no courage. He is afraid of displeasing his enemies."[25]

Péguy's bitterness was the result of years of frustrations nurtured by his growing sense that his devotion to Bergson was not appreciated fully by his master and his fear that, as Bergson's fame grew, so did the one-sidedness of their relationship. On February 27, 1914, Péguy wrote to Bergson:

> You never suspected the harm you did me the day you told me you no longer had time to read me. I consented to everything, to twenty years of increasing misery and solitude, as long as I was read by three or four people, you being the first. I work today in a tomb and you no longer even accompany in thought what has passed from you into me.

To this, Bergson replied: "Allow me to tell you that I understand nothing, absolutely nothing, of what you write to me. Overloaded with work, truly overwhelmed, I am obliged to narrow the circle of my reading more and more; but I read you regularly, always with the same interest and always with the same deep sympathy."[26]

But perhaps there was an element of truth to Péguy's accusation that by refusing to speak up for himself, Bergson was trying to keep his enemies at bay. Perhaps Bergson's reluctance to take part in the culture wars in which he was a central figure stemmed from a fear of repercussions. He may also have been wary of exacerbating both the frenzy that followed his every move and the growing hostility he was facing on several fronts.

Bergson defended his silence as a matter of principle. He could not comprehend why his opinion on all sorts of topics political, literary, moral, and so on—none of which had anything to do with his philosophical research—was of interest to journalists and the public. He felt that it was unreasonable to expect him to philosophise about all things, and on the spot, simply because he had produced what many deemed to be penetrating philosophical theories. The assumption was that social, political, and aesthetic applications of his thought, ready-made solutions to the burning issues of the day, should drop fully formed from his pen. But Bergson knew from his own experience of philosophising that each problem required him to start anew and to clean the slate of his mind completely:

> I have no general principle from which I deduce consequences, and which would allow me to answer any question on any subject. I am frequently asked my opinion on the most diverse questions and often I don't have any opinion on them at all.... It takes me ten years to write a book, to study a subject. And after finishing my first book, I wouldn't have been able to come up with the ideas I set out in the second. To write this second book, I needed prolonged contact with a new set of facts. No doubt the conclusions of this second work were in continuity with those of the first, but I could not have deduced them from the first.[27]

Bergson was not ashamed to admit that the number of problems he could confidently assert he had solved was laughably small (two, maybe three at most).[28] In fact, he believed that no serious person should expect to achieve much more in their lifetime.

Bergson was not being falsely modest. He had always been greatly irritated by those who used their intellectual platform to proclaim themselves experts on any given topic. He called these sophists who enjoyed the sound of their own voice more than anything else but whose words rang desperately empty to anyone who knew how to listen, *homo loquax*.[29] According to Benrubi, Bergson found the simple exercise of giving a toast at a dinner party incredibly difficult and tedious. When he had nothing to say, he preferred not to speak.[30] And so, when Bergson was asked about the practical, political, or moral applications of his theories, his response would be something like: "I have made it a rule never to put forward anything of which I am not certain: not only must I be convinced, but my conviction must be based on positive and communicable arguments discovered by me."[31]

Bergson was most notably silent on a matter about which almost everyone else living in France at the turn of the century had a very strong opinion. In the late months of 1894, Alfred Dreyfus, a Jewish captain in the French army, was accused and then convicted of treason for having allegedly shared French military secrets with Germany. The evidence against Dreyfus was insubstantial, and from the start, anti-Semitism had been a key factor in the most infamous miscarriage of justice in French history. For over a decade, between 1894 and 1906, when Dreyfus was finally rehabilitated, the affair radically split French opinion into two bitterly opposed camps. Right-wing nationalist newspapers like *La Libre parole* fanned the flames of the anti-Semitism that was already on the rise at all levels of society by publishing headlines like "The Traitor Convicted. Down with the Jews!"[32] In the pro-Dreyfus camp, Émile Zola published his famous open letter to the president "J'Accuse . . . !" in *L'Aurore*.[33]

If there was ever a matter of public opinion about which it was not possible to remain neutral, it was the Dreyfus affair. And yet Bergson, himself Jewish, said nothing. It is possible that, in an atmosphere of unbridled anti-Semitism, Bergson wished to avoid attracting attention to his own Jewishness. If Bergson had concerns about the violent anti-Semitism to which he had seen his coreligionist Dreyfus subjected, these concerns would have been legitimate. But other Jews—Benda, for instance—did find the courage to speak out in favour of Dreyfus.

In private, Bergson said that he had ultimately believed in Dreyfus's innocence, but that he had disliked the "methods of agitation" deployed in the name of justice. Above all, he had deplored the harm the affair had done to national unity and would have preferred it to play out within the law courts rather than in the court of public opinion.

Naturalised at eighteen, Bergson had spent his whole life becoming the most respectable philosopher he could be in the eyes of the French state, ticking off all the institutional boxes, amassing all the possible honours. His exemplary career, crowned by election to the Académie française, had been one long expression of reverence for the country and institutions that had raised him since he had left his parents' side at the age of ten. In the Dreyfus affair, Bergson's heart broke for France, his country, before breaking for the victim of state-sanctioned injustice.

Perhaps, as he claimed, Bergson was silent because of his principled conviction that an idea needed to mature before being spoken. Or perhaps, as Péguy said, Bergson's refusal to take part in any form of discourse beyond the limited scope of his philosophical interests ultimately boiled down to fear—the legitimate fear of antagonising his enemies even further, the fear of being taken out of context, the fear of creating more noise around himself. But the end result was the same: in the years leading up to the First World War, Bergson remained silent on the issues of his time. And yet, despite his general neutrality, despite his reserved, discreet personality, and despite his reverence for institutions and their rules, Bergson was perceived as wielding dangerous power.

PUT ON THE INDEX

In a 1912 article, Walter Lippmann wrote: "If I were interested in keeping churches, constitutions and customs fixed so they would not change, I should regard Bergson as the most dangerous man in the world. The spread of his teaching will put institutions on the defensive."[34] Two years later, Lippmann was proved right. In June 1914, three of Bergson's works—*Time and Free Will*, *Matter and Memory*, and *Creative Evolution*—were placed on the Vatican's *Index Librorum Prohibitorum*, the official list maintained between 1560 and 1966 of banned heretical publications. Bergson joined the likes of Blaise Pascal, René Descartes, Baruch Spinoza, Voltaire, and, after his time, Simone de Beauvoir.

In the early decades of the twentieth century, many disenchanted youths had started turning to religion. The historically secular École normale supérieure saw a sharp influx of Catholic students in these years. Jacques Maritain, the husband of Raïssa Maritain, who had found in Bergson such a liberating voice (see Chapter 8), and Péguy were prominent examples of young thinkers who had returned to religion as an antidote to what they viewed as rampant scientism and positivism. At the same time, there were many efforts in France to reconcile science and religion. Alfred Loisy was one of the main proponents of reconciling the teachings of the Catholic Church with new scientific discoveries. The label "modernist" was given to these progressive Catholics by a more conservative branch who disagreed with the movement. The conservatives had the Vatican on their side, and in 1907 Pope Pius X condemned modernism as "the synthesis of all heresies" and pushed for a more traditional approach founded on the more rationalist doctrine of Thomism. Bergson, the figurehead of the rebellion against rationalism and the philosopher favoured among the more progressive Catholics, was therefore associated with what has come to be known as "the Modernist crisis" in the Catholic Church.

This association was exacerbated by the fact that several of Bergson's most devoted followers, like Edouard Le Roy, Jacques Chevalier, and George Tyrrell, were linked with the modernist movement condemned by the Catholic Church. It also did not help that, in *Creative Evolution*, Bergson had painted a very unorthodox picture of God. The creativity of evolution did not, for Bergson, presuppose a creator in any traditional sense: "Everything is obscure in the idea of creation if we think of *things* which are created and a *thing* which created, as we habitually do, as the understanding cannot help doing."[35] As with all other aspects of his philosophy, Bergson's God should be conceived as process, as self-creating, as ever-changing, as change itself. In the words of the historian Charlotte Sleigh: "Instead of attempting to reinstate God as the designer behind [evolution], he deified the process itself."[36] In light of Bergson's untraditional representation of God, his associations with some of the main actors of the modernist crisis, and the fact that he was Jewish and, on top of it all, the most famous man in the world, it was no surprise that the philosopher came to be seen as a threat by the Vatican.

Bergson managed the impressive feat of inspiring fear on both the right and the left, in secularist rationalists as well as in the official representatives of the Catholic Church. Just as his admirers came from all areas of the political, ideological, and cultural spectrum, so too did his opponents, who formed a heterogeneous group motivated by a variety of different, often contradictory agendas.

In 1914, as Bergsonism's hegemony reached its peak, Bergson reached a breaking point. The excitement and increasingly vicious backlash surrounding his Académie française election, coupled with an ever-mounting list of obligations—such as the preparation of a series of lectures he delivered in Edinburgh in May—and little to no time off, all became too much.[37] Bergson asked to be replaced at the Collège de France and chose his friend and follower Le Roy to temporarily take his place. Bergson's career, like the situation in Europe, was about to change forever. Though he had no idea at the time, he would never return to the Collège de France, and the extraordinary events that led to the outbreak of war would push him to break the habit of a lifetime. For the first time, he would take a public stand on behalf of the country he had adopted as his own.

CHAPTER 19

WAR MISSIONS

"GERMANY DECLARES WAR ON FRANCE."[1]
On August 4, 1914, the headline jumped out as Bergson, on vacation with Louise and Jeanne in Switzerland, unfolded his copy of *Le Matin*. The family immediately made plans to return to Paris. Bergson had wanted to leave his wife and daughter in the safety and seclusion of L'Echappée, their holiday home built opposite Mont Blanc, but at such a critical moment, they had insisted on following him back home.[2]

In the weeks before the news broke, while talk of heightened tensions between neighbouring European countries was steadily seeping through the chatter, most people did not have war on their minds. The American author Edith Wharton recalled that, at a party near Paris at the end of June 1914, "a momentary shiver ran through the company" when somebody brought up the assassination of

Archduke Ferdinand. Soon the "talk wandered away to the interests of the hour ... the last play, the newest exhibition, the Louvre's most recent acquisitions."[3] Even for those more attuned to recent developments in international relations, the threat of war had not felt real until the news broke that it was. In the early days of the conflict, Bergson wrote to Xavier Léon:

> Sometimes I wonder if I'm dreaming. I had always believed and said that this war was inevitable, and now that it's here, I find it hard to believe that this is real, such is the magnitude of the event and the depth of the upheaval it will produce.[4]

This was the second time in Bergson's lifetime that his country had been at war. The first time had been during the lonely years of his childhood spent far from his parents in a Jewish boarding-house in Paris. After France's humiliating defeat by Prussia, Bergson and many of his generation had grown up with the abstract, yet ever-looming threat of a new conflict. Much later, Bergson described what he had experienced when decades of anxieties had finally materialised in 1914:

> I suddenly felt an invisible presence which all the past had prepared and foretold, as a shadow may precede the body that casts it. It was as though some creature of legend, having escaped from the book in which its story was told, had quietly taken possession of the room.... It was to intervene just at this moment, in this place, that it had been vaguely interlinked with my life-history.... I experienced what William James expresses, a feeling of admiration for the smoothness of the transition from the abstract to the concrete: who would have thought that so terrible an eventuality could make its entrance into reality with so little disturbance? The impression of this facility was predominant above all else.[5]

WAR SPEECHES

On July 31, 1914, a few days after Austria declared war on Serbia and a few days before Germany declared war on Russia and its allies, Bergson's old classmate Jean Jaurès, now a leading figure in international socialism, was dining in the Café du croissant on the rue Montmartre, close to the headquarters of his newspaper, *L'Humanité*.[6] Around half past nine, eighteen-year-old Raoul Villain, a supporter of Action Française, drew a gun and shot twice. One of the bullets lodged in Jaurès's head, killing him instantly.[7]

In the weeks preceding his assassination, Jaurès had been doing everything in his power to help cool the tensions mounting in Europe.[8] He and many others had hoped that the war could be prevented. Proust prayed "that some last-minute miracle" would "prevent the launching of the omni-death-dealing-machine."[9] On July 29, a few days before he was killed, Jaurès had delivered an antiwar speech in Brussels before a huge crowd. He ended with a warning: if war broke out, "dragging along the masses" in its unbridled violence, "men would turn to the German, French, Russian and Italian leaders and ask them: what reasons do you give us for all these corpses? And then the unchained Revolution would say to them: 'Go away and ask God and man for forgiveness!'"[10] He was met with resounding applause.

A week later, Germany had invaded Belgium. On August 8, Bergson, presiding over a session of the Académie des sciences morales et politiques, opened with a speech very different in spirit and tone from his old classmate's. He started by saluting Belgium, "a small nation with a great soul." Then he declared that the war against Germany was

a struggle of civilisation against barbarism. Everyone feels this, but our Academy has perhaps a particular authority in order to say it. Dedicated, mainly, to the study of psychological, moral and social questions, it carries out its simple scientific duty in pointing out

Germany's brutality and cynicism, and in its disdain for all justice
and all truth, a regression to a state of savagery.[11]

He ended his speech by proclaiming, "Long live the law! Long
live France," and was met with a standing ovation.[12] This was the
first in a series of propagandistic speeches that Bergson delivered
during the war. His nationalistic sentiments caused immediate
backlash and cost him several friendships with German philosophers.[13] In 1915, the German physiologist Wilhelm Wundt, in a
nationalistic speech of his own, deplored Bergson's surrender to
"chauvinism."[14] This accusation was repeated by many intellectuals after the war who felt that Bergson's stance had discredited him
as a thinker.

The war marked an important transmutation in Bergson's career.
He was no longer teaching at the Collège de France, having asked
to be replaced earlier in 1914, and now took on a very different kind
of mission. Rather than continue his disinterested contemplation of
metaphysics, he was acting on behalf of his country.

There was nothing unique about the rhetoric Bergson used in
his August 8 speech. When he had opened his copy of Le Matin
four days earlier and seen the headline announcing that Germany
had declared war on France, he would have also seen the article's
subtitle: "The holy war of civilisation against barbarism."[15] The
representation of the German camp as "barbaric" was consistent
with the propaganda deployed by French officials and intellectuals
throughout the war.[16] But what was unique about Bergson's war
speeches was that they mobilised his philosophical ideas, in particular notions he had developed in Creative Evolution, to address
the unfolding situation.[17] In his speeches, Bergson associated
France with civilisation and lawfulness and claimed that in its
very essence his nation was driven by a kind of internal creative,
self-replenishing force, something akin to the élan vital. Germany,
on the other hand, throughout its history, had come to embody
"savagery" and "barbarism," a "mechanisation of spirit."[18]

Bergson's war speeches were in stark contrast with the self-imposed rules—which he had followed throughout his career up until this point—that he would refrain from applying his philosophy to problems external to it and that he would exercise caution before expressing opinions or ideas that had not had time to fully mature. Now Bergson appeared to be doing the exact opposite— reacting in the heat of the moment and stretching his philosophical findings well beyond the scope he had originally delimited for them.

Emotions were running high. The war crimes perpetrated by German soldiers against civilians as they invaded Belgium at the start of the war had been well documented in France.[19] Bergson, in his own words, was raising "a cry of horror and indignation" in the face of "the crimes methodically committed by Germany: arson, pillage, destruction of monuments, massacre of women and children, and the breach of all the laws of war."[20] But anger and grief alone did not explain why Bergson was compelled to speak so explicitly when he had until that point been so determined to keep his opinions to himself.

When Bergson gave his first war speeches, he had recently been elected president of the Académie des sciences morales et politiques, a position that he felt imposed on him a "scientific duty" to work towards the progress of morality. Later in the war, after his presidency had ended, Bergson continued to speak in an official capacity, fulfilling various diplomatic and propaganda missions. Bergson later said he had been moved to do so by a "force beyond [his] control," an all-consuming sense of duty.[21] Since this sense of duty could not translate into action on the front (Bergson was now in his fifties), his verbal attacks against Germany and devotion to France were made all the fiercer. The day after his first speech, Bergson had written to Xavier Léon: "I'm annoyed at myself for only being able to speak, when so many young people are taking action, and doing so with such élan."[22] Perhaps, therefore, Bergson did not see his political involvement as breaching the rules he had previously imposed on himself because, in this instance, he believed he was speaking, not as a philosopher, but as a citizen, as a representative of his country in a state of emergency.

Charles Péguy was among the first to die, from a bullet in the head, during the first battle of the Marne in early September 1914. The battle that took his life along with so many others had saved Paris from German invasion. Barricades were erected around the city, which many, including Anna de Noailles and Proust, had fled.[23] But what the Germans had expected to be a swift victory turned into a drawn-out trench warfare in which a whole generation was lost. Bergson found out that Péguy had died about two weeks later and wrote to Murat:

> Péguy's death ... struck me like a thunderbolt. Not only did I admire him greatly, I loved him deeply. I have never known a higher soul. And it had to be him, one of the greatest, one of the best, who was cut down first! I cannot find the words to express what I feel.[24]

Their relationship had been strained for several years, but before Péguy had left for the front, Bergson had promised him that no matter what happened, his wife and children would be taken care of. He would remain true to his word. The loss of his close friend in a battle against the foreign enemy would only have heightened Bergson's feelings of national belonging.

Perhaps nationalism had also been a way for Bergson to assert his Frenchness after years of anti-Semitic campaigns directed against him. As the historian Johann Chapoutot noted: "The 1914 war was an opportunity for Jews, both French and German, to prove their attachment to the nation: those who ... were stigmatised as stateless could now reveal themselves to be fully patriotic."[25]

Bergson had always affirmed his patriotism. When he had started his education in France in the 1870s, he had been immersed in an atmosphere of resentment towards German science and culture in the aftermath of the defeat of France by Prussia. This might in part explain why he claimed that he was never much influenced by

German thinkers. In 1914, when Bergson experienced war for the second time, his devotion to his country was blind and absolute: "I was nothing. Nobody was anything anymore. There was only France."[26]

JOINING THE WAR EFFORT

During the war, Bergson took part in several propaganda missions. In 1915, he wrote a short history of French philosophy that was distributed at the San Francisco World's Fair. This tract painted French philosophy as the "initiator" of many of philosophy's greatest advances and as inherently inventive and original, inspiring many of the main German thinkers. Interestingly, as the Bergson scholar Caterina Zanfi pointed out, this depiction was in direct contradiction with Bergson's argument, in a talk delivered only four years earlier, "that philosophy could not be reduced to historical and national determinations."[27] When he reedited the text in the 1930s, Bergson had evidently moved back to this original position and away from his nationalistic propagandistic message: he removed the idea that French philosophy was somehow the most central and original philosophy in history and instead added that "French genius is not exclusive, but remains essentially human."[28]

In May 1916, Bergson and three other members of the Institut de France selected by the French government travelled to Spain. A few months earlier, Portugal had entered the war on the Allies' side, but it was unclear what Spain would do. The main event of the trip was to take place in Madrid, where Bergson and the others were scheduled to deliver talks and meet influential people, but a few extra stops along the way had been planned, one in San Sebastian and one in Burgos. Officially, this French delegation was meant to deliver a series of talks on different topics, but unofficially it was a propaganda mission, an attempt to rally important and influential figures to the Allies' side. Though Bergson had felt increasingly exhausted in the years leading up to the war, he felt obligated to accept the assignment. A few days before they departed, Bergson asked if he could skip the first step altogether and meet up with the delegation in Madrid:

> I am feeling extremely tired; I suffer from serious insomnia; I can only sleep by taking all sorts of precautions that would be impossible for me to take during our two or three days of preliminary travel, complicated by receptions, visits and so on. Between now and the moment when I will have to make a real effort, I need to have absolute calm. Otherwise, I run the risk of finding myself unable, once in Madrid, to give my lectures and to do the work that needs to be done.[29]

In his first talk, through a presentation of some of his philosophical ideas, Bergson attempted to convince his audience, a group of students, that there existed a profound link between the spirit of the French and the spirit of the Spanish. No nation, Bergson told the students, "is better suited [than France] to understand yours, to sympathise with the currents of thought and of feeling of the Spanish soul."[30] Before returning home, Bergson assured a journalist from *La Razon* that he believed France and Spain were "two noble nations, on the same level, with, if I may say so, the same moral altitude. And it seems to me that all their interests are aligned."[31] Despite the delegation's best efforts, Spain remained neutral for the rest of the conflict.

Later that year, Bergson wrote to an anxious Countess Murat:

> Instead of telling ourselves, "Today's news is bad, so it may turn out badly in the end," let us say, "Things are sure to turn out well in the end, so today's news cannot be as bad as it looks." No doubt the future is unpredictable; but there are possibilities and impossibilities, and I class the definitive success of the Germans among the absolute impossibilities,—unless we, ourselves, consent to this success, unless we lose heart, unless politicians come along and put obstacles in our way; but all this will depend on us.[32]

At this point, the battle of Verdun had been going strong for several months. It lasted from February until December 1916, claimed over three hundred thousand men, and injured countless others. Away from the trenches, in Paris, blackouts were imposed at night, restaurants and theatres closed, and the Grand Palais had been transformed into a military hospital. The City of Light was dark and quiet and Bergson's most important mission was yet to come.

BERGSON'S SECRET MISSION

War had broken out in Europe during the first half of Woodrow Wilson's first term as president of the United States. Two years into the conflict, he ran for a second term on a platform of neutrality—under the slogan "He has kept us out of the war"—and narrowly beat Republican Charles Evans Hughes. But on April 2, 1917, Wilson asked Congress to support his motion to declare war on Germany. The Senate backed the measure on April 4, and the House followed two days later.

Historians cite two major factors accounting for the 180-degree turn in Wilson's position on the war in Europe: Germany's submarine warfare, which impacted American civilians, and a telegram intercepted by British intelligence suggesting that Germany was trying to rally Mexico to its cause, against the United States.[33] But one other factor remains absent from all of these accounts. Between February and May 1917, as part of a mission that had been carefully crafted and prepared by the French government, Bergson met with the highest members of the American government, including President Wilson himself.

On January 11, 1917, Bergson had been summoned by Aristide Briand, the head of the French government, who presented him with a "great service" that his country required of him.[34] The goal was to communicate the French vision of the war to the Americans on both a political and ideological level. Bergson had to reassure Wilson that the Allies shared his desire for a Society of Nations and convince him that the war could not be resolved until the United

States entered it. His mission was to help dispel any hesitation Wilson might still have had about entering the conflict on the side of the Allies.

French authorities believed that sending a diplomat on official business to carry out this mission might be perceived as too aggressive and could backfire. But they hoped that Bergson, the famous philosopher, who had only a few years earlier delivered a highly successful series of lectures on American soil, might appeal to Wilson's academic sensibilities. Before he became president of the United States of America, Wilson had been president of Princeton University.

Bergson at first hesitated. He worried about leaving Louise and Jeanne for an indefinite period during such volatile times. He also doubted his ability to deliver the desired outcome:

> It was therefore with the vague intention of asking to be relieved of this mission that I went to see Jules Cambon, Secretary General of the Ministry of Foreign Affairs. . . . Now, I had not yet sat down in front of M. Cambon when he told me: "My duty is to inform you that we have just picked up and deciphered a German wireless, warning that from tomorrow there will be merciless submarine warfare, without distinction of nationality, etc. Your journey to America will therefore become most dangerous." These words were all it took. I had to leave. There was no room for hesitation.[35]

When Bergson crossed the Atlantic, the threat of German torpedoes was on everyone's mind. Faced with the possibility of total obliteration, Bergson and his shipmates were asked to keep their life jackets on at all times during the voyage, but very few complied. Bergson sensed a kind of silent resolve in his fellow passengers and admired the fact that they refused to treat danger as an unwanted guest but rather welcomed it as a remedy for the guilt they had been feeling since the start of the war.[36] They were not the ones fighting in the trenches. They had been living comfortably, reading about the mounting death toll in the newspapers. And so Bergson too decided he would rather drown than suffer the indignity of a life jacket.

Before leaving, Bergson had been thoroughly briefed on the US economy, trade, public opinion, diplomacy, and the cost of the war. Upon arrival, he would have to build networks, seek out influential figures, and convince them of the need for the United States to join the war.

Bergson had hoped he would arrive on US soil without fanfare, but journalists soon found out he was in the country and rushed to his hotel. The philosopher did his best to fend them off, but by arriving unannounced, he had inadvertently created a sense of intrigue that made his appearance even more newsworthy.[37] For obvious reasons, it was very important that the true motivations behind his visit remain unknown. For a long time after the war, he would keep his mission secret, mainly because he did not want the many friends he had made during that time to feel betrayed and used.[38] Though he may have felt sincere friendship towards his new acquaintances, he had nevertheless been following a secret ulterior motive, which was to persuade them to comply with what his government needed them to do.

The French government had been correct in assuming that an esteemed philosopher like Bergson would be better received than an official figure. Bergson was able to form meaningful connections with some of the most influential people in New York and Washington. On one occasion, Theodore Roosevelt invited him to breakfast in his hotel on Fifth Avenue. During their two-and-a-half-hour conversation, Roosevelt criticised Wilson and claimed he would go to France with twenty thousand men and fight. Bergson later reflected: "He would have gone straight to the front, to our trenches. Most likely he would have been killed. And that would have been very noble, but what good would it have done us?"[39]

Bergson was able to meet with Wilson's innermost circle. He befriended Franklin Lane, who was in charge of the Council of National Defence and one of Bergson's readers and admirers. He and Bergson sometimes met in the evenings for conversations during which the philosopher pleaded the case for France and the Allies. The gist of these talks was then fed back by Lane to Wilson.

Bergson also befriended the Texan diplomat Edward M. House, known as Colonel House (though the title was merely honourary), who had become one of Wilson's closest advisers after managing his 1912 presidential campaign. Bergson described his first encounter with House as one of those occasions when two strangers immediately bond through the mysteries of human chemistry. But the affinity between the diplomat from Texas and the Parisian philosopher may not have been as spontaneous as Bergson recounted. The philosopher played a clever and calculated game, commenting to Thomas R. Marshall, the vice president, that House "reminded him of the old Romans who lived their lives wholly for the advancement . . . of their country." House was flattered and wrote about the philosopher's remark in his diary. There is little doubt that Bergson had intended for this comment to find its way back to his new influential friend.[40]

As part of his mission, Bergson investigated the real reasons for Wilson's hesitation to join the war. He found that those reasons were "at least in large part, religious and philosophical."[41] Wilson worried that God would never forgive him for the loss of American lives. But House, possibly under Bergson's influence, argued to Wilson that far more lives would be lost if nothing was done.

A few weeks into his trip, Bergson was granted an audience with Wilson himself. No records of the meeting exist, but Bergson's preparatory notes tell us that his arguments leaned on Wilson's philosophical proclivities. It is likely that Bergson argued that the United States would need to participate in the war to have a say in postwar negotiations. He knew that Wilson was in favour of a League of Nations to ensure future peace and democracy. Bergson suggested that Wilson could thus become the first to realise Plato's dream of a philosopher king and that France was prepared to support him.

When Wilson finally announced that the United States was joining the war effort, he cited the survival of democracy as a decisive factor. The vision of the war that Bergson communicated to Wilson was in fact the vision that Wilson embraced and for which he is remembered.

Two decades later, Bergson wrote in his characteristically self-deprecating tone, "I do not claim to have had much to do with the decision that was finally taken."[42] But House and Lane remembered things differently. House described Bergson as his "guide, philosopher and friend, during some never-to-be-forgotten days," and Bergson remembered Lane telling him, "You had more to do with the President's decision than you think" (to which Bergson immediately added: "That was probably an exaggeration").[43]

All that ultimately mattered to Bergson was that his country had prevailed:

> I lived through unforgettable hours during that time. Humanity appeared to me as if transfigured. Above all, the beloved France, the France which, if it had been crushed, would have dragged the best of civilisation down with it, the France which, despite the confidence I had always tried to spread around me, I felt was threatened in its very existence, France was saved. It was the greatest joy of my life.[44]

The war had pushed Bergson beyond the limits he had up until then set for himself. He had used his own philosophical ideas to paint a simplistic picture of the conflict as a battle between good and evil. Almost two decades after his first war speech, Bergson reflected on the "'exaltation of a people at the outbreak of a war,' which could 'perhaps' be explained as a 'defensive reaction against fear.'" As Mark Sinclair notes, here Bergson was "perhaps engaging in an implicit self-critique: the mobilisation of his philosophy in the service of the French war effort ... was to a degree a function of a bellicose, perhaps fearful, but certainly partially closed mind."[45] However, even during war times, Bergson had opposed the nationalistic calls some of his colleagues were making to remove some of the foreign members of the Academie des sciences morales et politiques.[46] In the years that followed the war, Bergson leaned into this spirit of openness, focusing his efforts on bringing about the vision of international collaboration he had sold Wilson. But the uncharacteristic virulence and simplistic thinking he had displayed during those pivotal years would contribute to his complete fall out of fashion during the interwar period.

CHAPTER 20

DISAPPEARING FROM MEMORY

On November 11, 1918, bells rang all over Paris, and posters appeared on the walls of the city announcing the end of the war:

> Victory, triumphant victory on all fronts is ours! The defeated enemy has laid down its arms and the bloodshed will now cease.[1]

Parisians celebrated the armistice for three days, but their world had been altered beyond recognition. In addition to the 1.4 million young French men who had died, many more had been mutilated. The dreams and aspirations of the Belle Epoque had also vanished in the cataclysm. Proust described with sadness how distant the spirit and energy of the prewar times now felt: "It is like a collection of beautiful antique fans on a wall. You admire them, but there is no hand now to bring them alive. The very fact that they are under glass proves that the ball is over."[2]

UNFASHIONABLE

The special kind of optimism that once moved Bergson's followers had evaporated. "Bergsonism" had been a philosophy of hope, of transgression, of freedom, but after 1918 the very meaning of those terms had changed. The noisy and heated debates around Bergson's philosophy had subsided or taken on new forms in which his ideas no longer had a place. As the Bergson scholar Mary Ann Gillies explains: "After the war, people were less interested in things that had been popular before it, regarding them as leftovers of an age that could not, and should not, return. Bergsonism thus became unfashionable."[3]

In 1919, a young philosopher called Raymond Lenoir used the publication of *L'Energie spirituelle*, a collection of Bergson's essays and talks from the 1901–1913 period, as an opportunity to ask whether the philosopher was indeed as "original" and "profound" as his admirers had always claimed.[4] Had it all been, "on the contrary, a fad, an epochal caprice that would not survive the test of war?" Lenoir's diagnosis was unequivocal: Bergson's philosophy "no longer meets the vital needs of the new age."[5]

The changes in cultural mood precipitated by the war were not the only factor at play in Bergson's fall out of fashion. To the general audience, much of Bergson's draw had come from his "magnetic appeal" in his public lectures.[6] But since Bergson had stopped lecturing at the Collège de France in 1914, his magnetism was no longer on display.[7]

On January 24, 1918, Bergson had finally taken his seat at the Académie française, his induction having been pushed back several times because of his war missions. His speech was followed by a five-minute standing ovation.[8] Bergson, who had twice been rejected by the Sorbonne, was finally recognised as a national hero by his peers, but he had lost the transgressive appeal that had attracted the youthful, rebellious, avant-garde audience of the prewar years. Increasingly, Bergson was perceived as a figure of the establishment and no longer as a subversive voice of radical freedom and creativity. What's more, many of his supporters on the left would never forgive the chauvinistic tone of his war speeches. The picture he had painted of the creativity of life had been tainted when he had summoned the *élan vital* in nationalistic war propaganda.

In the 1920s, as Bergson-mania was dying down, one event in particular, Bergson's final public polemic, precipitated his fall into oblivion.

"THE TIME OF THE PHILOSOPHER"

Albert Einstein was awarded a Nobel Prize in November 1922, but not for his theory of relativity. The president of the Nobel committee explained that, while relativity had been at the centre of many important discussions, these had been epistemological, "the subject of lively debate in philosophical circles," rather than scientific. To illustrate their point, the committee noted that one of Einstein's main opponents in the relativity debates had been a philosopher, the most notorious philosopher in fact: "It will be no secret that the famous philosopher Bergson in Paris has challenged this theory." And so Einstein was rewarded, not for his work on relativity, but for his more indisputably scientific (according to the committee) "discovery of the law of the photoelectric effect."[9]

Earlier that year, in the spring of 1922, Einstein had travelled to Paris to give a series of talks. He had been invited at the request of a fellow physicist, the Collège de France professor Paul Langevin. Einstein had hesitated at first to accept the invitation. The anti-German sentiments that had been lingering in France since the 1870 war had been fully revived in 1914, and many French scientists endorsed a boycott of German scientists.[10] Einstein was also Jewish, and he had been on the receiving end of much anti-Semitism, and even some death threats, both at home and in the same French newspapers that had been attacking Bergson for years.[11] Thus, his decision to expose himself to the nationalists of Paris was an act of bravery, one that he hoped could contribute to reuniting broken scientific communities.

When Einstein arrived at the Gare du Nord in Paris, "photographers, reporters, cinematographers, official and diplomatic personalities awaited him in impressive numbers," in a scene reminiscent of Bergson's glory days.[12] But the physicist escaped the crowd by crossing the tracks with Langevin and using a different exit.

The French physics society did not acknowledge the presence of the eminent German scientist in the capital, and so the main event of Einstein's trip took place on April 6, 1922, at a meeting of the Société française de philosophie before an audience of philosophers and physicists.

The philosopher Xavier Léon opened the proceedings by reminding the audience that one of the society's missions from its inception had been to bridge the gap not only between different philosophical schools but also between philosophers and scientists. Langevin then launched into a presentation of Einstein's theories before opening the floor to questions and comments. Einstein responded to difficult questions about various aspects of his theory, including a lengthy question from the philosopher Léon Brunschvicg about the links between relativity and Kant's conception of science. Einstein answered tactfully that "each philosopher has their own Kant," then added, "I cannot answer what you have just said, because the few indications you have given are insufficient for me to know how you interpret Kant."

Einstein's answers were often a lot shorter than the questions, and Léon, keen to keep the conversation flowing, asked Bergson's friend and follower Edouard Le Roy to say a few words. Le Roy was embarrassed: "Our friend Xavier Léon is determined that I should speak. Given his kind insistence, I cannot refuse. But really, I have nothing to say." Le Roy stitched together a short reflection about space, time, and scientific measurement that inevitably led him to his master: "In particular, I believe that the problem of time is not the same for M. Einstein as it is for M. Bergson."

At this point in time, Einstein's theory had been on Bergson's mind for over a decade, ever since he had heard Langevin give a presentation about relativity at a conference in Bologna. As he later explained, Bergson had felt that he could not ignore Einstein's theories, that it was his "duty" to examine *durée* in the light of relativity. Bergson believed that time and space should be considered separately, while Einstein combined them in a four-dimensional space-time in which past, present, and future coexisted all at once. About a year before Bergson and Einstein met, Bergson told his friend Chevalier that he had "returned" to the study of mathematics, which he had so enjoyed during his youth, and that he wished to write something to show that, despite appearances, his and Einstein's theory were not contradictory, that his idea of *durée* was not incompatible with relativity. For Bergson, the physicist's ideas had raised all sorts of questions and reflections, but that day at the meeting of the Société française de philosophie, he had not anticipated being brought into the discussion.[13] So when he heard Le Roy mention his name, his heart probably sank. Bergson believed that no good could ever come from public debates, "because no one will ever accept to admit publicly to a mistake. But there's a deeper reason: in a dispute, you force your opponent to objectify thoughts that would otherwise have remained unconscious or at least inconsistent, and that's an additional obstacle you raise."[14]

Le Roy, who had himself been forced into the discussion, passed on the burden. Since "Bergson is among us," perhaps it would be more appropriate, he pointed out, for the philosopher of *durée* "himself to take the floor."[15] Bergson reluctantly stood up and modestly insisted, "I came here to listen. I had no intention of speaking." He knew, however, that there was no possible escape, so he continued by paying tribute to the physicist and celebrating the theoretical avenues he had opened up: "Let me begin by saying how much I admire Einstein's work. It seems to me to demand the attention of philosophers as well as scientists. I see in it not only a new physics, but also, in some respects, a new way of thinking." And he joked: "Since it would be wrong to talk about time without considering the time, and since it is now late, I will confine myself to brief comments on one or two points." Bergson then spoke for about half an hour.[16]

Central to Bergson's improvised presentation was the idea that Einstein's conception of time and his own conception of *durée* were not incompatible: "I have no objection to your definition of simultaneity, any more than I have to the theory of Relativity. . . . What I want to establish is simply this: once the theory of Relativity has been accepted as a physical theory, all is not finished." Einstein's French was adequate but not excellent, and so he missed many of the subtleties of Bergson's exposé. His response was much shorter than Bergson's, and his conclusion was a lot more memorable: "The time of the philosopher does not exist."[17]

The two men had talked past each other: they both believed that their discipline should have the last word. In his short but devastating rebuttal, Einstein asserted the supremacy of physics, leaving no room for philosophy when it came to the question of time. Bergson, on the other hand, believed that, while the mathematics of relativity did not need to be challenged, "we still have to determine the philosophical significance of the concepts it introduces."[18]

At the time of his public disagreement with Einstein, Bergson had already written a whole book that directly addressed these issues, *Duration and Simultaneity: With Reference to Einstein's Theory*.[19] What was fundamentally at stake for Bergson was the question of the relationship between science and philosophy. He argued that Einstein's theory as a whole rested upon unconscious and unsophisticated metaphysical foundations that, if left unexamined, could lead philosophers and physicists astray in their analyses of time. Therefore, even after the physicist was done speaking, the philosopher still had a lot to say.

But as always seemed to be the case when Bergson chose to delve into the scientific matters of his day, he was represented as scientifically illiterate. Even though Bergson repeated again and again that he neither rejected relativity as a theory nor challenged its mathematical framework, he was accused of dismissing a theory he supposedly did not understand. Several physicists, including Jean Becquerel, Lorentz, and Einstein himself, accused Bergson of having made crucial mistakes in his reading of Einstein's theory, in particular regarding the famous "twin paradox" thought experiment.[20] A drawn-out back-and-forth ensued. In the appendix to the second edition of *Duration and Simultaneity*, Bergson expressed his frustration about being misunderstood, but he was not heard, and especially not by Einstein, who supported the idea that Bergson was simply mistaken and, as a philosopher, ill equipped to deal with such complex scientific issues. Like the majority of people at his time, Bergson may not have grasped all of the subtleties of Einstein's theoretical apparatus, but he did study the physicist's work carefully and with sufficient knowledge and understanding to engage seriously with the material. Einstein, on the other hand, certainly had not taken the time to understand Bergson. The philosopher complained to Chevalier:

> I doubt that he was familiar enough with philosophy and especially with French to have read my book. . . . Einstein therefore had to rely on some French physicist who did not understand me, and who, lacking the philosophical preparation necessary to understand me, remained resistant to all my explanations.[21]

Bergson, who had been battling the misconception that he was anti-science and scientifically uneducated since the start of his philosophical career, had grown weary of having to defend himself. He ended up removing himself from the relativity debate, and after all the criticism he had received, he distanced himself from *Duration and Simultaneity* altogether. That did nothing to challenge the perception that the rising star of physics had ultimately won and that the aging philosopher was out of touch.[22] This perception, combined with the shift in the general mood after the war, contributed to Bergson's disappearance from the public eye.

Einstein and Bergson's fraught relationship escaped from the theoretical realms of physics and metaphysics and spilled over into the very practical world of international diplomacy. A few months after their public debate, both men were invited to join the International Committee on Intellectual Cooperation (ICIC), which had been created as an advisory organisation for the recently formed League of Nations.

Though members were said to have been selected, "without any discrimination as to nationality," Einstein immediately resented what he perceived to be the anti-German sentiments of some members.[23] The physicist did not attend the first meeting in 1922 and resigned soon after.

The original twelve-member committee, which, in addition to Bergson, included the philosopher and statesman Sarvepalli Radhakrishnan, the classicist Gilbert Murray, and the physicists Marie Curie and Hendrik Lorentz, was tasked with debating a great number of questions, such as the preservation of world heritage, copyright law, the value of Esperanto, and how to fund exchange programs between universities. Bergson, who had hoped after the relativity debacle to return to his own research, was elected as the ICIC's first chairman. He felt he had no choice but to accept, and found himself completely submerged by this new task, which he described to Chevalier as "a fireball" that crashed into his life "already organised so tightly that there was no room left even for a single hairpin."[24]

Nevertheless, Bergson took his role very seriously. Around this time he was also appointed to a French committee formed to determine whether to modernise the French education system or to lean more into the classics. (Bergson was of the latter opinion.)

After the war, after the debate with Einstein, after decades of noise, Bergson finally could endure no more. In the mid-1920s, at the age of sixty-five, his health sharply declined, and on August 15, 1925, he stepped down from his position as chairman of the ICIC. Not only was Bergson resigning from his presidential duties, but he was also removing himself entirely from public life, and after this, he slowly disappeared from collective memory.

CHAPTER 21

"GENTLEMEN, IT IS FIVE O'CLOCK. CLASS IS OVER."

It had started in the early months of 1925 with a swelling and an unfamiliar numbness in his foot. Within a few years, Bergson would find himself periodically unable to move, sometimes for days at a time, or too exhausted and feverish to have a simple conversation. For years he had suffered from bouts of severe fatigue and insomnia, but this was different.

Two years before his first symptoms, Bergson had written to Floris Delattre: "I am extremely tired. For twelve or fifteen years I have not taken a day, not even a half day of proper rest."[1] Worn out by nearly two decades of uninterrupted work and intense public scrutiny, strained by the recent war and the high stakes of his international missions, and crumbling under the pressure of his various diplomatic roles, the philosopher's body had given in.

At first, Bergson's "obscure illness" left doctors puzzled.[2] In the early days of his disease, they were his only visitors. He would later joke that his condition could not be too serious if he had managed to survive more than fifteen of them and their various treatments. Over the years, he was advised to subject himself to boiling hot mud baths, hydrotherapy, electrotherapy, massages, gold salt injections, bee venom, and the warmth of the sun. One doctor attempted to stimulate Bergson's sympathetic nervous system by tickling the back of his nose. Bergson joked about the patent absurdity of his predicament but soon had to terminate the treatment because it caused painful heart problems.[3] Specialists eventually determined that Bergson was suffering from a severe case of rheumatoid arthritis. From the mid-1920s until his death in 1941, Bergson's life was punctuated by intense pain, fevers, a progressive loss of mobility, and countless remissions and relapses. During this time, Bergson's wife and daughter, Louise and Jeanne, devoted all their energy to caring for him.

In his drawn-out final years, Bergson's joints became swollen and his fingers deformed. A simple meal took him hours to finish, and the energy required to think and write came to him only in short and increasingly rare bursts, scattered throughout the day. He often worried that his days of philosophising were over. He resigned himself to the idea that the various treatments he received could only delay the progression of his disease but would never cure him. He also believed that the fevers and infections he repeatedly suffered and survived were simply nature's attempts at ending a long life that had run its course. By the late 1930s, he felt he had overstayed his welcome on earth.[4]

Yet, despite his poor health, in the final decade and a half of his life Bergson managed to produce what many consider his best philosophical work. As he prepared for his own death, and as Europe once again descended into darkness, Bergson explored new spiritual avenues as he thought about the future of humanity.

"BERGSONISM IS DEAD"

In the late 1920s and 1930s, Bergson received the most prestigious honours of his life: he was promoted to the highest rank of the Légion d'honneur, and in 1927 he was awarded the Nobel Prize in Literature "in recognition of his rich and vitalizing ideas and the brilliant skill with which they have been presented."[5] But at the same time, the philosopher had lost most of his influence.

In the years leading up to World War I, many of Bergson's followers had viewed his philosophy as a disruptive force for progress. But by the late 1920s, he was seen as an embodiment of the philosophical orthodoxy, a defender of the status quo, a relic from a lost time.[6] In the words of the French philosopher Raymond Aron, Bergson had become a "classic," that is, "someone that everyone knows, that a few read, that almost no one sees as a contemporary."[7] According to the historian François Azouvi, Bergson's "concepts were no longer of any help to most of those who were inventing new ways of thinking, writing, behaving or painting."[8]

During this time, Bergson was attacked by prominent left-wing thinkers who represented him as a member of the old philosophical guard and accused him of upholding conservative bourgeois values. They also criticised the nationalism he had displayed in his war speeches, which disqualified, they said, his philosophy as a whole. Among these thinkers were Julien Benda (who had made a career out of denigrating the thinker of *durée*) and the Communist Paul Nizan. But the most influential among them was the Marxist philosopher Georges Politzer, who in 1929 published an anti-Bergsonian pamphlet.[9] In the first pages Politzer stated:

It is immediately apparent that Mr. Bergson is continuing the tradition of those philosophers who profess to understand, and who, in fact, understand nothing. Bergson's philosophy has always been a zealous ally of the state and the class of which it is the instrument. M. Bergson was openly in favour of the war and, in effect, against the Russian Revolution. At no time did he ever utter the slightest word of revolt.[10]

His conclusion delivered the final blow: "Mr. Bergson is as yet still dying, but Bergsonism is in fact dead."[11]

It was true that many of the prewar Bergsonisms had disappeared. Bergson had once had followers on both ends of the political spectrum. Now, on the left, the mood had turned resolutely against him, and Bergson found most of his support among Catholic thinkers and on the right. Even the far-right group Action Française published a relatively positive article on his Nobel win showing that they no longer perceived the philosopher as a threat.[12]

Emblematic of this interwar Bergsonism was Bergson's close friend, the Catholic philosopher Jacques Chevalier. In the early 1900s, Chevalier had been among the hundreds who attended Bergson's Collège de France lectures each week, and it was around this time that the professor and the student had met. Decades later, when the Nazis occupied half of France, Chevalier served three months as minister for education in Pétain's collaborationist government.

From Chevalier's student days until Bergson's death in occupied Paris, the two men and their families bonded and frequently met and corresponded. The final decades of Bergson's life can be glimpsed through Chevalier's careful notes of their conversations and through his publications, which he usually had Bergson pre-approve. Their friendship had blossomed around Bergson's gradual move towards Catholicism.

A few years after publishing *Creative Evolution*, in a letter to one of his critics, the Jesuit theologian Joseph de Tonquédec, Bergson had explained that from *durée* to the *élan vital*, his research had revealed "a free and creative God, generative of both matter and life, and whose creative effort is continued in life by the evolution of species and by the constitution of human personalities."[13] Bergson was not interested in following the doctrines of the Church. He had come to faith and religion through a slow and solitary process of philosophical maturation. A few years before he died, he told Chevalier:

> For me, there was no conversion in the sense of sudden enlighten-
> ment. I came gradually to ideas which, probably, had never been
> totally absent from me, but of which I was not fully aware, about
> which I did not concern myself. I came to them little by little. Nev-
> ertheless, there was a trigger: it was reading the mystics.[14]

In the 1910s, as part of his research for a new project whose contours he could not yet make out, Bergson had started reading about
different systems of ethics and was eventually led to the Christian
mystics. In 1911, he excitedly told Péguy's friend, the writer Joseph
Lotte, "I have discovered a new world."[15]

These new reflections would take two and a half decades to materialise into Bergson's final work. Despite his illness, despite his
exhaustion, and despite having become profoundly unfashionable,
the book Bergson published in 1932, *The Two Sources of Morality
and Religion*, "was warmly received as the crowning moment of [his]
philosophical work."[16]

A "SUPPLEMENT OF SPIRIT"

Aside from his response to Einstein and *Mind-Energy*, a collection of
talks and essays published in 1919, Bergson had not produced a major
philosophical work since *Creative Evolution* appeared in 1907. When
he had still been the most famous philosopher in the world, there had
been rumours that he was preparing a new book on the subject of ethics, or perhaps aesthetics. One interviewer noticed that when asked
about his new project, Bergson's whole demeanour had changed: "His
face took on an expression of weariness, of discouragement."[17]

By 1932, those who still followed Bergson had given up on waiting for a new book by the septuagenarian philosopher. But then
"one fine day," recalled Bergson's old student, the philosopher
Jacques Maritain, "without any publicity, without any press release,

without anyone, even among the author's closest friends, having been informed, the work that had been anticipated for twenty-five years appeared in bookstores."[18]

True to old habits, Bergson had kept his new ideas to himself. Chevalier was one of the only people who had seen the manuscript before it was published, and even then, it was at a stage when it was too late to make any revisions. Close to the publication date, Bergson confessed that he was unhappy with the final product, that he had mainly written it "for himself," and that he had almost abandoned the idea of publishing it:

> It would have taken very little, a slight observation that barely amounted to criticism, to make me abandon the idea of publication. This is one of the reasons why I haven't shown anyone anything, either the proofs or the manuscript.... Anyway, come what may. This absurd illness will have prevented me from saying things the way I wanted to say them. At least I will have said them. And I think I will be able to leave this world with more peace of mind.[19]

The way Bergson normally produced a book was to absorb as many insights on a topic as he possibly could, reading almost everything there was to read, until he knew what he wanted to say. Then he could write, a very short process in comparison. *Creative Evolution* had taken him years to research but only a few months to write.[20] But because of the many responsibilities he had taken on during and after the war, followed by his debilitating illness, Bergson could only muster the energy to research and write his new book in short bursts.

Bergson's approach to morality and religion was quite novel for the time. He argued that they should be studied as manifestations of "Life itself."[21] In this sense, the book built upon the findings of *Creative Evolution* but also expanded the reach of the *élan vital* beyond what most would consider the purely biological and into the realms of the social and even the mystical.

According to Bergson, all societies tend towards closure; that is, in the words of the historians of philosophy Alexandre Lefebvre and Nils F. Schott, "they limit moral, political, and religious concern, along with the rights and obligations that flow from it, to an exclusive group of people. This group can be as small as a family or tribe, or as large as a country or group of nations."[22] It is above all out of habit that our obligation compels us in a closed society. As Lefebvre and Schott point out, Bergson's characterisation of closedness was not all negative. A tight-knit group has an evolutionary advantage in terms of survival, and such social dynamics nurture what many consider to be overall positive traits such as "discipline and self-sacrifice, obedience, solidarity and fellowship, loyalty, security, and patriotism."[23] But in its inward-looking attitude, in the "us vs. them" distinction it draws, the natural outcome of a closed society is war. One of Bergson's aims in his new book was to determine how to escape the bind of our natural tendency towards closure.

In an ideal world, we would be able to extrapolate the love and sense of obligation we feel towards our family and extend it to all the members of our social group, and then finally to humanity as a whole.[24] But this is not how things play out in reality. Even countries that uphold the value of universal human rights, like France, are able to put such values aside for various reasons, including war. Such a society, Bergson observed with irony, "says that the duties it defines are indeed, in principle, duties toward humanity, but that under exceptional circumstances, regrettably unavoidable, they are for the time being suspended in practice."[25]

Bergson's conclusion that, left in the hands of nature, societies' tendency towards closure doomed them to war is not as pessimistic as it seems. According to him, no society is entirely closed. There exists an opposite tendency towards openness in which moral duty is not limited to the group but expands to humanity as a whole, and beyond.

For Bergson, in the same way that there are artistic and scientific geniuses, some exceptional men and women are "moral geniuses," and he named a few: "the Christian saints, ... the Greek sages, the prophets of Israel, the Buddhist Arahants and many others." These exemplary figures act on their own aspiration rather than in reaction to external pressures and inspire others to follow their lead.[26] As Sinclair notes: "This aspect of morality ... does not repeat and reproduce, like habit, constantly turning around itself in a circle, but rather pushes forward into the open, breaking new moral ground."[27]

Parallel to the open-closed distinction regarding morality and society, Bergson distinguished between "static" and "dynamic" religion. On its static side, religion is an evolutionary solution like any other. More precisely, in the same way that laughter protects society against the rigidification of behaviours and attitudes (see Chapter 9), the creation of religious myths and fables protects us from some of the more antisocial tendencies of our intellect that may pose a threat to social unity.[28] For instance, distress about the certainty of death is assuaged with the prospect of an afterlife, and the anxiety caused by the unpredictability of the outcomes of our actions can be tempered by the promise that some higher power has a master plan.

On its dynamic side, religion is no longer merely an evolutionary solution to a human problem; it is a mystical experience, which Bergson understood as "the establishment of a contact, consequently of a partial coincidence, with the creative effort of which life is the manifestation."[29] The great mystic enters into direct contact with the process of life itself, "extending the divine action," continuing the work of creation, pushing humanity beyond the limits of its nature.[30]

Bergson's extensive study of different kinds of mystical experiences over different periods and cultures led him to believe that mysticism finds its ultimate expression in the Christian mystics.[31] But all great mystics, wrote Bergson,

> prove to be great men of action, to the surprise of those for whom mysticism is nothing but visions, and raptures and ecstasies. That

240

which they have allowed to flow into them is a stream flowing down and seeking through them to reach their fellow-men; the necessity to spread around them what they have received affects them like an onslaught of love ... so that ... other men will open their souls to the love of humanity.[32]

In the final section of the book, "Final Remarks: Mechanics and Mysticism," Bergson reflected on the future of humanity. A decade before the start of the Manhattan Project, which developed the first nuclear weapons, Bergson was already worried about the destructive capabilities of technology developing too fast for our ethics to be able to keep up. In the acceptance speech he had sent to the Nobel committee a few years earlier, he expressed the anxieties that haunted him in his old age:

If the nineteenth century made tremendous progress in mechanical inventions, it too often assumed that these inventions ... would raise the moral level of mankind. Increasing experience has proved, on the contrary, that the technological development of a society does not automatically result in the moral perfection of the men living in it, and that an increase in the material means at the disposal of humanity may even present dangers unless it is accompanied by a corresponding spiritual effort. ... To take only the most striking example: one might have expected that the use of steam and electricity, by diminishing distances, would by itself bring about a moral *rapprochement* between peoples. Today we know that this was not the case and that antagonisms, far from disappearing, will risk being aggravated if a spiritual progress, a greater effort toward brotherhood, is not accomplished.[33]

In *The Two Sources*, Bergson mused that population growth and scarcity of resources would no doubt require us to eat less meat. He hoped for equality between the sexes and for the "decline in the pursuit of superfluous luxuries."[34] But above all, Bergson believed that a "supplement of spirit" would be needed to balance out the blind expansion of technology.[35] We would need what Bergson calls a kind of "spiritual reform."[36] For Bergson there is no technology in opposition to life, no culture in opposition to nature, only moral and material creation as expressions of the same evolutionary movement, the same history.

A few years before he died, nearly a decade after he published *The Two Sources*, Bergson was still formulating new ideas:

> I am still working as best I can but those who say I am preparing a new book are wrong. The truth is that I would rather, before leaving this world, form opinions on certain issues, and do this for myself. It is unlikely that a book will come out of this.[37]

THE FINAL LESSON

The will Bergson drafted in 1937 contained a controversial passage that has since been much discussed and dissected:

> My reflections have led me closer and closer to Catholicism, in which I see the complete fulfilment of Judaism. I should have become a convert, had I not seen in preparation for years (in great part, alas, through the fault of a certain number of Jews entirely deprived of moral sense) the formidable wave of anti-Semitism which is to sweep over the world. I wanted to remain among those who tomorrow will be persecuted.[38]

One Bergson expert interprets the remark about the anti-Semitism of the 1930s being "the fault of a certain number of Jews" as a reference to Jewish participation in the Bolshevik revolution, which drew anti-Semitic reactions.[39] It is difficult to know exactly what Bergson had in mind when writing these words targeting some of his coreligionists, but when his wife Louise authorised the publication of certain parts of his will, she removed the contentious passage, knowing that it could lead to all sorts of interpretations. She may also have wanted to avoid giving the impression that the solidarity Bergson expressed towards his own people was not genuine. Bergson had told Chevalier in private that he found himself unable to "abandon this Judaism in which I was brought up. . . . I would find it very painful if [my conversion] were to provide an argument to the persecutors of my race."[40]

In the end, the social aspect of conversion, honouring the doctrines and the dogmas, was less important to Bergson than his personal conversion, his intimate understanding of his own faith. The only ritualistic aspect of Catholicism that Bergson wished to honour was to have a Catholic priest present at his funeral. Another important instruction Bergson left his family was that he did not want any of his correspondence, lectures, or anything else that he had not authorised to be published, and for good measure he asked Louise to burn all his unpublished papers.[41] When World War II broke out in September 1939, Bergson was about to turn eighty and he told Chevalier, "I await death with a lively sense of curiosity."[42]

On June 14, 1940, Nazis paraded down the Champs-Élysées. A week later, in the heart of the Compiègne forest, Marshal Philippe Pétain signed an armistice with Germany. All over France, huddled around radios, people listened in stunned silence as the terms of the agreement with the enemy were read out. The country was divided into two halves: the occupied zone which included Paris; and a so-called *zone libre*, which would be placed under the jurisdiction of Pétain's government based in Vichy.

That summer Bergson had been in Dax for treatments. The city fell into the occupied zone, and soon German soldiers started appearing. The Bergsons scrambled to make plans to return to their Parisian home, where the philosopher spent his final months.[43]

Some of Bergson's friends reported that a few weeks before he died, the eighty-one-year-old philosopher had stepped outside into the biting cold, and then, leaning on the arm of his valet, had waited in line for several hours to register as a Jew. This was probably, they believed, how he contracted the pulmonary congestion that killed him.[44] Bergson could have chosen not to comply with the occupiers' degrading demands. In fact, he was one of the few who retained the luxury of choice. A lifetime of honours and services to the French nation had earned the philosopher a pass from the collaborationist Vichy government. Bergson was offered an exemption from the oppressive measures to which other French Jews were violently subjected. But he refused the special treatment and instead braved the cold both outside and within his own home. Bergson, who had always valued the honours his country was willing to bestow on him, refused this time and he did not live to see the end of the war.

Bergson died of pneumonia during the fourth night of 1941 in his poorly heated Parisian apartment. Coal was difficult to come by in Nazi-occupied Paris. In his final hours, a priest had been summoned to his bedside.

For a man who had once been considered one of the most important thinkers in the world, Bergson's funeral was an underwhelming affair. The sparsely attended service took place during a snowstorm at the Garches cemetery a few kilometres outside of Paris.[45] But this is what Bergson would have wanted—no fanfare, just family, a sober affair.

In the weeks after Bergson's death, strange details about the philosopher's final moments started emerging. For a long time, Bergson had been fascinated with the idea that in the moments before we die, we experience something like total memory: our entire history unfolds in a panorama that typically "flashes" in sequence before our eyes. Bergson had read about various instances of this phenomenon recounted by people who had survived drowning, or who had tried and failed to end their lives. These testimonies confirmed one of his most important theories: that no memory is ever entirely lost. The memories most useful to us in everyday life remain close to the surface of our consciousness, but we carry all of our ever-expanding lived experience with us at all times. Our experience grows like a snowball rolling down a hill. Our most deeply buried memories resurface only in the rare moments when we relax our focus and turn our attention away from the pressing demands of being alive, such as in a deep sleep, or in a state of hypnosis, or when we realise we are about to die.

If, in his final instants, Bergson had seen his whole existence flash by, his panoramic vision would have opened with the sounds of a melody played on the piano by his father in a room swelling with the warmth of each note. He would have perhaps revisited his debates with Jaurès in the halls of the École normale supérieure or relived his discovery of *durée*. He might have once again seen Louise's face for the first time or held his infant daughter Jeanne in his arms. The mounting pressure of fame and the years of frenzy and noise he had once endured would have perhaps been condensed into one confusing impression of prolonged chaos.

But in his final moments, Bergson's life did not flash before his eyes. Instead, he retreated into an activity he knew well:

In the bedroom of his Parisian home, Bergson had been in a coma for twelve hours. Those who witnessed his agony sensed that the end was near when, all of a sudden, the illustrious philosopher began to speak. He gave a lecture, a philosophy lecture, for an hour. He pronounced the words very distinctly. His sentences were clear. His lucidity overwhelmed those who listened to him. And then he said, "Gentlemen, it is five o'clock. Class is over." And he expired.[46]

EPILOGUE

There exists only one recording of Bergson's voice. It was made in his home on a warm summer afternoon in 1936, using a portable device. Bergson, who would turn seventy-seven later that year, was too ill and frail to leave his study. Of the interview recorded that day, all that has survived is the sound check. For just under two minutes, we hear Bergson read from one of his own books, *Laughter*, a passage about the meaning of art. Listening to the tremors and slow cadence of the elderly philosopher's voice through the crackling noises of the almost ninety-year-old recording, it is not at first obvious what was supposedly so captivating about him as a speaker. But as the recording progresses, the listener becomes aware of the musical inflexions in Bergson's voice, his emphasis on certain words, and the dramatic tension he injects into the few paragraphs. The listener is left with an impression of having heard the philosopher's ideas come to life. Bearing in mind that at the height of his fame, Bergson was several decades younger than in this recording, and that he mostly improvised his lectures and talks instead of reading from a script, it becomes possible to intuit just how enchanting his Collège de France lectures must have been for the hundreds in attendance.

In the early twentieth century, Bergson was one of the most famous people alive. The exact reasons for his immense success remain difficult to pinpoint. Yes, he was original, but originality in the field of philosophy does not always equate to international stardom. There was obviously something special about Bergson, not only about his ideas but, more importantly perhaps, about the way he said them and where he said them—inside the walls of an institution of open learning before much larger audiences than are usually present in academic settings.

Bergson never sought out fame, but in his drive to succeed within the French academic system, fame found him. This quiet yet ambitious man ended up, one might say in spite of himself, voicing the mood of a generation. Perhaps Walter Lippmann put it best when he wrote:

> The reason for his stupendous reputation lies, it seems to me, in this: that Bergson is not so much a prophet as a herald in whom the unrest of modern times has found a voice. He is popular because he says with splendid certainty what thousands of people have been feeling vaguely.[1]

Bergson's capacity to express what most were unable to voice made him feel as though his ideas no longer belonged to him, that they had escaped him, taking on meanings he had never intended. His readers and listeners tried to fit Bergson's philosophy into frameworks for which it had not been made. But after hearing Bergson's voice in that short recording, I cannot blame them for wanting to take something so alive and make it their own.

REMEMBERING BERGSON

In a Monty Python sketch from 1970, a cheesy game show host (John Cleese) asks an ill-tempered, racist, uncooperative old lady contestant (Terry Jones) a ludicrously challenging question. The exchange unfolds as follows:

Cleese: What great opponent of Cartesian dualism resists the reduction of psychological phenomena to physical states?

Jones: I don't know that!

Cleese: Well, have a guess.

Jones: Henri Bergson.

Cleese: Is the correct answer!

Jones: Ooh, that was lucky. I never even heard of him!

The sketch plays on the incongruity of the old lady plucking this unfamiliar name from the air.

Three decades after Bergson died, and six decades after he brought Broadway to a halt, the Pythons could safely assume that the French philosopher's name would come across as particularly obscure to an anglophone audience.[2]

Bertrand Russell is partly to blame for Bergson's fall into oblivion in the English-speaking world. Like Bergson, Russell eventually enjoyed great popular success (though never at Bergson's level) and his bestseller *A History of Western Philosophy* cemented the idea in the minds of several generations of anglophone readers that Bergson was not philosophically meaningful.

But in recent years there has been a kind of Bergson revival in the anglophone world. Could it be because there is a need for a return to his ideas? In many ways, the concerns of people at the beginning of the twentieth century echo our twenty-first-century anxieties, and Bergson might well offer some solutions.

Quantification is seeping into the most intimate realms of our psyches via algorithms that purport to anticipate our desires in a consumerist, capitalist society. New attempts are made to mechanise our consciousness. Some AI engineers believe that they will be able to replicate human consciousness in machines, while critics point out that current so-called artificial intelligence programs simply rehash preexisting materials without ever displaying the creativity and freedom inherent in human consciousness.

In his final book, *The Two Sources of Morality and Religion*, Bergson wrote about the need to inject more spirit—meaning more humanity—into our technology, which is progressing too fast for our ethical concerns to keep up. He also wrote about our need to find ways to open up societies that close up on themselves and retreat into increasing authoritarianism and xenophobia. The thinker of *durée* still has a lot to say to the present moment.

ACKNOWLEDGEMENTS

Writing a book is a terribly solitary exercise. Victor, Aline, Sirius, and Maddy, you helped me feel less isolated in the process, and for that you deserve my eternal love and gratitude. Thank you for tolerating my existential crises, and for making me laugh every day.

There is no doubt in my mind that I owe this book to a mother whose faith in me has never once wavered, a father who has read almost every sentence I have ever drafted, and grandparents who have regularly reminded me to sit down and write. I am also indebted to my (so-called) Uncle Duncan who helped me remain sane throughout both my PhD and this project, and to all the other Herrings, Wilkinses, Mourses, and Edmondses who have supported me in many important ways.

Thank you also to the friends who have consistently kept my heart warm by cheering me on, sometimes from afar. Alice, Nathan, Hannah, Oliver, Jade, Sam, Coreen, Richard, Laura, Steve, Nick, Christina, Alex, Niamh, Vishnu, Janet, Florian, Marion, Bérénice, Coralie, and Mathilde, I am looking at you.

I am incredibly grateful to those who took time out of their busy lives to provide feedback on various drafts, with special thanks to Mathilde Tahar and Caterina Zanfi, who helped me remain as faithful as possible to Bergson's thought. Thank you also to my love Victor Mours (who must have read at least six different versions of the book), my dad David Herring, Jeremy Dunham, Alice Murphy, Hannah Robson, Laura Sellers, and Coreen McGuire.

I owe special thanks to my different mentors over the years: Laurent Loison and Greg Radick, whose patient advice and encouragement shaped my thinking and writing, and Nigel Warburton, who urged me to take on this project in the first place.

Finally, I must acknowledge the patience and enthusiasm of my brilliant editors Sarah Caro and Brandon Proia, and the invaluable advice and support of my agent Sophie Scard.

NOTES

INTRODUCTION: THE MOST FAMOUS PHILOSOPHER IN THE WORLD

1. Maire 1935, p. 189, my translation.
2. Grogin 1988, p. ix.
3. Chevalier 1928, p. 7, my translation.
4. Bergson 1915, p. 251, my translation.
5. Bergson 1972, p. 1555, my translation.
6. Chevalier 1959, p. 98, my translation.
7. Ibid., p. 143.
8. Edman cited by P.A.Y. Gunter in Canales 2015, p. 31.
9. Cited in Droit 1997, my translation.
10. Benrubi 1942, p. 136, my translation.
11. Marcel 1941, p. 30, my translation.
12. Bergson 1935, p. 275.

CHAPTER 1: ON THE ORIGIN OF HENRI

1. Cited in Schivelbusch 1977, p. 100.
2. Descartes 1993, p. 21.
3. Ibid.
4. Bergson 1946, p. 17.
5. Bergson 2023, p. 14.
6. I am using the Polish spelling of Bergson's father's name. Other sources use the spellings Michaël or Michel.
7. Different sources use different spellings of Bergson's mother's first name, such as Cate, Catherine, and Käte.
8. Soulez and Worms 2002, p. 15.
9. Ibid.
10. Ibid., p. 22.
11. Mossé-Bastide 1955, p. 15.

12. "Qui va à la chasse perd sa place" can be loosely translated as "You snooze you lose."

13. Soulez and Worms 2002, p. 24.

14. Ibid., p. 25.

15. Some records speculate that Bergson might not have even been aware of these events because he was bedridden with a nasty bout of measles (ibid., p. 34).

16. Bergson 1972, pp. 1038–1039, my translation.

CHAPTER 2: A "MERE" PHILOSOPHER

1. Desboves 1878, pp. i–iii.

2. "Etant donné trois cercles, trois points, trois lignes, trouver un cercle qui, touchant les cercles et les points, laisse sur les lignes un arc capable d'angle donné" (cited in Millet 1974, p. 36).

3. Mossé-Bastide 1955, p. 8, my translation.

4. Chevalier 1928, p. 7, my translation.

5. Soulez and Worms 2002, pp. 30, 31. The authors hypothesise that Bergson was in fact writing about himself.

6. Mossé-Bastide 1955, p. 18, my translation.

7. Desboves 1878.

8. Chevalier 1959, pp. 37–40, my translation.

9. Ibid., p. 38.

10. Bergson 1972, pp. 1502–1503, my translation.

11. Harpe 1941, p. 358, my translation.

12. Bergson 1972, p. 258, my translation.

13. Ibid.

14. Chevalier 1959, p. 57, my translation.

15. Lippmann 1912a.

16. Russell 1912a, p. 326.

17. Canales 2015, p. 9.

18. Huxley 1923, p. 33.

CHAPTER 3: "HE HAS NO SOUL"

1. McAuliffe 2011, p. 78.

2. "Social Darwinism" is the idea that natural selection also applies to human societies and therefore that governments, acknowledging this natural state of things, should encourage the survival of the fittest, including not intervening to help the less fit.

3. Cited in Alglave 1878, p. 1141, my translation.

4. Du Bos 1946, p. 63, and Chevalier 1959, pp. 37–40, my translation.

5. Pfister 1928, p. 4. Bergson was naturalised as a French citizen at the age of eighteen.

6. Although Bergson and Jaurès were both famous during their lifetimes, one vastly outlived the other in posthumous fame. It is not always easy to predict which historical figures will be commemorated and celebrated by future generations and which ones will fall into obscurity. One reliable measure (often taken posthumously) of their cultural importance is the number of streets, schools, airports, libraries, and other landmarks bearing their name. At the top of the current leaderboard in France we find

World War II hero Charles de Gaulle, followed by the father of modern vaccination, Louis Pasteur, *Hunchback of Notre Dame* author Victor Hugo, and, in fourth place, Jaurès. Once again, Bergson does not even appear on the leaderboard, and only a handful of places today bear his name: a small square in Paris, a school in the town where he first taught, and an avenue bordering the cemetery where he is buried.

7. Lévy-Bruhl 1928, p. 1, my translation.

8. Pfister 1928, p. 4, my translation.

9. Lévy-Bruhl 1928, p. 1.

10. Bergson 2024a, my translation.

11. Soulez and Worms 2002, p. 24, my translation.

12. Chevalier 1959, pp. 38–39, my translation.

13. Ibid., p. 39.

14. At the École, Bergson followed the lectures of Émile Boutroux, who had been deeply marked by the Kantianism of the German philosophers he had met during his studies (Soulez and Worms 2002, p. 45). As Frédéric Worms and Philippe Soulez underline, another of Bergson's teachers, a Catholic philosopher named Léon Ollé-Laprune, did not appear to belong to either of these two camps, but his belief that philosophers should study the sciences no doubt spoke to Bergson's Spencerian penchants.

15. Mossé-Bastide 1955, pp. 23–24, my translation. The philosophy that Bergson would develop in the following years can be described as an attempt to reconcile the requirements of both spiritualism and positivism. As Bergson scholar François Azouvi (2007, p. 26, my translation) puts it: "Bergson's success was, in part, due to his ability to simultaneously camp on both shores, by, on the one hand, accomplishing the scientistic project of an experimental, therefore positivistic, metaphysics, and on the other hand, fulfilling the desire for a reunification with the notion of 'spirit.'"

16. Guitton 1960, p. 21, my translation.

17. Du Bos 1946, p. 66, my translation.

CHAPTER 4: TIME IS NOT SPACE

1. When I was a student at the Sorbonne, one of my professors used this story to introduce us to Bergson. I later wrote to him to ask if he remembered where he had read this, but he simply replied, "I am sure of the accuracy of the anecdote, but I don't know where I found it. I am afraid I cannot help you." The anecdote is partly reported in Mossé-Bastide 1955, pp. 51–52.

2. Bergson 1972, pp. 765–766, my translation.

3. Bertoldi 2000, my translation.

4. Chevalier 1959, p. 228.

5. Bergson 2002, p. 8, my translation.

6. Ibid., p. 7.

7. Cited in Soulez and Worms 2002, pp. 49–50, my translation.

8. Bergson 1972, p. 1039, my translation.

9. Ibid.

10. Bardy 1990, p. 18.

11. Evrard 2021, p. 238, my translation.

12. Bardy 1990, p. 17, my translation.

13. Bergson and Kahn 2003, p. 68. While Bergson was preparing for the entry exams for the École, he gave private lessons to Albert Kahn, who at the time was preparing for the baccalaureate. The two men remained friends. In the late 1890s, after Kahn became extremely wealthy working in South African diamond mines, he asked Bergson to help him found a charity called the "Autour du Monde" scholarships to fund travel for young scholars to experience the world in a humanitarian perspective.

14. Guerlac 2006, p. 70.

15. Bergson 1910, p. 134.

16. Maire 1935, p. 28.

17. Lévy-Bruhl 1928, my translation.

18. *La Montagne* 1941, p. 2.

19. Bergson rarely cited the philosophers who had most influenced him. When he did cite sources, it was usually to criticise them. He believed that the history of philosophy should not aim to uncover the intellectual genealogy of ideas, but instead should determine what is truly novel in each thinker. Therefore, the search for "influences" made little sense (see Benrubi 1942, p. 19).

20. Du Bos 1946, pp. 63–64, my translation.

21. Bergson 1946, p. 10.

22. "Science cannot deal with time and motion except on condition of first eliminating the essential qualitative element—of time, duration, and of motion, mobility" (Bergson 1910, p. 115).

23. "Mechanics . . . always expresses something already done" (ibid., p. 119).

24. "For in these equations, the symbol *t* does not stand for a duration, but for a relation between two durations, for a certain number of units of time, in short, for a certain number of simultaneities: these simultaneities, these coincidences would still take place in equal number: only the intervals which separate them would have diminished, but these intervals never make their appearance in our calculations" (ibid., p. 193).

25. Ibid., pp. 193–194.

26. See Guerlac 2006, chap. 3.

CHAPTER 5: THE MELODY OF DURÉE

1. Maritain 1942, p. 84, my translation.

2. Joussain 1911, p. 487, my translation.

3. Bergson 2002, p. 412, my translation.

4. Guerlac 2006, p. 52.

5. Joussain 1911, p. 487, my translation.

6. In later publications, Bergson would show that consciousness is not the only realm of *durée* and that, to a certain degree, there is *durée* in inert matter. As Mark Sinclair (2020, p. 223) writes: "The third chapter of *Creative Evolution* accounts for the relation of matter and life by showing that matter and the space in which it appears are the result of the relaxation of duration: extension is the ex-tension of duration. Matter is, thus, a tendency of durational life itself, just as life is a tendency of matter."

7. Bergson 2023, p. 9.

8. Ibid.

9. Bergson 2002, p. 412, my translation.

10. Ibid., p. 413.

11. As Bergson wrote in 1903: "There are no two identical moments in the life of the same conscious being. Take the simplest sensation. . . . The consciousness which will accompany this sensation cannot remain identical with itself for two consecutive moments, because the second moment always contains, over and above the first, the memory that the first has bequeathed to it" (Bergson 1912a, p. 12).

12. Bergson 2023, p. 11.

13. Ibid., p. 10.

14. Cited in Mossé-Bastide 1955, p. 54, my translation.

15. Du Bos 1946, p. 68, my translation.

Chapter 6: The Enchanter

1. Taine cited in Guerlac 2006, p. 24.

2. Bourget cited in Myers 1893, pp. 88–89.

3. Moore 1912, p. 371.

4. Mallarmé cited in Azouvi 2007, p. 68, my translation.

5. France cited in Grogin 1988, p. 38. On the occult revival, see ibid., chap. 3. On Bergson's sister Moina Mathers, see Herring 2021 and Maoilearca 2022.

6. Grogin 1988, p. 38.

7. Cited in ibid., p. 5.

8. Bergson 1972, p. 1599.

9. Mossé-Bastide 1955, p. 29.

10. *Revue de l'enseignement secondaire et de l'enseignement supérieur* 1890, p. 131, my translation.

11. Mossé-Bastide 1955, p. 29.

12. Cited in Du Bos 1946, p. 64. Bergson also told Du Bos, "I realised that in this first version, I had not taken Kant—who had never spontaneously exerted a very great ascendancy on my mind—into account." To have any hope of being taken seriously in the French philosophical climate, Bergson had no choice but to include a discussion of the philosopher from Königsberg. Guerlac (2006, p. 21) writes, "Kant's critique of dogmatic metaphysics (which aspired to knowledge of the absolute) legitimized the relative knowledge of appearances that, according to the critical philosopher, is framed transcendentally through the *a priori* conditions of space and time. Thanks to Kant, then, knowledge is guaranteed by the mechanisms of thought. Neo-Kantianism provided the epistemological basis for the distinctly modern intellectual culture of positivism. It was the dominant current of thought in the French university system when Bergson decided to become a philosopher. Bergson's first major philosophical work, the *Essai sur les données immédiates de l'expérience*, as its title already suggests, launches a powerful critique of Kant."

13. Guerlac 2006, p. 64.

14. I rely heavily on Suzanne Guerlac's illuminating explanations here. For a detailed summary of Bergson's argument, see Guerlac 2006; Sinclair 2020; Allen 2023. See also Bergson 1910.

15. Laplace 1951, p. 4.

16. See Guerlac 2006, chap. 2.

17. As Čapek (1971, p. x) notes, "The view that matter and its spatio-temporal frame-work would be stripped of their classical mechanistic features"—a theme that Bergson would especially develop in his second book *Matter and Memory*—was held by only a "few heretically daring minds. Bergson was one of these."

18. Guerlac 2006, pp. 86, 89.

19. Bergson cited in Guerlac 2006, pp. 99–100.

20. Bergson 2023, pp. 10–14. In the words of the historian Richard Grogin (1988, p. 28): "[For Bergson,] the free act arises when the self, reflecting the whole personality and all of its past experiences, forces its way to the surface of consciousness piercing the outer self of habit and ready-made ideas, and takes a decisive action."

21. Mossé-Bastide 1955, p. 29.

22. *Revue de l'enseignement secondaire et de l'enseignement supérieur* 1890, p. 129, my translation.

23. Fargue cited in Azouvi 2007, p. 48, my translation.

24. James 1909, p. 227.

Chapter 7: Memory Matters

1. Bois 1913, p. 4.

2. Chevalier 1959, p. 138.

3. Ibid., p. 216.

4. Bergson 1911a, p. 206.

5. Ibid., p. 262.

6. The totality of matter, according to Bergson, can be conceived, in the words of Bergson scholar Suzanne Guerlac (2006, p. 109), as a "dynamic energy system in which each point is always acting on all the others."

7. Bergson 1911b, pp. 151–152.

8. Bergson 1911a, p. 23.

9. Guerlac 2006, p. 112.

10. Cited in ibid., pp. 111–112.

11. Bergson 2023, p. 12.

12. Bergson 1911a, pp. 69–70.

13. Wharton 1934, pp. 170–171.

14. Guerlac 2006, p. 125.

15. Ibid., p. 127.

16. Ibid., p. 125.

17. Bergson 1911a, p. 95.

18. Bergson 2023, pp. 11–12.

19. Ibid., p. 12.

20. Bergson 1972, p. 1062.

21. Wharton 1934, pp. 170–171.

22. Jaloux 1941, my translation.

23. Guitton cited in *In Memoriam: Jeanne Bergson, 1893–1961*, 1963.

24. Bergson, letter of March 25, 1935; see Crait + Müller (auction house), https://www.crait-muller.com/lot/90041/8690920.

25. Guitton cited in *In Memoriam: Jeanne Bergson, 1893–1961*, 1963.

Chapter 8: Snowballing

1. Maritain 1942, pp. 77–78.
2. Ibid., p. 39.
3. Ibid., p. 63.
4. Bergson 2002, p. 79.
5. Azouvi 2007, p. 41, my translation.
6. Chevalier 1959, pp. 223–224, my translation.
7. Ibid., p. 178.
8. Christen-Lécuyer 2000, pp. 35–50.
9. Cited in Azouvi 2007, p. 47, my translation.
10. Ibid., p. 185.
11. Jacob 1898, p. 201, my translation.
12. Soulez and Worms 2002, p. 78.
13. Pétrement 1959, p. 12.
14. Bergson 2002, p. 36, my translation.
15. Ibid., p. 37.
16. Turquet-Milnes 1921, p. 214; Azouvi 2007, p. 90.
17. Bergson 2002, p. 47, my translation.
18. Bergson's critique of psychophysics in *Time and Free Will* and his research on aphasia in *Matter and Memory* were two instances cited of his "originality."
19. Bergson 2002, p. 49, my translation.
20. No trace remains of Bergson's inaugural lecture at the Collège de France. We do know that Proust and Péguy were present, and that the number of attendees was modest.
21. Agathon 1911, pp. 22–23, my translation.
22. Azouvi 2007, pp. 77–89.
23. Underhill cited in Douglass 1986, p. 11.
24. Maritain 1942, pp. 83–85.
25. Bergson cited in Bernstein 1913, p. 95.
26. James 1920, pp. 178–179.
27. After James died in 1910, Bergson kept a portrait of his American friend on his desk until the end of his life.
28. This nightmare is recounted by Bergson in his talk on dreams. Bergson 1972, p. 457.

Chapter 9: Laughter Is Vital

1. Bergson 2002, p. 39, my translation.
2. Ibid., p. 42.
3. Parts of this chapter are taken from an article I published with *Aeon* (Herring 2020).
4. Bergson 1911b, p. 1.
5. Ibid., p. 2.
6. Ibid., p. 3.
7. Ibid., pp. 4–5.

8. Ibid., p. 6.
9. Ibid., p. 8.
10. Bergson 2023, p. 117.
11. Bergson 1911b, p. 18.
12. Ibid., pp. 21, 37.
13. Ibid., p. 10.
14. Ibid., p. 174.
15. Ibid., p. 135.
16. *New York Times* 1912a, p. 118.
17. Russell 1912b, p. 194.
18. Adès 1949, p. 12, my translation.
19. Visan 1911, pp. 424–427.

CHAPTER 10: LIFTING THE VEIL

1. Cited in *In Memoriam: Jeanne Bergson, 1893–1961,* 1963.
2. Bergson 1911b, p. 151.
3. Ibid., pp. 151, 157.
4. Bergson 1972, p. 894. This sentiment is similar to the one expressed in a quote attributed to Oscar Wilde: "Before Turner, there was no fog in London." Wilde was not actually referencing Turner when he expressed the idea from which the misattributed quote materialised: "At present, people see fogs, not because there are fogs, but because poets and painters have taught them the mysterious loveliness of such effects" (Wilde 1905, p. 41).
5. Azouvi 2007, p. 61, my translation.
6. Cited in Guerlac 2006, p. 52.
7. Jaurès cited in Azouvi 2007, p. 64, my translation.
8. Ibid., chap. 3.
9. Bergson 2024a, my translation.
10. Later, in his autobiography, Russell (1998, p. 465) deplored that "I was sometimes accused by reviewers of writing not a true history but a biased account of the events that I arbitrarily chose to write of. But to my mind, a man without bias cannot write interesting history—if, indeed, such a man exists."
11. Russell 1931, p. 82.
12. As the science fiction author H. G. Wells remarked: "When one says chair, one thinks vaguely of an average chair. But collect individual instances of armchairs and reading-chairs, and dining-room chairs and kitchen chairs, chairs that pass into benches, chairs that cross the boundary and become settees, dentists' chairs, thrones, opera stalls, seats of all sorts, those miraculous fungoid growths that cumber the floor of the Arts and Crafts Exhibition, and you will perceive what a lax bundle in fact is this straightforward term. In co-operation with an intelligent joiner I would undertake to defeat any definition of chair or chairishness that you gave me." Cited in Lippmann 1913, p. 119.
13. "Even concepts that do not generalise per se, but designate individual realities—for instance, the concept 'the moon' refers to our one moon—still generalise what all the different states, perceptions, changing phases of the moon have in common under one term." Bergson 2016, p. 56.

14. Bergson 1911b, p. 153.

15. Bergson 2014, p. 350.

16. Bergson 1912a, p. 9.

17. Benrubi 1942, pp. 27–28.

18. Bergson 1972, p. 62.

19. Bergson 1912a, p. 8.

20. Ibid.

21. Ibid., pp. 3–4.

22. In this sense, Bergson argues, against Kant, that absolute knowledge is possible.

23. Ibid., p. 65.

24. Ibid., p. 69.

25. Tyrrell 1908, p. 435.

26. Russell 1946, p. 857.

27. Le Dantec 1912, p. 84.

28. Bergson 1946, p. 306n26.

29. Bergson 1912, p. 21.

CHAPTER 11: THE STRANGE CASE OF EUSAPIA PALLADINO

1. Courtier 1908, p. 479.

2. Bernstein 1913, p. 99.

3. Benrubi 1942, p. 369.

4. No correspondence appears to have survived between Bergson and his sister Moina. According to his brother-in-law, MacGregor Mathers, Bergson was not the least bit interested in magic: "I have shown him everything that magic can do and it has had no effect on him." Cited in Grogin 1988, p. 43.

5. Natale 2016.

6. Bennett 1903, p. 7.

7. Evrard 2016, p. 230.

8. Cited in Bergson 1972, p. 510, my translation.

9. Ibid.

10. Evrard 2016, p. 234.

11. Grogin 1988, p. 51.

12. Cited in Evrard 2016, p. 242, my translation.

13. Ibid., p. 238.

14. Ibid., p. 241.

15. Bergson 1972, p. 607.

16. The main conclusion of the article had less to do with the incredible phenomenon and more to do with the nature of the hypnotic state itself. Bergson and Robinet had observed that the subjects, when asked to read the hypnotist's mind, did everything they could to do as they were told. Since they could not actually read anyone's mind, they did the next best thing: they pretended to be reading the hypnotist's thoughts when they were instead reading his retina. According to Bergson, in this state, they weren't even aware they were cheating (Bergson 1886).

17. Darlu 1887, p. 571, my translation.

18. De Rochas 1901.

19. Meunier 1910, pp. 81–107.
20. *Manchester Guardian* 1913, p. 9.
21. Meunier 1910, p. 99, my translation.
22. Labaune 2021.

CHAPTER 12: CINEMATOGRAPHIC INTELLIGENCE

1. Coissac 1925, p. 190, my translation.
2. Chevalier 1959, p. 163, my translation.
3. Bergson 2023, p. 264.
4. Ibid., p. 265.
5. Ibid.
6. Bergson 2024a.
7. Bergson 2023, p. 127.
8. Ibid.
9. Ibid., p. 1.
10. Ibid., p. 2.
11. Ibid.
12. Ibid., p. 4.
13. Ibid., p. 149.
14. Ibid., p. 138.
15. François 2010, p. 6, my translation.
16. Russell 1912a, p. 323.
17. "It is less at its ease in the organized world, where it treads its way with an assured step only if it relies upon physics and chemistry; it clings to the physico-chemical in vital phenomena rather than to what is really vital in the living" (Bergson 1946, p. 42).
18. Bergson 2023, p. 160.
19. Ibid.
20. Bergson 1912a, p. 74.

CHAPTER 13: ECLIPSING DARWIN

1. Carr 1924, p. 104.
2. Ibid.
3. James 1920, p. 290.
4. Ibid., pp. 290–291.
5. For instance, the Darwinian explanation, in Bergson's telling, was typical of mechanistic thinking, which thought of the evolution of organs such as the eye as similar to the construction of a machine through the progressive assemblage of parts and the progressive selection of minute changes. Bergson made a common critique of Darwinism: that natural selection understood as a destructive process—that is, as the survival of the fittest and the elimination of the unfit—could account for neither the emergence of structures as complex as, for instance, the eye or the vertebrate nor the emergence of similar structures in different lineages (Bergson 2023, pp. 59–81).
6. "The neo-Darwinians are probably correct, I would say, when they teach that the essential causes of variation are differences inherent in the germ that the individual carries, and not in the activities this individual undertakes in the course of its career."

Mutationism indicates "that at a given moment, and after a long period of time has gone by, the entire species is seized by a tendency to change. As such the *tendency* to *change* is not accidental." Eimer's theory introduced the "hypothesis according to which the variations of different characteristics continue from generation to generation in definite directions," and certain forms of neo-Lamarckism "appeal to a cause of psychological nature" (ibid., pp. 82–83).

7. Ibid., pp. 81–82.

8. Ibid., p. 82.

9. Huxley 1912, pp. vii–viii.

10. Huxley 1923, p. 33. For a study of Huxley's Bergsonism, see Herring 2018.

11. Bergson 2023, p. 93.

12. Some parts of this chapter are taken from a chapter I published in *The Bergsonian Mind* (Herring 2022), and other parts are taken from an article I published in the *Times Literary Supplement* (Herring 2023).

13. Bergson 1912a, p. 69.

14. Bergson 2023, p. 30.

15. Ibid., p. 52.

16. Ibid., p. 33.

17. Bergson 1912b, p. 41.

18. "The thought which is only thought, the work of art which is only in the conceptual state, the poem which is only a dream, costs as yet no effort: what requires an effort is the material realisation of the poem in words, of the artistic conception in a statue or a picture" (ibid.).

19. In the words of philosopher Mathilde Tahar (2022, p. 12), "Organisms are not a composition of matter and spirit: they are material objects whose organisation cannot be explained in the same way as inert matter, because in them, the tendency towards inertia of matter is counteracted by the tendency towards indeterminacy."

20. Bergson 2023, p. 216.

21. Ibid.

22. Ibid., p. 163.

23. Ibid., p. 223.

24. Ibid.

25. Ibid., p. 231.

26. Driesch 1908a.

27. Driesch 1908b.

28. Bergson 2023, pp. 44–46.

29. Tahar 2022, p. 12. For more on Bergson's relationship to vitalism, see Tahar 2022.

30. Darbishire 1917, p. 92.

31. Ibid., p. 36.

32. Bergson 2023, pp. 21–22.

33. For Bergson, though opposed to life, matter also endures. As Tahar (2022, p. 10) writes: "The *élan vital* goes in an opposite direction to matter, without life and matter being two substantially distinct forces. Rather, they are two rhythms of duration, which Bergson conceives as opposite energetic movements."

34. Russell 1917.

35. Russell 1911, p. 217, my translation. A very similar argument was made by one of Russell's mentors, the Scottish zoologist and science populariser John Arthur Thomson (1911, p. 127).

36. Hulme 1911b.

37. Patrick 1911, p. 582.

38. Hulme 1911b.

39. Bergson 2023, p. 93.

CHAPTER 14: DELUGED

1. *Le Petit Parisien* 1910a.

2. *Le Petit Parisien* 1910b.

3. Carter 2000, p. 489.

4. Azouvi 2007, p. 140.

5. Cited in ibid., my translation.

6. Weber cited in Azouvi 2007, p. 138; Darbishire 1917, pp. 90–91.

7. Carter 1911, pp. 43–45.

8. Maire 1935, p. 187, my translation.

9. Bergson 2002, pp. 180–181, my translation.

10. Ibid., p. 166.

11. Benrubi 1942, p. 15.

12. Ibid., p. 96, my translation.

13. Bergson 2024a, my translation.

14. Maire 1935, p. 187, my translation.

15. Cited in Antliff 1993, p. 4.

16. Cited in Jones 1960, pp. 81–82.

17. Bergson 2002, p. 550, my translation.

18. Ibid., p. 473.

CHAPTER 15: THE BERGSON BOOM

1. Hulme cited in Jones 1960, p. 86.

2. Deng 2023; Sugimura 2023; Gemert 2022.

3. Gillies 1996, p. 28.

4. *Nature* 1911, p. 399.

5. *Aberdeen Daily Journal* 1911, p. 2.

6. *New York Times* 1912b.

7. Balfour 1911, p. 23.

8. Hulme 1911a, p. 39.

9. Tyrrell 1908, pp. 435–436.

10. James 1909, p. 226.

11. The publishing house Henry Holt & Co. (1911) published a note in the *New York Times*: "Ever since the French edition of Henri Bergson's 'Creative Evolution' appeared, we have been having inquiries about our translation. These French writers are marvels at making fairly fascinating a subject that others would make heavy. The late 'William James' was probably not far out when he said that Bergson was a 'real magician.'"

12. Bergson 2002, p. 196, my translation.

13. Ibid., p. 250.

14. *New York Times* 1911.

15. Bergson 1911c, p. 24.

16. Bergson 1912b, p. 32.

17. *Citizen* 1911.

18. *The Times* 1911.

19. Hulme cited in Jones 1960, pp. 86, 87.

20. Husband 1912, p. 465.

21. Morrell 1963, p. 183.

22. Russell cited in Monk 1996, 233.

23. "Owing to Bergson I shall have to begin my Aristotelian paper while I am here" (Russell cited in ibid.).

24. Ibid., p. 238.

25. Ibid., p. 235.

26. The Humanist Heritage Project describes the Cambridge Heretics Club as "a society formed at the University of Cambridge in 1909, in opposition to compulsory worship, and in celebration of humanist values. Members and speakers devoted themselves to the rejection of assumed authority and religious creed, presenting and discussing papers on themes of religion, philosophy, and art" (Humanist Heritage Project, n.d.).

27. The society was divided between a group represented by its secretary, Wildon Carr, an ardent Bergsonian, and its chairman, G. E. Moore, one of the chiefs of the analytic school to which Russell belonged (Jones 1960, p. 76).

28. Cited in Monk 1996, p. 238.

29. Ibid.

30. Russell cited in Vrahimis 2022, p. 30.

31. Ibid., p. 31.

32. Russell 1946, p. 831.

33. *Le Temps* 1912.

34. May 1959, pp. 229–230.

CHAPTER 16: A PHILOSOPHER FOR WOMEN

1. Parts of this chapter are taken from an article I published with *Aeon* (Herring 2019).

2. Gratton 1911.

3. *Le Temps* 1914.

4. *The New Age* 1914a.

5. Visan 1911, p. 428.

6. L'Alouette 1914.

7. Lecoq 1914.

8. Cited in Conley 2019.

9. *The New Age* 1914b.

10. Dard, Leymarie, and McWilliam 2010, p. 92.

11. Cited in Canales 2015, p. 34; see Grogin 1988, pp. 186–188.

12. Menaud 1996.

13. Eliot 1917, p. 10.
14. Menaud 1996.
15. Lermina 1912.
16. D.L.B. 1915.
17. Bard 1995, p. 538.
18. Miropolsky 1913.
19. Cox 1913, p. 551.
20. Bernstein 1913, p. 102.
21. Bergson 1972, p. 944, my translation.
22. Bernstein 1913, pp. 102–103.
23. *La Vie Parisienne* 1912a.
24. Mignot-Ogliastri 1986, p. 242, my translation.
25. *La Vie Parisienne* 1912a, my translation.
26. Sylvaire 1913, my translation.

CHAPTER 17: BLOCKING BROADWAY

1. Slosson 1916, pp. 67–68.
2. McGrath 2013, p. 614.
3. Bergson 2002, p. 495, my translation.
4. *La Vie Parisienne* 1912b.
5. Wells 1906, pp. 28–29.
6. Ibid., p. 30.
7. Slosson 1916, pp. 44–45.
8. May 1959, p. 228.
9. Ibid.
10. "Pragmatism was part of it, but the freewheeling, radically pluralist pragmatism of the late James, not the practical problem-solving of the social scientists. European naturalism was acceptable, but usually it was turned upside down, and made into pantheism: nature was all, but nature had come alive. Aestheticism was fully a part of the new credo, but not the tired aestheticism of the nineties; rather the dawn of a new art that would transform life. On the whole the Liberation was not a movement of outsiders; its headquarters were the centers of the older culture, Chicago and New York, its American leaders mostly members of the dominant minority. If they were social radicals, vaguely socialist or (more characteristically) anarchist, it was out of generous emotion rather than disaffection." Ibid., p. 220.
11. Bergson 1972, pp. 992–993, my translation.
12. Ibid.
13. Bergson to Butler, cited in McGrath 2013, p. 601.
14. *The Sun* 1913a.
15. Ibid.
16. *The Outlook* 1913, pp. 467–468.
17. *New York Times* 1913.
18. Bernstein 1913, p. 94.
19. Ibid., p. 96.
20. Ibid., p. 100.

21. Sinclair 2020, p. 180.

22. Azouvi 2008, p. 93.

23. Cited in Rainey 2009, p. 93.

24. Cited in Azouvi 2007, p. 222, my translation.

25. Ibid., p. 224.

26. Ibid.

27. Ibid., p. 225.

28. Beaunier 1907.

29. Slosson 1916, p. 82.

30. Sorel 1908.

31. Levine 1913.

32. Ibid.

33. Benrubi 1942, p. 20, my translation.

34. *The New Age* 1914c.

35. Russell 1956, p. 78. Sorel too believed that Bergson did not understand the implications of his own philosophy (see Jones 2011, p. 79).

36. Jones 2011, p. 78.

37. *New York Times* 1911b.

38. Péguy 1914, pp. 17–18, my translation.

39. Moore cited the following passage as particularly (retrospectively) Bergsonian: "It seems to me that we require something like a mental gyration of the heel. We need so rapid a revolution of all things about the point of sight, that while the minutiae vanish altogether, even the more conspicuous objects blend into one" (Poe cited in Moore 1912, p. 371).

40. Ibid.

41. Gide 1948, pp. 782–783, my translation.

42. Bergson cited in McGrath 2013, p. 602. At the same time, Bergson cared very much about being recognised as original, believing that metaphysicians had to start from scratch with each new problem. Philosophy had to be original; otherwise, it was not true philosophy.

CHAPTER 18: "THE MOST DANGEROUS MAN IN THE WORLD"

1. *Excelsior* 1914.

2. Durkheim 1938.

3. Cited in Azouvi 2007, p. 204, my translation.

4. Cited in Canales 2015, p. 34.

5. Azouvi 2007, p. 168, my translation.

6. Cited in Grogin 1988, p. 188.

7. Ibid.

8. Azouvi 2007, p. 205, my translation.

9. Benda 1912, p. 59, my translation.

10. Benda 1927, p. 253, my translation.

11. Cited in Grogin 1978, p. 226.

12. Ibid.

13. Cited in Azouvi 2007, p. 205, my translation.

14. Cited in *Current Opinion* 1914.
15. Benda 1914, p. 169, my translation.
16. Cited in Douglass 1986, p. 14.
17. Grogin 1988, p. 182.
18. Maire 1935, p. 216.
19. Bergson 2002, p. 547, my translation.
20. Benrubi 1942, p. 52, my translation.
21. Adès 1949; Chevalier 1959.
22. Grogin 1988, p. 148.
23. Péguy 1914, p. 93, my translation.
24. Lippmann 1912b.
25. Cited in Guyot 1950, p. 275, my translation.
26. Bergson 1972, pp. 1041–1042, my translation.
27. Ibid., p. 940.
28. Adès 1949, pp. 144–145.
29. Bergson 1946, p. 100.
30. Benrubi 1942, p. 28.
31. Chevalier 1928, p. 57, my translation.
32. *La Libre parole* 1899.
33. *L'Aurore* 1898.
34. Lippmann 1912a, p. 101.
35. Bergson 2023, p. 218.
36. Sleigh 2009, p. 244.

37. Bergson delivered only the first half of his lecture series on "The Problem of Personality." The second half was indefinitely postponed after the war broke out. The lectures were later published in *Mélanges* (Bergson 1972, pp. 1051–1086).

CHAPTER 19: WAR MISSIONS

1. *Le Matin* 1914b.
2. Bergson 2002, p. 591.
3. Wharton cited in McAuliffe 2014, p. 270.
4. Bergson 2002, pp. 591–592.
5. Bergson 1935, pp. 133–134.
6. Becker 2013, p. 103.
7. *Le Matin* 1914a.

8. Jaurès was convinced that "wars were the result of capitalist rivalries. It was therefore up to the workers' movement to oppose the war." An international general strike, he said, should be called to prevent the conflict. This opened him up to death threats and vicious attacks in the press. The young nationalist who shot Jaurès claimed that he had acted to "eliminate an enemy of his country." In a shocking verdict after the war, in an atmosphere of unbridled patriotism, Villain was acquitted, as it was deemed that if Jaurès's plans had succeeded, France would never have prevailed (Becker 2013, p. 104, my translation).

9. Proust cited in McAuliffe 2014, p. 272.
10. Becker 2013, p. 112, my translation.

11. Bergson 1972, p. 1102; see also Sinclair 2016, p. 468.

12. Bergson 1972, p. 1102.

13. Zanfi 2013.

14. Cited in Sinclair 2016, p. 468.

15. *Le Matin* 1914b.

16. Zanfi 2013, p. 123.

17. Sinclair 2016.

18. Cited in Sinclair 2016, pp. 468, 474. Bergson's war speeches can be found in Bergson 1972.

19. In October, ninety-three prominent German scientists, Nobel laureates, intellectuals, and artists signed "The Manifesto of the Ninety-Three." They defended the brutal invasion of the Belgian city of Leuven and denied that the well-documented war crimes committed there had occurred, presenting them instead as calumnious lies by their enemies. They affirmed an opposite image to the propaganda against Germans: they were not the aggressors, and "neither the people, the Government, nor the Kaiser wanted war." Albert Einstein was among the few German figures solicited who refused to sign. "The Manifesto of the Ninety-Three," August 4, 1914, available at https://web.tohoku.ac.jp/modern-japan/wp-content/uploads/Manifesto-of-the-93.pdf.

20. Bergson 1972, p. 1107, my translation.

21. Ibid.

22. Bergson 2002, pp. 591–592, my translation.

23. McAuliffe 2014, p. 279.

24. Bergson 2002, p. 595, my translation.

25. Chapotout 2008, p. 298.

26. Bergson 1972, p. 1570, my translation.

27. Zanfi 2013, pp. 71–72, my translation.

28. Ibid., p. 132.

29. Bergson 2002, p. 663.

30. Bergson 1972, p. 1198, my translation.

31. Ibid., p. 1236, my translation.

32. Bergson 2002, p. 667, my translation.

33. In this final section, I rely heavily on Philippe Soulez's research in his *Bergson Politique* (1989).

34. See "Mes Missions" in Bergson 1972, pp. 1554–1570.

35. Bergson 1972, p. 1564, my translation.

36. Ibid., p. 1565.

37. Soulez 1989, pp. 90–91.

38. Bergson 1972, p. 1558.

39. Ibid., p. 1563.

40. House's diary cited in Soulez 1989, p. 103.

41. Bergson 1972, p. 1560, my translation.

42. Ibid., p. 1556.

43. Ibid., pp. 1556–1557.

44. Ibid., p. 1564.

45. Sinclair 2020, p. 246. Bergson later appeared to have moved away from the radical position he expressed in 1914, although, in republishing his most virulent anti-German speech at the start of World War II, he does not seem to have completely disavowed it (Bergson 1972, p. 1593).

46. Soulez and Worms 2002; Bergson 1972, p. 1104.

CHAPTER 20: DISAPPEARING FROM MEMORY

1. *Le Matin* 1918, p. 2, my translation.

2. Albaret 2003, p. 159.

3. Gillies 1996, p. 27. François Azouvi (2007, p. 293, my translation) makes a similar point: "What had made before 1914 [Bergson's] extraordinary success appears to have magically evaporated as early as 1918: when cubists, futurists, modernist Catholics, or revolutionary syndicalists identified as Bergsonian, it was not because they worshiped an immortal idol. Rather, Bergson's ideas helped them conceptualise their own movements that were too novel to be clearly defined. During the inter-war period, the tables had turned: Bergson was recognised as a national hero, but his concepts were no longer of use to those who were inventing new ways of thinking, writing, behaving, and painting."

4. An English translation was published in 1920 under the title *Mind-Energy: Lectures and Essays* (Bergson 1920).

5. Lenoir 1919, pp. 1078, 1088, my translation.

6. Grogin 1988, p. 205.

7. Bergson 2002, p. 917, my translation. He officially announced his retirement in 1921: "I see no other way of continuing the work for which [my colleagues] once so kindly judged me worthy to take my place among them."

8. Brousson 1918, p. 2.

9. Canales 2015, p. 3.

10. See ibid., p. 16.

11. Einstein 1968, p. 43.

12. Cited in Canales 2020.

13. For an in-depth study of the debate between Bergson and Einstein, see Canales 2015 and During 2015.

14. Chevalier 1959, p. 83, my translation.

15. Cited in Canales 2016.

16. Ibid.

17. Bergson 1972, pp. 1340–1347, my translation.

18. Ibid., p. 1345, my translation.

19. Bergson 1965.

20. According to the historian Jimena Canales (2005, p. 1171): "Bergson's controversial statement was part of a much larger argument that has been forgotten. In fact, Bergson *did* acknowledge that the twins' times would differ under most circumstances. His statement only held true under quite special circumstances—circumstances that did not allow for *any* differences in the twins' situations, not even differences in acceleration. Explicitly focusing only on movement which was 'straight and uniform,' he demanded that '[t]heir situations be identical.' In every other case, Bergson accepted that the twins'

clock-times would differ. In the first appendix to the second edition of his book, Bergson expressed irritation against readers who overlooked this aspect of his argument and who claimed that he denied the retardation of the traveling clock."

21. Chevalier 1959, p. 69, my translation.

22. In her 2015 book *The Physicist and the Philosopher*, Jimena Canales argues that the notion that Einstein "won" the debate with Bergson is tied to the victory of our current-day conception of knowledge—according to which quantitative, mathematised science has more authority than all other fields of research combined—and that this conception of knowledge is historically situated.

23. Laqua 2011, p. 224.

24. Chevalier 1959, p. 42.

Chapter 21: "Gentlemen, It Is Five O'clock. Class Is Over."

1. Cited in Mossé-Bastide 1955, p. 346, my translation.

2. Delattre 1941, p. 134, my translation.

3. Chevalier 1959, pp. 169–170.

4. Delattre 1941, p. 137.

5. Because Bergson's health did not permit him travel to Sweden to accept the award in person, he wrote to the Nobel Committee: "I would have liked to be able to express the feelings I have in person. . . . From the bottom of my heart I thank the Swedish Academy. It has done me an honour that I would not have dared to claim. . . . I am even more touched when I think that this distinction conferred on a French writer can be considered as a mark of sympathy given to France" (Bergson 1972, p. 1488, my translation).

6. See Azouvi 2007, chap. 10.

7. Cited in ibid., p. 318, my translation.

8. Ibid., p. 293.

9. *Fin d'une parade philosophique: Le Bergsonisme* was originally published in 1929 under Politzer's pen name, François Arouet.

10. Politzer 1967, pp. 10–11.

11. Ibid., p. 188.

12. Azouvi 2007, p. 248.

13. Cited in Sinclair 2020, p. 203.

14. Chevalier 1959, pp. 272–283, my translation.

15. Bergson 1972, p. 881, my translation.

16. Sinclair 2020, p. 29.

17. Bergson 1972, pp. 880–881, my translation.

18. Cited in Sinclair 2020, p. 28.

19. Bergson 2002, p. 1363, my translation.

20. Adès 1949, pp. 13–15.

21. Cited in Lefebvre and Schott 2022, p. 256. For this section, I rely heavily on Lefebvre and Schott's remarkably clear chapter in Sinclair and Wolf's *The Bergsonian Mind* (2022) and on Sinclair's chapter on the *Two Sources* in his *Bergson* (2020, chap. 10).

22. Lefebvre and Schott, p. 251.

23. Ibid., p. 254.

24. This was Bergson's old École classmate Durkheim's position, which he criticised in *The Two Sources of Morality and Religion*.

25. Cited in Lefebvre and Schott 2022, pp. 253–254.

26. Cited in Sinclair 2020, p. 238.

27. Ibid.

28. As Sinclair noted: "Bergson's interpretation of religion is faithful to the etymological sense of the word as *binding again* or *reattachment*" (ibid., p. 243).

29. Bergson 1935, p. 188.

30. Cited in Sinclair 2020, p. 243.

31. "The mystical aspects of ancient Greek thinking, for example, were still all too intellectual. In the East, Buddhism lacked warmth in failing to belief in the efficacy of human action, while Hinduism, with Ramakrishna or Vivekananda, focused on charity only with the influence of Christianity" (ibid., p. 244).

32. Bergson 1935, p. 81.

33. Bergson 1972, pp. 1488–1490.

34. Sinclair 2020, p. 247.

35. Cited in ibid.

36. Bergson 1935, p. 274.

37. Cited in Benrubi 1942, p. 133, my translation.

38. Cited in Oesterreicher 1952, p. 43.

39. Soulez 1989, p. 326.

40. Chevalier 1959, p. 282, my translation.

41. In the decades that followed Bergson's death, however, his wishes were eventually put aside. The *Mélanges* volume (Bergson 1972) contains many of his letters, and in 2002 the first volume of his correspondence was published. A second volume is due to be published in 2024.

42. Chevalier 1959, p. 140, my translation.

43. Actor Sacha Guitry, who happened to be staying in a hotel nearby provided a surprising and no doubt slightly unreliable account of the events. He recalled that Bergson had asked him for help obtaining the new mandatory travel documents. Guitry, who also wished to leave Dax and return home, went to collect the papers from city hall. Back at the hotel, he found some German officers and asked for their signature. They appeared surprised as they read the names. Both Guitry and Bergson were internationally renowned. The highest-graded officer asked Guitry: "Are you Monsieur Sacha Guitry? . . . And is this Monsieur Bergson the great philosopher?" Guitry replied that it was so, and he was instructed to wait. He spent the afternoon worried that he had outed Bergson as a Jew and created trouble for the old man. But later that day he was presented with the signed documents. Bergson's read: "Mr. Henri Bergson is allowed to return to Paris by car. He is to be given 100 litres of petrol at the start of his journey which he is permitted to renew on the way home, and he is to be treated with the respect due to a representative of French culture." On the day of their departure, still according to Guitry's account, as Bergson was leaving the hotel, being carried in his chair, twelve German solders saluted him, a mark of respect for a Nobel laureate and world-renowned thinker. Guitry recalled: "Word spread very quickly, and the news spread throughout Paris. It was significant and, as such, it calmed many apprehensions. So much so, in fact, that it was commented on in

various ways. An imprudent or mischievous newspaper reported it and 48 hours later, on Radio-Paris, a voice, unfortunately French, formally denied what it called an absurd legend, protesting that German soldiers would never have honoured a Jew in this way" (Guitry 1947, pp. 120–123, my translation).

44. Soulez and Worms 2002, p. 264.

45. Chevalier sent a telegram to Louise Bergson offering his condolences. The official character of the telegram, which presented condolences in the name of the collaborationist Vichy government to a mourning Jewish family, did not sit well with some of the other government members. Chevalier claims that he brought up this issue with Pétain himself, who "held Bergson in particularly high regard" and who agreed that to remain silent on Bergson's death would be a dishonour. Some of Chevalier's colleagues retaliated against this decision in the press, and a month later Chevalier was forced to resign (Chevalier 1959, pp. 299–301).

46. *Candide* 1941. This deathbed story was corroborated by the eminently serious philosopher Léon Brunschvicg: "On the final night, he thought he was at the Collège de France; he was lecturing, he said 'it is five o'clock, I have to end here' and he died" (Bergson 1972, p. 1629).

EPILOGUE

1. Lippmann 1912a.

2. This section is taken from my *Aeon* article (Herring 2020).

A BEGINNER'S GUIDE TO BERGSON

ENGLISH TRANSLATIONS OF BERGSON'S WORKS

Translations of works published during Bergson's lifetime:

1889. *Essai sur les données immédiates de la conscience.*

1910. *Time and Free Will. An Essay on the Immediate Data of Consciousness.* Translated by F. L. Pogson. New York: The Macmillan Co.

1896. *Matière et mémoire.*

1911. *Matter and Memory.* Translated by N. M. Paul and S. Palmer. London: George Allen and Unwin LTD.

1900. *Le Rire.*

1911. *Laughter. An Essay on the Meaning of the Comic.* Translated by Cloudesley Brereton and Fred Rothwell. New York: The Macmillan Company.

1903. "Introduction à la métaphysique."

1910. *Introduction to Metaphysics.* Translated by T. E. Hulme. New York: Putnam's Sons.

1907. *L'Évolution créatrice.*

2023. *Creative Evolution.* Translated by Donald Landes. Abingdon: Routledge.
The first translation of this book by Arthur Mitchell was published in 1911. While Bergson oversaw the original translation, I recommend 21st century readers use Landes's updated version which is, in many ways, closer to the text.

1919. *L'Énergie spirituelle.*

1920. *Mind-Energy: Lectures and Essays.* Translated by Wildon Carr. New York: Henry Holt and Company.

1922. *Durée et simultanéité.*

1965. *Duration and Simultaneity.* Translated by Leon Jacobson. Indianapolis: The Bobs-Merrill Company INC.

1932. *Les Deux sources de la morale et de la religion.*

1935. *The Two Sources of Morality and Religion.* Translated by R. Ashley Audra and Cloudesley Brereton. London: Macmillan and Co.

1934. *La Pensée et le mouvant.*

1946. *The Creative Mind.* Translated by Mabelle L. Andison. New York: The Philosophical Library.

Bergson's lectures

An English translation of Bergson's Collège de France lectures is in the works with the first volume published in 2024:

Freedom: Lectures at the Collège de France, 1904–1905. Edited by Nils F. Schott and Alexandre Lefebvre and translated by Leonard Lawlor.

A selection of untranslated works compiled after Bergson's death:

1972. *Mélanges.* Edited by André Robinet. Paris: PUF.

2002. *Correspondances.* Edited by André Robinet. Paris: PUF.

2024. *Correspondances volume 2.* Edited by Florent Serina and Caterina Zanfi. Paris: PUF.

A SELECTION OF ANGLOPHONE STUDIES OF BERGSON'S PHILOSOPHY

Introductions to Bergson's philosophy

Allen, Barry. 2023. *Living in Time: The Philosophy of Henri Bergson.* Oxford: Oxford University Press.

Ansell-Pearson, Keith. 2018. *Bergson: Thinking Beyond the Human Condition.* London: Bloomsbury Academic.

Ansell-Pearson, Keith and John Ó Maoilearca (eds.). 2002. *Henri Bergson: Key Writings.* New York: Continuum.

Deleuze, Giles. 1988. *Bergsonism.* Translated by H. Tomlinson. New York: Zone Books.

Guerlac, Suzanne. 2006. *Thinking in Time: An Introduction to Henri Bergson.* Ithaca: Cornell University Press.

Jankelevitch, Vladimir. 2015. *Henri Bergson.* Translated by Nils F. Schott. Durham (North Carolina): Duke University Press.

Moore, F. C. T. 1996. *Bergson: Thinking Backwards.* Cambridge: Cambridge University Press.

Mullarkey, John. 2000. *Bergson and Philosophy: An Introduction.* Notre Dame: University of Notre Dame Press.

Sinclair, Mark. 2020. *Bergson*. London and New York: Routledge.

Sinclair, Mark and Yaron Wolf (eds.). 2022. *The Bergsonian Mind*. London and New York: Routledge.

FURTHER READING

Ansell-Pearson, Keith. 2002. *Philosophy and the Adventure of the Virtual: Bergson and the Time of Life*. London and New York: Routledge.

Antliff, Mark. 1993. *Inventing Bergson: Cultural Politics and the Parisian Avant-Garde*. Princeton: Princeton University Press.

Ardoin, Paul, S. E. Gontarski and Laci Mattison (eds.). 2013. *Understanding Bergson, Understanding Modernism*. New York: Bloomsbury.

Burwick, Frederick and Paul Douglass (eds.). 1992. *The Crisis of Modernism: Bergson and the Vitalist Controversy*. Cambridge: Cambridge University Press.

Canales, Jimena. 2015. *The Physicist and the Philosopher. Einstein, Bergson and the Debate That Changed Our Understanding of Time*. Princeton: Princeton University Press.

Čapek, Milič. 1971. *Bergson and Modern Physics*. Dodrecht: D. Reidel Publishing Company.

Douglass, Paul. 1986. *Bergson, Eliot, and American Literature*. Lexington: The University Press of Kentucky.

Gillies, M. A. 1996. *Henri Bergson and British Modernism*. Montreal: McGill-Queen's University Press.

Grogin, R. C. 1988. *The Bergsonian Controversy in France 1900–1914*. Alberta: The University of Calgary Press.

Gunter, Pete A. Y. 2023. *Getting Bergson Straight: The Contributions of Intuition to the Sciences*. Wilmington: Vernon Press.

Hirai, Yasushi (ed.). 2023. *Bergson's Scientific Metaphysics*. London: Bloomsbury.

Kelly, Michael R. (ed.). 2010. *Bergson and Phenomenology*. London: Palgrave.

Lawlor, Leonard. 2003. *The Challenge of Bergsonism: Phenomenology, Ontology, Ethics*. London: Continuum Press.

Lefebvre, Alexandre. 2013. *Human Rights as a Way of Life: On Bergson's Political Philosophy*. Stanford: Stanford University Press.

Lefebvre, Alexandre and Nils F. Schott (eds.). 2019. *Interpreting Bergson*. Cambridge: Cambridge Univeristy Press.

Lefebvre, Alexandre and Melanie White (eds.). 2012. *Bergson, Politics, and Religion*. Durham (North Carolina): Duke University Press.

Maoilearca, John Ó. 2022. *Vestiges of a Philosophy: Matter, the Meta-Spiritual, and the Forgotten Bergson*. Oxford: Oxford Studies in Western Esotericism.

Moravec, Matyáš. 2024. *Henri Bergson and the Philosophy of Religion: God, Freedom, and Duration*. London and New York: Routledge.

Mullarkey, John (ed.). 2006. *The New Bergson*. Manchester: Manchester University Press.

Pilkington, A. E. 1976. *Bergson and His Influence: A Reassessment*. Cambridge: Cambridge University Press.

Posteraro, Tano S. 2022. *Bergson's Philosophy of Biology: Virtuality, Tendency and Time*. Edinburgh: Edinburgh University Press.

Quirk, T. 1990. *Bergson and American Culture: The Worlds of Willa Cather and Wallace Stevens*. Chapel Hill: University of North Carolina Press.

Scharfstein, Ben-Ami. 1942. *The Roots of Bergson's Philosophy*. New York: Columbia University Press.

Vrahamis, Andreas. 2022. *Bergsonism and the History of Analytic Philosophy*. London: Palgrave.

BIBLIOGRAPHY

Aberdeen Daily Journal. 1911. "The Philosophy of Bergson." *Aberdeen Daily Journal,* July 4, p. 2.

Adès, Albert. 1949. *Adès chez Bergson: Reliques inconnues d'une amitié.* Paris: Edmone Albert Adès.

Agathon. 1911. *L'Esprit de la nouvelle Sorbone: La Crise de la culture classique, la crise du français.* Paris: Mercure de France.

Albaret, Céleste. 2003. *Monsieur Proust,* translated by Barbara Bray. New York: New York Review Books.

Alglave, E. 1878. "Herbert Spencer à Paris: Un banquet philosophique." *Revue scientifique de la France et de l'étranger: Revue des cours scientifiques* 1: 1141–1142.

Allen, Barry. 2023. *Living in Time: The Philosophy of Henri Bergson.* Oxford: Oxford University Press.

L'Alouette, J. 1914. "Questions de méange." *Le Petit Journal,* March 8, p. 1.

Ansell-Pearson, Keith. 2002. *Philosophy and the Adventure of the Virtual: Bergson and the Time of Life.* London: Routledge.

———. 2018. *Bergson: Thinking Beyond the Human Condition.* London: Bloomsbury Academic.

Ansell-Pearson, Keith, and John Ó Maoilearca, eds. 2002. *Henri Bergson: Key Writings.* New York: Continuum.

Antliff, Mark. 1993. *Inventing Bergson: Cultural Politics and the Parisian Avant-Garde.* Princeton, NJ: Princeton University Press.

Ardoin, Paul, S. E. Gontarski, and Laci Mattison, eds. 2013. *Understanding Bergson, Understanding Modernism.* New York: Bloomsbury.

Arouet, François [Georges Politzer]. 1967. *La Fin d'une parade philosophique: Le Bergsonisme.* Utrecht: J. J. Pauvert.

Azouvi, François. 2007. *La Gloire de Bergson: Essais sur le magistère philosophe.* Paris: Gallimard.

———. 2008. "Le Magistère bergsonien et le succès de l'élan vital." In *Annales bergsoniennes IV: L'Évolution créatrice 1907–2007: Épistémologie et métaphysique,* edited by

Anne Fagot-Largeult and Frédéric Worms. Paris: Presses Universitaires de France, pp. 85–93.

Balfour, Arthur. 1911. "Creative Evolution and Philosophic Doubt." *Hibbert Journal: A Quarterly Review of Religion, Theology, and Philosophy* 10: 1–23.

Bard, Christine. 1995. *Les Filles de Marianne: Histoire des féminismes 1914–1940*. Paris: Fayard.

Bardy, Jean. 1990. "Bergson à Clermont-Ferrand: Lieux et atmosphère autour d'une pensée qui se cherche et s'affirme." In *Bergson Naissance d'une philosophie: Actes du Colloque de Clermont-Ferrand (17–18 novembre 1989)*, edited by Centre national de la recherche scientifique (CNRS). Paris: Presses Universitaires de France, pp. 13–22.

Beaunier, André. 1907. "Les Syndicalistes." *Le Figaro supplément littéraire du dimanche*, March 16, p. 3.

Becker, Jean-Jacques. 2013. *L'Année 14*. Paris: Armand Colin.

Benda, Julien. 1912. *Le Bergsonisme, ou, Une philosophie de la mobilité*. Paris: Mercure de France.

———. 1914. *Sur le succès du bergsonisme: Précédé d'une réponse aux défenseurs de la doctrine*. Paris: Mercure de France.

———. 1927. *La Trahison des clercs*. Paris: Grasset.

Bennett, Edward T. 1903. *The Society for Psychical Research: Its Rise and Its Progress and a Sketch of Its Work*. London: R. Brimley Johnson.

Benrubi, Isaak. 1942. *Souvenirs sur Henri Bergson*. Neuchâtel and Paris: Delachaux et Niestlé.

Bergson, Henri. 1886. "De la simulation inconsciente dans l'état d'hypnotisme." *Revue philosophique de la France et de l'étranger* 22: 525–531.

———. 1910. *Time and Free Will: An Essay on the Immediate Data of Consciousness*, translated by F. L. Pogson. New York: Macmillan Co.

———. 1911a. *Matter and Memory*, translated by Nancy Margaret Paul and W. Scott Palmer. London: George Allen and Unwin Ltd.

———. 1911b. *Laughter: An Essay on the Meaning of the Comic*, translated by Cloudesley Brereton and Fred Rothwell. New York: Macmillan Co.

———. 1911c. *La Perception du changement: Conférences faites à l'université d'Oxford les 26 et 27 mai 1911*. Oxford: Oxford University Press.

———. 1912a. *An Introduction to Metaphysics*, translated by T. E. Hulme. London: G. P. Putnam's Sons.

———. 1912b. "Life and Consciousness." *Hibbert Journal: A Quarterly Review of Religion, Theology, and Philosophy* 10: 24–44.

———. 1915. "La Philosophie française." *La Revue de Paris* 22 (3): 236–256.

———. 1920. *Mind-Energy: Lectures and Essays*, translated by Wildon Carr. New York: Henry Holt and Co.

———. 1935. *The Two Sources of Morality and Religion*, translated by R. Ashley Audra and Cloudesley Brereton. London: Macmillan and Co.

———. 1946. *The Creative Mind*, translated by Mabelle L. Andison. New York: Philosophical Library.

———. 1965. *Duration and Simultaneity*, translated by Leon Jacobson. Indianapolis: Bobbs-Merrill Co.

———. 1972. *Mélanges*, edited by André Robinet. Paris: Presses Universitaires de France.

———. 2002. *Correspondances*, vol. 1, edited by André Robinet. Paris: Presses Universitaires de France.

———. 2014. *Key Writings*, edited and translated by Keith Ansell-Pearson and John O'Maoilearca. New York: Bloomsbury.

———. 2016. *Histoire de l'idée de temps: Cours au collège de France 1902–1903*. Paris: Presses Universitaires de France.

———. 2023. *Creative Evolution*, translated by Donald Landes. Abingdon, UK: Routledge.

———. 2024a. *Correspondances*, vol. 2, edited by Florent Serina and Caterina Zanfi. Paris: Presses Universitaires de France.

———. 2024b. *Freedom: Lectures at the Collège de France, 1904–1905*, edited by Nils F. Schott and Alexandre Lefebvre and translated by Leonard Lawlor. London: Bloomsbury.

Bergson, Henri, and Albert Kahn. 2003. *Correspondances*, edited by Sophie Coeuré and Frédéric Worms. Strasbourg: Desmaret.

Bernstein, Herman. 1913. *With Master Minds*. New York: Universal Series Publishing Co.

Bertoldi, Sylvain. 2000. "La Catho célèbre ses cent vingt-cinq ans." Archives Ville d'Angers, September. https://archives.angers.fr/chroniques-historiques/les-chroniques-par-annees/1996-2000/la-catho-celebre-ses-cent-vingt-cinq-ans/index.html (accessed December 15, 2023).

Bois, Elie-Joseph. 1913. "À la Recherche du temps perdu." *Le Temps*, November 13, p. 4.

Brousson, Jean-Jacques. 1918. "La Réception de M. H. Bergson à l'Académie française." *Excelsior: Journal illustré quotidien* 9 (2628): 2.

Burwick, Frederick, and Paul Douglass, eds. 1992. *The Crisis of Modernism: Bergson and the Vitalist Controversy*. Cambridge: Cambridge University Press.

Canales, Jimena. 2005. "Einstein, Bergson, and the Experiment That Failed: Intellectual Cooperation at the League of Nations." *Modern Language Notes* 120 (5): 1168–1191.

———. 2015. *The Physicist and the Philosopher: Einstein, Bergson, and the Debate That Changed Our Understanding of Time*. Princeton, NJ: Princeton University Press.

———. 2016. "This Philosopher Helped Ensure There Was No Nobel for Relativity." *Nautilus*, April 18. https://nautil.us/this-philosopher-helped-ensure-there-was-no-nobel-for-relativity-235898/ (accessed February 11, 2024).

———. 2020. "Einstein, du Collège de France à la Société française de philosophie." In *Einstein au Collège de France*, edited by Antoine Compagnon and Céline Surprenant. Paris: Collège de France.

Candide. 1941. "La Mort de Bergson." *Candide*, February 19, p. 2.

Čapek, Milič. 1971. *Bergson and Modern Physics*. Dordrecht: D. Reidel Publishing Co.

Carr, Herbert Wildon. 1919. *Henri Bergson: The Philosophy of Change*. London: T. C. and E. C. Jack Ltd.

———. 1924. "Idealism as a Principle in Science and Philosophy." In *Contemporary British Philosophy: Personal Statements*, 1st and 2nd series, edited by John Henry Muirhead. London: Allen and Unwin Ltd., pp. 102–126.

Carter, C. William. 2000. *Marcel Proust: A Life*. New Haven, CT: Yale University Press.

Carter, Huntly 1911. "The 'Blue Bird' and Bergson in Paris." *The New Age* 9 (2): 43–45.

Chapoutot, Johann. 2008. "La Trahison d'un clerc? Bergson, la Grande Guerre, et la France." *Francia* 35: 295–316.

Chevalier, Jacques. 1928. "Henri Bergson." *Les Nouvelles littéraires* 7 (4, August 4): 7.

———. 1959. *Entretiens avec Bergson*. Paris: Plon.

Christen-Lécuyer, Carole. 2000. "Les Premières étudiantes de l'Université de Paris." *Travail, genre, et sociétés* 2 (4): 35–50.

Citizen. 1911. "Bergson." *Citizen*, October 5, p. 5.

Coissac, Georges-Michel. 1925. *Histoire du cinématographe: De ses origines à nos jours*. Paris: Éditions du "Cinéopse."

Conley, John. 2019. "Madeleine de Scudéry." *Stanford Encyclopedia of Philosophy*, Fall 2019. https://plato.stanford.edu/archives/fall2019/entries/madeleine-scudery (accessed March 1, 2024).

Courtier, Jules. 1908. *Rapport sur les séances d'Eusapia Palladino à l'Institut général psychologique en 1905, 1906, 1907, et 1908*. Paris: Institut général psychologique.

Cox, Marian. 1913. "Bergson's Message to Feminism." *The Forum* 49: 548–559.

Current Opinion. 1914. "The Threatened Collapse of the Bergson Boom in France." *Current Opinion* 3 (56): 370–371.

Darbishire, Arthur D. 1917. *An Introduction to a Biology: And Other Papers*. New York: Funk and Wagnalls.

Dard, Olivier, Michel Leymarie, and Neil McWilliam, eds. 2010. *Le Maurrassisme et la culture: L'action française, culture, société*, vol. 3. Lille: Presses Universitaires du Septentrion.

Darlu, A. 1887. "La Liberté et le déterminisme selon M. Fouillée." *Revue philosophique de la France et de l'étranger* 12 (1): 561–581.

De Rochas, A. 1901. "Le Rêve." *Annales des sciences psychiques* 10 (3): 160–172.

Delattre, Floris. 1941. "Les Dernières années d'Henri Bergson." *Revue philosophique de la France et de l'étranger* 66 (1): 125–138.

Deleuze, Giles. 1988. *Bergsonism*, translated by Hugh Tomlinson and Barbara Habberjam. New York: Zone Books.

Deng, Gang. 2023. "L'Intuition, la vie: Réception et influence du bergsonisme dans la philosophie chinoise." *Bergsoniana* 3: 13–33.

Desboves, Adolphe. 1878. *Étude sur Pascal et les géomètres contemporains: Suivie de plusieurs notes scientifiques et littéraires*. Paris: Librairie Ch. Delagrave.

Descartes, René. 1993. *Meditations on First Philosophy*, translated by Donald A. Cress. Indianapolis: Hackett Publishing Co.

D.L.B. 1915. "Compulsory Service." *The Bystander* 47 (605): 22–24.

Douglass, Paul. 1986. *Bergson, Eliot, and American Literature*. Lexington: University Press of Kentucky.

Driesch, Hans. 1908a. *The Science and Philosophy of the Organism: Gifford Lectures Delivered at Aberdeen University, 1907*, 2 vols. London: Adam and Charles Black.

———. 1908b. "Bergson: Der biologische Philosoph." *Zeitschrift für des Ausbau der Entwicklungslehre* 2: 48–55.

Droit, Roger-Pol. 1997. "La Dernière leçon d'Henri Bergson." *Le Monde*, April 25.

Du Bos, Charles. 1946. *Journal, 1921–1923*. Paris: Corrêa.

During, Elie. 2015. *Bergson et Einstein: La querelle du temps*. Paris: Presses Universitaires de France.

Durkheim, Émile. 1938. *The Rules of Sociological Method*, translated by Sarah A. Solovay and John H. Mueller. New York: Free Press.

Einstein, Albert. 1968. *Einstein on Peace*. New York: Schocken Books.

Eliot, T. S. 1917. *Prufrock and Other Observations*. London: The Egoist Ltd.

Evrard, Renaud. 2016. *Enquête sur 150 ans de parapsychologie*. Paris: Éditions Trajectoire.

———. 2021. "Bergson et la télépathie: À propos d'une correspondance inédite." *Bergsoniana* 1: 237–255.

Excelsior. 1914. "On écoute aux fenêtres le cours de M. Bergson." *Excelsior: Journal illustré quotidien* 1187: 1.

François, Arnaud, ed. 2010. *L'Évolution créatrice de Bergson*. Paris: Vrin.

Gemert, Ties van. 2022. "The Early Reception of Bergson's Philosophy in the Netherlands (1890–1909)." *Bergsoniana* 2: 179–197.

Gide, André. 1948. *Journal, 1889–1939*. Paris: Gallimard.

Gillies, Mary Ann. 1996. *Henri Bergson and British Modernism*. Montreal: McGill-Queen's University Press.

Gratton, T. 1911. "Bergson Lecturing." *The New Age* 10 (1): 15.

Grogin, Richard C. 1978. "Rationalists and Anti-Rationalists in Pre–World War I France: The Bergson-Benda Affair." *Historical Reflections* 5 (2): 223–231.

———. 1988. *The Bergsonian Controversy in France, 1900–1914*. Alberta: University of Calgary Press.

Guerlac, Suzanne. 2006. *Thinking in Time: An Introduction to Henri Bergson*. Ithaca, NY: Cornell University Press.

Guitry, Sacha. 1947. *Quatre ans d'occupations*. Paris: L'Elan.

Guitton, Jean. 1960. *La Vocation de Bergson*. Paris: Gallimard.

Gunter, Pete A. Y. 2023. *Getting Bergson Straight: The Contributions of Intuition to the Sciences*. Wilmington, DE: Vernon Press.

Guyot, Charlie. 1950. "Péguy et Bergson." *Revue d'histoire et de philosophie religieuses* 30 (4): 273–289.

Harpe, Jean de la. 1941. "Souvenirs personnels d'un entretien avec Bergson." In *Henri Bergson: Essais et témoignages inédits*, edited by Albert Béguin and Pierre Thévenaz. Neuchâtel: Editions de la Baconière, pp. 357–364.

Henry Holt & Co. 1911. "Philosophy's Popularity." *New York Times*, April 16, 1911.

Herring, Emily. 2018. "'Great Is Darwin and Bergson His Poet': Julian Huxley's Other Evolutionary Synthesis." *Annals of Science* 75 (1): 40–54.

———. 2019. "Henri Bergson, Celebrity." *Aeon*, May. https://aeon.co/essays/henri-bergson-the-philosopher-damned-for-his-female-fans/ (accessed March 1, 2024).

———. 2020. "Laughter Is Vital." *Aeon*, July. https://aeon.co/essays/for-henri-bergson-laughter-is-what-keeps-us-elastic-and-free/ (accessed February 28, 2024).

———. 2021. "Moina Mathers—High Priestess of the Belle Époque." Engelsberg Ideas, May 28. https://engelsbergideas.com/portraits/moina-mathers-high-priestess-of-the-belle-epoque/ (accessed February 2, 2024).

———. 2022. "The Vital Impulse and Early 20th-Century Biology." In *The Bergsonian Mind*, edited by Mark Sinclair and Yaron Wolf. London: Routledge, pp. 251–263.

———. 2023. "Thinking with Élan." *Times Literary Supplement*, May 5, p. 12.

Hirai, Yasushi, ed. 2023. *Bergson's Scientific Metaphysics*. London: Bloomsbury.

Hulme, T. E. 1911a. "Mr. Balfour, Bergson, and Politics." *The New Age* 10 (2): 38–40.

———. 1911b. "Bax on Bergson." *The New Age* 9 (14): 329.

Humanist Heritage Project. n.d. "The Cambridge Heretics." https://heritage.humanists .uk/the-cambridge-heretics/.

Husband, Mary Gilliland. 1912. "Creative Evolution." *International Journal of Ethics* 22 (4): 462–467.

Huxley, Julian. 1912. *The Individual in the Animal Kingdom*. Cambridge: Cambridge University Press.

———. 1923. *Essays of a Biologist*. New York: Alfred A. Knopf.

In Memoriam: Jeanne Bergson, 1893–1961. 1963. Exhibition of drawings and engravings, Galerie Bernheim-Jeune, Paris, March 13.

Jacob, Benjamin. 1898. "La Philosophie d'hier et celle d'aujourd'hui." *Revue de métaphysique et de morale* 6(2): 170–201.

Jaloux, Edmond. 1941. "Souvenirs sur Henri Bergson." *Journal de Genève*, February 2, p. 1.

James, William. 1909. *A Pluralistic Universe*. London: Longmans, Green and Co.

———. 1920. *The Letters of William James*, vol. 2. Boston: Atlantic Monthly Press.

Jankelevitch, Vladimir. 2015. *Henri Bergson*, translated by Nils F. Schott. Durham, NC: Duke University Press.

Jones, Alun R. 1960. *The Life and Opinions of T. E. Hulme*. Boston: Beacon Press.

Jones, Donna V. 2011. *The Racial Discourses of Life Philosophy: Négriture, Vitalism, and Modernity*. New York: Columbia University Press.

Joussain, André. 1911. "L'Idée de l'inconscient et l'intuition de la vie." *Revue philosophique de la France et de l'étranger* 36 (1): 467–493.

Kelly, Michael R., ed. 2010. *Bergson and Phenomenology*. London: Palgrave.

Labaune, Christophe. 2021. "Bergson au Collège de France (exposition virtuelle)." Colligere, March 25. https://archibibscdf.hypotheses.org/8177 (accessed February 8, 2024).

Laplace, Pierre-Simon. 1951. *A Philosophical Essay on Probabilities*, translated by F. W. Truscott and F. L. Emory. New York: Dover Publications.

Laqua, Daniel. 2011. "Transnational Intellectual Cooperation, the League of Nations, and the Problem of Order." *Journal of Global History* 6 (2): 223–247.

Lawlor, Leonard. 2003. *The Challenge of Bergsonism: Phenomenology, Ontology, Ethics*. London: Continuum Press.

Le Dantec, Félix. 1912. *Contre la métaphysique: Questions de méthode*. Paris: Félix Alcan.

Lecoq, J. 1914. "Les 'Snobinettes' et la philosophie." *Le Petit Journal*, January 25, p. 1.

Lefebvre, Alexandre. 2013. *Human Rights as a Way of Life: On Bergson's Political Philosophy*. Stanford, CA: Stanford University Press.

Lefebvre, Alexandre, and Nils F. Schott, eds. 2019. *Interpreting Bergson*. Cambridge: Cambridge University Press.

———. 2022. "Closed and Open Societies." In *The Bergsonian Mind*, edited by Mark Sinclair and Yaron Wolf. London: Routledge, pp. 251–263.

Lefebvre, Alexandre, and Melanie White, eds. 2012. *Bergson, Politics, and Religion*. Durham, NC: Duke University Press.

Lenoir, Raymond. 1919. "Réflexions sur le bergsonisme." *Nouvelle revue française* (December): 1077–1089.

Lermina, Jules. 1912. "Bavardage." *L'Aurore*, September 11, p. 1.

Levine, Louis. 1913. "The Philosophy of Henry [*sic*] Bergson and Syndicalism." *New York Times*, January 26, p. 4.

Lévy-Bruhl, Lucien. 1928. "Henri Bergson à l'École normale." *Les Nouvelles littéraires* 7 (323, December 15): 1.

La Libre parole. 1899. "Le Traître condamné: Dix ans de détention et la dégradation." *La Libre parole*, September 10, p. 1.

Lippmann, Walter. 1912a. "The Most Dangerous Man in the World." *Everybody's Magazine* 27: 100–101.

———. 1912b. "Bergson's Philosophy: It Is Necessary for One to Become a Bergsonian Before One Can Thoroughly Understand Bergson." *New York Times*, November 17, p. 21.

———. 1913. *A Preface to Politics*. New York: Mitchell Kennerley.

Maire, Gilbert. 1935. *Bergson mon maître*. Paris: Éditions Bernard Grasset.

Manchester Guardian. 1913. "M. Bergson on Psychical Research: Presidential Address." *Manchester Guardian*, May 29, p. 9.

"The Manifesto of the Ninety-Three." 1914. August 4. Available at: https://web .tohoku.ac.jp/modern-japan/wp-content/uploads/Manifesto-of-the-93.pdf.

Maoilearca, John Ó. 2022. *Vestiges of a Philosophy: Matter, the Meta-Spiritual, and the Forgotten Bergson*. Oxford: Oxford Studies in Western Esotericism.

Marcel, Gabriel. 1941. "Grandeur de Bergson." In *Henri Bergson: Essais et témoignages inédits*, edited by Albert Béguin and Pierre Thévenaz. Neuchâtel: Éditions la Baconière, pp. 29–38.

Maritain, Raïssa. 1942. *We Have Been Friends Together*. New York: Longmans, Green and Co.

Le Matin. 1914a. "L'Assassinat de Jaurès." *Le Matin*, August 2, p. 2.

———. 1914b. "L'Allemagne déclare la guerre à la France." *Le Matin*, August 4, p. 1.

———. 1918. "Un Appel du conseil municipal de Paris." *Le Matin*, November 12, p. 2.

May, Henri F. 1959. *The End of American Innocence: A Study of the First Years of Our Own Time, 1912–1917*. New York: Alfred A. Knopf.

McAuliffe, Mary. 2011. *Dawn of the Belle Epoque*. Plymouth, UK: Rowman and Littlefield.

———. 2014. *Twilight of the Belle Epoque*. Plymouth, UK: Rowman and Littlefield.

McGrath, Larry. 2013. "Bergson Comes to America." *Journal of the History of Ideas* 74 (4): 599–620.

Menand, Louis. 1996. "Eliot and the Jews." *New York Review of Books* 43 (10, June 6): 12.

Meunier, Georges. 1910. *Ce qu'ils pensent du Merveilleux*. Paris: Éditions Albin Michel.

Mignot-Ogliastri, Claude. 1986. *Anna de Noailles: Une Amie de la Princesse Edmond de Polignac*. Paris: Fondation Singer-Polignac.

Millet, Jean. 1974. *Bergson et le calcul infinitésimal*. Paris: Presses Universitaires de France.

Miropolsky, Hélène. 1913. "Le Suffrage des femmes." *Le Temps*, February 7, p. 3.

Monk, Ray. 1996. *Bertrand Russell: The Spirit of Solitude, 1871–1921*. New York: Free Press.

La Montagne. 1941. "Henri Bergson enseigna la philosophie au lycée Blaise Pascal." *La Montagne*, January 6, p. 2.

Moore, Charles Leonard. 1912. "The Return of the Gods." *The Dial: A Semi-Monthly Journal of Literary Criticism, Discussion, and Information* 53: 371–372.

Moore, F.C.T. 1996. *Bergson: Thinking Backwards*. Cambridge: Cambridge University Press.

Moravec, Matyáš. 2024. *Henri Bergson and the Philosophy of Religion: God, Freedom, and Duration*. London: Routledge.

Morrell, Ottoline. 1963. *The Early Memoirs of Lady Ottoline Morrell*. London: Faber and Faber.

Mossé-Bastide, Rose-Marie. 1955. *Bergson Educateur*. Paris: Presses Universitaires de France.

Mullarkey, John. 2000. *Bergson and Philosophy: An Introduction*. Notre Dame: University of Notre Dame Press.

———, ed. 2006. *The New Bergson*. Manchester: Manchester University Press.

Myers, Frederic W. H. 1893. *Science and a Future Life, with Other Essays*. London: Macmillan and Co.

Natale, Simone. 2016. "The Medium Goes to America." *History Today* 66 (5, May). https://www.historytoday.com/history-matters/medium-goes-america (accessed December 18, 2023).

Nature. 1911. "The International Philosophical Congress at Bologna." *Nature* 86 (2168): 399.

The New Age. 1914a. "Readers and Writers." *The New Age* 14 (16): 498–499.

———. 1914b. "Views and Reviews." *The New Age* 15 (17): 399.

———. 1914c. "Unedited Opinions. The Popularity of Bergson." *The New Age* 15 (1): 12.

New York Times. 1911. "Students Flock to Bergson to Learn New Philosophy." *New York Times*, August 27.

———. 1912a. "What Makes Us Laugh? Bergson Answers S. S. Cox's Old Question in a Brilliant Essay." *New York Times*, March 3, p. 118.

———. 1912b. "Henri Bergson." *New York Times*, May 26, p. 321.

———. 1913. "Tea for Henri Bergson." *New York Times*, February 20, p. 11.

Oesterreicher, John M. 1952. *Walls Are Crumbling: Seven Jewish Philosophers Discover Christ*. New York: Devin-Adair.

The Outlook. 1913. "Professor Bergson at the City College." *The Outlook* 103: 467–468.

Patrick, George T. W. 1911. "Creative Evolution." *Journal of Educational Psychology* 2 (10): 582–583.

Péguy, Charles. 1914. "Note sur M. Bergson." *Cahiers de la quinzaine* 8(15): 17–97.

Le Petit Parisien. 1910a. " C'est un véritbale déluge." *Le Petit Parisien*, January 21, p. 1.

———. 1910b. "Une Catastrophe sans exemple." *Le Petit Parisien*, January 27, p. 1.

Pétrement, Simone. 1959. *Henri Bergson: Exposition du centenaire*. Paris: Bibliothèque Nationale de France.

Pfister, Christian. 1928. "Bergson élève de l'École normale." *Les Nouvelles littéraires* 7 (323, December 15): 4.

Pilkington, A. E. 1976. *Bergson and His Influence: A Reassessment*. Cambridge: Cambridge University Press.

Posteraro, Tano S. 2022. *Bergson's Philosophy of Biology: Virtuality, Tendency, and Time*. Edinburgh: Edinburgh University Press.

Quirk, Tom. 1990. *Bergson and American Culture: The Worlds of Willa Cather and Wallace Stevens*. Chapel Hill: University of North Carolina Press.

Rainey, Lawrence, Christine Poggi, and Laura Wittman, eds. 2009. *Futurism: An Anthology*. New Haven, CT: Yale University Press.

Revue de l'enseignement secondaire et de l'enseignement supérieur. 1890. "Thèses et soutenance de M. Henri Bergson, ancien élève de l'École normale supérieure, professeur de philosophie au collège Rollin (27 décembre 1889)." *Revue de l'enseignement secondaire et de l'enseignement supérieur* 7 (13): 129–134.

Russell, Bertrand. 1912a. "The Philosophy of Bergson." *The Monist* 22: 321–347.

———. 1912b. "The Professor's Guide to Laughter." *Cambridge Review* 33: 193–194.

———. 1931. *The Scientific Outlook*. London: George Allen and Unwin Ltd.; New York: W. W. Norton.

———. 1946. *A History of Western Philosophy and Its Connection with Political and Social Circumstances from the Earliest Times to the Present Day*. London: George Allen and Unwin Ltd.

———. 1956. *Portraits from Memory, and Other Essays*. New York: Simon & Schuster.

———. 1992. *The Collected Works of Bertrand Russell: Logical and Philosophical Papers, 1909–1913*, vol. 6, edited by John Slater and Bernd Frohmann. London: Routledge.

———. 1998. *Autobiography*. London: Routledge.

Russell, Edward Stuart. 1911. "Le Vitalisme." *Scientia* 9: 207–225.

———. 1917. Letter from Russell to D'Arcy Thompson, January 1, 1917, ms16399–ms16400, D'Arcy Wentworth Thompson Papers, University of St Andrews.

Scharfstein, Ben-Ami. 1942. *The Roots of Bergson's Philosophy*. New York: Columbia University Press.

Schivelbusch, Wolfgang. 1977. *The Railway Journey: The Industrialization of Time and Space in the Nineteenth Century*. Berkeley: University of California Press.

Sinclair, Mark. 2016. "Bergson's Philosophy of Will and the War of 1914–1918." *Journal of the History of Ideas* 77 (3): 467–487.

———. 2020. *Bergson*. London: Routledge.

Sinclair, Mark, and Yaron Wolf, eds. 2022. *The Bergsonian Mind*. London: Routledge.

Sleigh, Charlotte. 2009. "Plastic Body, Permanent Body: Czech Representations of Corporeality in the Early Twentieth Century." *Studies in History and Philosophy of Biological and Biomedical Sciences* 40: 241–255.

Slosson, Edwin Emery. 1916. *Major Prophets of To-Day*. Boston: Little, Brown and Co.

Sorel, Georges. 1908. *Réflexions sur la violence*. Paris: Marcel Rivière.

Soulez, Philippe. 1989. *Bergson politique*. Paris: Presses Universitaires de France.

Soulez, Philippe, and Frédéric Worms. 2002. *Bergson*. Paris: Presses Universitaires de France.

Sugimura, Yasuhiko. 2023. "Transplanter le bergsonisme dans le 'lieu du néant': Bergson et 'l'École de Kyoto.'" *Bergsoniana* 3: 55–70.

The Sun. 2013a. "Bergson Fills Hall at First Lecture." *The Sun*, February 4, p. 7.

———. 2013b. "Bergson's Second Lecture: Thousands Try in Vain to Hear French Philosopher." *The Sun*, February 5.

Sylvaire, Dominique. 1913. "Le Dernier vendredi de M. Bergson." *Excelsior: Journal illustré quotidien*, March 3, p. 3.

Tahar, Mathilde. 2022. "Bergson's Vitalisms." *Parrhesia* (36): 4–24.

Le Temps. 1912. "Une Philosophie nouvelle." *Le Temps*, July 19, p. 4.

———. 1914. "Le Cours de M. Bergson." *Le Temps*, February 7, p. 6.

Thomson, John Arthur. 1911. "Is There One Science of Nature?" *Hibbert Journal: A Quarterly Review of Religion, Theology and Philosophy* 10: 110–129, 308–327.

The Times. 1911. "University Intelligence." *The Times*, June 24, p. 5.

Turquet-Milnes, Gladys. 1921. *Some Modern French Writers: A Study in Bergsonism*. New York: McBride and Co.

Tyrrell, George. 1908. "Review of *L'Évolution créatrice*." *Hibbert Journal* 6: 435–442.

La Vie Parisienne. 1912a. "Choses et autres." *La Vie Parisienne*, January 20, p. 50.

———. 1912b. "Perplexité." *La Vie Parisienne*, July 20, p. 509.

Visan, Tancrède de. 1911. *L'Attitude du lyrisme contemporain*. Paris: Mercure de France.

Vrahimis, Andreas. 2022. *Bergsonism and the History of Analytic Philosophy*. London: Palgrave.

Wells, H. G. 1906. *The Future in America: A Search After Realities*. New York: Harper and Brothers Publishers.

Wharton, Edith. 1934. *A Backward Glance*. New York: D. Appleton-Century Co.

Wilde, Oscar. 1905. *Intentions*. New York: Brentano's.

Zanfi, Caterina. 2013. *Bergson et la philosophie allemande, 1907–1932*. Paris: Armand Colin.

Zola, Émile. 1898. "J'Accuse . . . ! Lettre au président de la République." *L'Aurore*, January 13, p. 1.

INDEX

perception
  Bergson, H., on evolution and, 71
  brain and, 71–72
  uninterrupted tension in, 75
"La Perception du Changement" ("The
    Perception of Change") lecture, of
    Bergson, H., 165
personality, durée and, 57
PhD thesis, of Bergson, H.
  defence of, 62–67
  determinism and, 64–65
  Fechner and, 63–64
  Janet, Boutroux, Waddington
    examiners of, 47, 58, 61, 62
  Laplace and, 64
  on psychophysics illusion, 65
  secondary on Aristotle, 62–63
philosophy, of Bergson, H. See also durée;
    élan vital
  anti-science agenda misconceptions
    on, 27
  Carter on, 154–155
  Einstein on, 27
  Huxley, J., on, 27
  intuition concept of, 4, 106–109,
    135–137, 195, 200–201
  James, W., praise of, 140, 163–164,
    187, 188
  Jaurès on, 103
  Lenoir on, 226
  life and consciousness defining, 10
  Lippmann on, 27
  Péguy on, 195
  Russell, B., on, 27
  science and, 42, 49–50, 136–137
  on science and metaphysics, 27, 106
  stability of reality, 14–15
  static symbolism of science critique, 10
  time is not space, 41–52
  U.S. response to, 188
  women and, 173–183
"Philosophy and Common Sense" lecture,
    of Bergson, H., 190
philosophy of science, of Bergson, H., 42,
    49–50, 136–137

"The Philosophy of Yesterday and Today,"
    on Bergson, H., 84
phrenology, Broca on, 70
Physics (Aristotle), 63
Picasso, Pablo, 192
Pius X (pope), modernism condemned
    by, 208
Plato, 165
  Heraclitus idea of instability criticism,
    13–14
Plotinus, 114
Poe, Edgar Allan, 195
Poetics (Aristotle), on laughter, 94
poetry
  Bergson, H., characterisation with,
    110, 143
  Mallarmé on, 61–62
  Wharton and, 73, 75
Politzer, Georges, 235–236
Pont des Arts, 154
positivism, 30, 40
  Comte, Renan and Taine on, 38
  of Russell, B., 188
  scientific methods applied in, 60
Pound, Ezra, 192
Les Précieuses ridicules play, of Molière,
    175
précieuse term, for women, 175–176, 182
pre-Socratic, 13, 94
propaganda missions, of Bergson, H.
  with Institute de France travel to Spain,
    217–218
  San Francisco World's Fair tract, 217
Proudhon, Pierre-Joseph, 1
Proust, Marcel, 154, 213, 216
  Bergson, H., letter on art to, 103–104
  on memory and mind, 67–68
provinces, Bergson, H., teaching position
    in, 43–47
Prussia, defeat of France by, 17, 30,
    212, 216
psychical research, 113–116. See also
    Society for Psychical Research
  Curie, P., and, 117–118
  dangerous experiments and, 119–123

299

Index

Emily Herring is a writer based in Paris. She received her PhD in the history and philosophy of science from the University of Leeds, and her writing has appeared in *Aeon* and the *Times Literary Supplement*.